The Fate of the Dollar

Also by Martin Mayer

Selected Nonfiction

Fiction

THE
FATE
OF THE
DOLLAR

Martin Mayer

A Truman Talley Book

𝕿𝖎𝖒𝖊𝖘 BOOKS

New York

332.45

Published by Truman Talley Books • Times Books,
a division of Quadrangle/The New York Times Book
Co., Inc., 3 Park Avenue, New York, N.Y. 10016

Published simultaneously in Canada by
Fitzhenry & Whiteside, Ltd., Toronto

Library of Congress Cataloging in Publication Data

Mayer, Martin, 1928-
    The fate of the dollar.
    "A Truman Talley book."
    Includes index.

    1. International finance. 2. Dollar, American.
I. Title.
HG3881.M385 1980   332.4'52'0973   79-66845
ISBN 0-8129-0880-5

Manufactured in the United States of America

for Henry Reuss
whose twenty years of carefully planned
and intelligently conducted hearings on
this subject made it possible to piece
together the story

Contents

PART ONE

1 / From Power and Glory to Glut

It is difficult to believe that there can ever have been another case of a country where the demand of the rest of the world for its products was so urgent and its demand for the products of the world so indifferent.

—Geoffrey Crowther, editor of *The Economist,* speaking of the United States (1957)

* * *

Solomon told me when he had been in office only a few months, "I don't like the idea of the value of the dollar abroad being at the mercy of the central banks." I said, "Good. Then finance the deficit yourself."

—Otmar Emminger, President, Deutsche Bundesbank, speaking of the Under Secretary of the Treasury of the United States and his problems (1979)

* * *

"I left the Federal Reserve Bank of New York in 1957," said Paul Volcker, an immensely tall, round-shouldered, fifty-one-year-old economist and cigar-smoker who returned to the New York Fed as its president and then left again to be chairman of the Federal Reserve Board. "All was quiet at that point. I went over and became an economist at Chase. One day George Champion called me into his office, which was a startling event—I'd never been called into the president's office at the Fed.

"Mr. Champion said, 'Sit down, young man. I want to talk to you about this balance of payments problem. I'm worried. I'm afraid we're going to begin losing gold. What do you think about it?'

THE FATE OF THE DOLLAR

"So I explained to him all the good economist's reasons why there couldn't be any trouble. He listened, and he said, 'Well, that's very interesting, young man,' and I went back to my office.

"Six months later, there was the first upside breakout on the London gold market. It taught me that there may be things that a man out in the market knows that nobody in government or a university knows. He may not know *why* he knows it, but he does."

1

At this distance in time, it is all but impossible to reconstruct the intellectual and attitudinal atmosphere that surrounded the international role of the United States dollar for the first dozen years after the end of World War II. Those who were tourists in Europe in the 1950s find it hard to credit perfectly accurate recollections of how much an American dollar could buy—at the legal rate of exchange. And often enough there were shady characters around who would offer a much better black-market rate, or shopkeepers who would knock down an already low price if the customer paid in American currency.

All over Europe, governments had seized control of their citizens' dollars or dollar-denominated assets. Banks, hotels, and restaurants that might receive dollars, and companies that were exporting their products to the United States, were required to convert their proceeds immediately to the local currency by turning over the dollars to the government. Only a very few companies or official agencies, engaged in what were considered vital importing activities, were permitted to make their own decisions about how dollars could be spent. For everyone except Americans, there was a "dollar shortage."

The expectations that planners and thinkers had held for the postwar economy had proven false in ways that benefited the United States and disadvantaged everyone else. America had geared up for war production more effectively than any other nation (Hitler's Germany never devoted as large a proportion of its Gross National Product to the war as the United States did in 1943 and 1944), and had financed its war effort in large part by printing money. Conventional analysis, remembering the period immediately after World War I and the Great Depression, foresaw a surge of inflation and then severe economic decline with high unemployment because there would not—could not—be sufficient demand to absorb for peaceful uses the product of the expanded industrial plant built for war purposes, or the labor of millions of returning servicemen.

Instead, the work force was heavily employed and the factory space quickly converted to peaceful uses by a burst of consumer demand fueled with previously unspendable savings accumulated during the war. A Europe physically more devastated and emotionally more disabled by the war than had been realized relied upon America for everything from food and fuel supplies to machine tools. The European nations had almost no reserves to use for such purchases; the winners had spent what they possessed in the early years before the United States became a partner, the losers had been expropriated by legal action or force. More than two-thirds of the world's monetary gold was American property, "buried at Fort Knox." The European productive capacities that had survived the war could not generate the exports that might pay for required imports—and even if they could have, the distribution systems nobody ever thinks about in normal times had decayed beyond men's memory of ways to restore them. These were the realities more hidden than explained by abstractions like "the dollar shortage."

To use terms that have only recently come into the headlines, the recovery of the war-damaged nations required that the United States have a "trade surplus" with them—that we export to them what we produced and they needed, even though we could not import enough from them to balance the ledgers. To provide the dollars the Europeans would need to make their purchases, America officially or privately would have to make enough gifts, loans, and investments to cover the gap. Given the great profitability of investment in booming America in the years right after the war—and the many risks (not least political risks) that shadowed investment in Europe during those years—private capital was unwilling to invest anything like the required quantities. The result, after the catastrophic winter of 1946–47 had revealed how small the margins of European survival had become, was the Marshall Plan and official American participation in directing the paths of redevelopment in Europe.

Aid that might be enough to cover the Europeans' deficit in their trade with the United States was not enough to manage their overall problem. Europe also needed—and had no way to pay for—Argentine and Uruguayan beef, Chilean and Congolese copper, Brazilian coffee, Egyptian cotton, Bolivian tin, Malayan rubber, Turkish tobacco, Indian jute; lamb and mutton from the Antipodes, bananas from Central America, oil from the Persian Gulf. Some of these countries could afford to sell on credit; most could not. Dollars to cover the European and Japanese deficits with others, as well as their deficits with the United States, would have to be made available by Americans, through aid or loans or military expenditures outside the United States.

More. Most European trade had been between the nations of Europe themselves, but their economies were not such that straight barter deals between the two countries could reestablish the patterns by which the different countries and climates and stocks of natural resources specialized in what each did best. This trade, severely disrupted even before the war by depression and nationalism, was now sinking in a whirlpool of reduced production and thus reduced uses for the foreign currencies each country might acquire by exporting. The pounds Italy might earn by selling Sicilian oranges to England did not buy the steel Italy needed to rebuild bridges because England had no surplus steel to export—and France would not accept English pounds in payment for French steel. So the Italians would seek to convert their pounds to dollars, which could be used everywhere. The Bank of

England didn't have the dollars; Americans didn't want the pounds. The oranges stayed on the trees, or sold for very low prices near home; British children did without Vitamin C, French steel production stagnated, and the Sicilian economy, already in terrible shape, got even worse.

The catastrophic severity of the dollar shortage was first revealed, in fact, through the failure of the American attempt to revive intra-European trade in 1946 through direct support of the British pound, a "stabilization loan" of almost $4 billion (with another $1 billion from Canada) designed to make it possible for London to resume its prewar functions as the financing center that arranged money flow among the European countries and between Europe and its colonies. The dollars supplied to make a $4.20 pound "convertible" to and from other currencies drained off to other hands in five frantic weeks in 1947, leaving the pound as close to useless in international trade as it had been before the loan.

If Europe were to revive, the scale of American aid, loans, investments and military expenditures abroad would have to be much larger than the amounts needed to close the trade gap. Simply to oil the operation of the money system, to supply credit for seasonal variations in trade flows, to make it possible for the European countries to convert each other's currencies and thus restore their willingness to export to each other would take a great outpouring of American money. The "trade surplus" would have to become a "payments deficit," with an annual increase of American dollars held by foreigners.

Even so, the dollar shortage would continue, because the need was so great. One of the key tasks of the Organization for European Economic Cooperation set up to administer the spending of Marshall Plan aid was the establishment of a stable stock of dollars to provide a European monetary reserve at the base of a European Payments Union which would make possible increasing trade across borders in the smallest continent. The United States kicked in $350 million to get the payments union started.

By the summer of 1949, it was obvious that official aid alone would not be enough to turn the trick. The costs involved in re-starting the economic engines of Europe were too great for Euro-pean production to be competitive on the world markets. Despite high tariffs on imports and quotas designed to prevent luxury im-ports, despite export subsidies designed to boost the profits of manufacturers who directed their attention abroad, despite the growing flow of Marshall Plan aid and the heavy expenditures of the American military establishment abroad, the Europeans con-tinued to lose what reserves they had. Recession in America re-duced U.S. imports by a devastating 5 percent. Trade among the European countries was diminishing, and production was stag-nant. Urged ahead by Truman's Treasury Secretary John Snyder and led by Britain's Sir Stafford Cripps (an austere Socialist who was thought rather to like the idea that he was condemning his countrymen to a life without luxuries), Europe in September 1949 took a step of deliberate impoverishment, drastically reducing the value of its currencies by comparison with the dollar.

The Continent became the paradise for the American tourist-shopper now so wistfully remembered by the middle-aged. De-mand for European goods revived worldwide, when they were available, simply because they had become so much cheaper than American goods. Most important of all, American investors began to find irresistible the bargain prices at which new factories could be built, and existing installations acquired, by American companies with dollars to spend. By 1950, European holdings of gold and dollars, which despite all the aid had dropped by $6 bil-lion in 1946–48, had begun to rise—and the European Payments Union came into existence. By 1953, the flow of private dollars to Europe (plus expenditures by the American military in Europe) had risen to the point where even before official aid moneys were counted in, the European stock of dollars was growing.

We are now in position to triangulate the course of the great armada of getting and spending set on the seas of the postwar world by the leaders of the 1940s:

(1) The United States would continue to generate large food surpluses and would be the predominant source of the "inno-

vative" manufactured goods (electronic equipment, medical apparatus, construction and road-building machinery, communications devices) demanded in the second half of the twentieth century. Its exports would far exceed its imports, despite their high prices, simply because innovative America would forever be producing things other countries couldn't make.

Thus the dollar could safely be "overvalued" as an international money—that is, goods produced elsewhere would be cheap to people with dollars; goods produced in America would be expensive for people who had to buy with other currencies. In cases where there was a danger that foreigners would prefer American goods even at what were for them, in their currencies, extravagant prices, the United States would wink at import controls in violation of international treaties and agreements. Transatlantic freight charges were arranged with the actual connivance of American authorities to make the shipment of goods more expensive in an easterly than in a westerly direction.

(2) The rest of the world would receive American goods to a greater apparent value than the goods exported to America (*apparent* value because in fact American goods were overpriced: thanks to the perceived shortage of dollars, an American hospital X-ray machine would command more champagne—a Chevrolet would buy more coffee—than might have been true prewar). The gap between what the rest of the world had to pay for American exports and what it received from American imports would be made up through a combination of aid to the poor countries detaching themselves from European imperialism (especially food aid), private American loans and investments in the countries that were moving ahead economically, and military expenditures where policy wished to emplace the signs of American power.

(3) When the books were balanced every year, the outflow of dollars for aid, military expenditures, and investments would be greater than the gap between the values of American exports and imports. The American "trade surplus" would become a "payments deficit," supplying an increasing stock of dollars to be used by other nations as backing for their currency and financing for

their trade. "It is essential," a staff report to Eisenhower's Commission on Foreign Economic Policy proclaimed in 1954, ". . . that we maintain a high and *rising* flow of dollars to the rest of the world through our imports of goods and services and through our private and public investment." The trade surplus would keep the dollar overvalued while the payments deficit would help prevent inflation in America by pulling dollars out of the country. The buildup of reserves abroad would create inflationary pressures on the undervalued currencies, but the inflation would be perceived, not inaccurately, as associated with economic growth. In general, as an International Monetary Fund economist puts it, "the dollar as a low-inflation currency would give its stability to the rest of the world."

Charles Kindleberger, an MIT economics professor who spent the early 1950s on Marshall Plan work in Paris, noted shrewdly that this American "payments deficit" was really an artifact of the bookkeeping. What was happening was that the Europeans, punished and terrified by the lack of internationally spendable money right after the war, were happy to accept immediate "liquidity" (a growing stock of dollars in their hands) as payment for long-term assets (the factories and mines and hotels the Americans were buying with those dollars). In effect, America had become the world's banker, with short-term liabilities (dollars sent abroad by the payments deficit, held by foreigners like checking accounts in a bank) matched against long-term assets (loans and investments that would not pay off for some time). And this was a dark cloud off on the horizon toward which the economic armada sailed, because a bank that funds long-term investments with short-term deposits always bears a risk that depositors will one day run to take their money out. In 1950, however, the cloud had a glorious golden lining; nearly $25 billion of monetary gold was ready to back the bank, and pay off the depositors, if a storm struck.

Anyway, it was almost impossible to pay attention to such a cloud in the early 1950s. Looking back on the statistics, we can easily see today that the venture was well and truly en route by

1950, the preconditions of European recovery in place, the first stirrings of reconstruction (buttressed by the start of the Korean War) animating Japan. At the time, the rest of the world seemed to be perpetually on the edge of renewed and bad trouble.

In 1951, renewed arms production for the war in Korea split the seams of the American economy and loosed the monster of inflation—but for the Europeans, the result was to price beyond their reach raw materials needed for their economy, imperiously requisitioned by the United States.

In 1954, the first signals of weakness from an American recession reduced European exports to the point where the American balance of payments threatened to turn positive again, depriving the world of its annual fix of dollars. Some French wag explained that "when America sneezes, Europe catches pneumonia."

In 1957, trade disruptions following the Anglo-French-Israeli attack on Egypt and the blocking of the Suez Canal created an almost unmanageable crisis for the pound and the franc.

As the annual reports of the Council of Economic Advisers inadvertently but very publicly demonstrate, economics is mostly a science of the post hoc. (President Carter, making a speech at Disney World in fall 1978, expressed regret at his inability to visit Fantasyland, "where my economic advisers are getting their advice.") By the mid-1950s, the economists had found their explanation of the relative weakness of the European recovery from the war; and that explanation proved that the dollar shortage was a permanent phenomenon, destined to interfere at regular intervals with income growth in the rest of the world.

The difficulty, the economists said, was structural. As incomes rose elsewhere, the demand abroad for the innovative American goods, the modern luxuries, would grow rapidly. But America imported mostly staples and a handful of raw materials—coffee, sugar, bananas, tin, bauxite, rubber—for which demand grew only slowly with rising income. To use a piece of economist's jargon which happens to be effective shorthand, the world's "income elasticity of demand" for American exports was much greater than the American elasticity of demand for imports. Hence, prosperity itself would rouse again for Europe the economic horrors of the late 1940s.

Worse. What really stimulated American "innovation," that dog in the international manger, was the appearance of foreign merchandise that threatened to take away a share of the U.S. market. American innovation concentrated on "import substitutes," and soon produced both cheaper and better jet engines than the British, silkier rayon than the Italians, faster photographic film than the Germans. "It is difficult to believe," Geoffrey Crowther of *The Economist* of London told a Harvard audience in 1957, "that there can ever have been another case of a country where the demand of the rest of the world for its products was so urgent and its demand for the products of the world so indifferent."

All this, and managerial skills, too—really, America was invulnerable, could follow whatever domestic economic policies it chose. In 1957, the annual report of the Office of European Economic Cooperation still showed the United States with a payments surplus "financed by special means." A report to the Bureau of the Budget on American balance of payments statistics eight years later noted that "not until the middle 1950s was it widely appreciated that the extension by the U.S. Government of foreign grants and loans and the expenditures of U.S. military forces abroad were regular and continuing features of international transactions." Such things had never been before; they were beyond the ken of economic analysis. There would always be a dollar shortage.

For a young economist like Paul Volcker, summoned to his boss's office only a few months after Crowther's speech, that was the received and demonstrable wisdom of his discipline. Almost the only dissenter was the maverick and sometimes emotional Robert Triffin, a Belgian-born, Harvard-doctored eclectic who had worked for the Federal Reserve during the war and for the International Monetary Fund and various American and European Marshall Plan agencies in Paris from 1947 to 1951. Triffin, who had moved on to an endowed professorship at Yale before his fortieth birthday, was considered a man of impressive political acumen as well as brilliance. He had provided the operating solutions for what all the sophisticates found intractable problems in setting up the European Payments Union. But he had failed to identify himself with any school of economists, thus acquiring a reputation as theoretically unformed, and he had a weakness for telling other economists and political leaders what fools they were. And his output consisted mostly of rather garrulous memos to the monetary and political authorities, which he would then assemble into books that were stitched together of their parts rather than argued straight through. His argument was that meeting the world's need for international reserves through American payments deficits and dollar outflows was an unsafe course to eventual shipwreck.

That was what George Champion had sensed in his office at Chase. Volcker reassured him that the dollar was healthy and the gold market was unimportant. "One of the most embarrassing incidents of my life," Paul Volcker says today.

2

There is some question whether the word "glut" has any meaning in economics, which is by its very name the study of scarcity, the "dismal science." Thomas G. Moore, director of the domestic division of the Hoover Institution, said recently and scornfully in a discussion of monetary matters, "Just let the price go down. When it gets low enough, you'll find buyers." But the balancing of supply and demand that is implied by the pricing mechanism assumes production (with its associated costs) and consumption (with the resulting disappearance of what was produced). The cost of producing dollars is virtually nil—a touch on a key at the Federal Reserve will do the trick. And the dollars are never consumed: they circulate, passing from hand to hand. Working off an oversupply of dollars takes a long time—and after a quarter of a century of American payments deficits that left dollars in the hands of foreigners, there is quite a supply to be worked off. Moreover, if the price of the dollar goes down in terms of foreign currencies, it will also go down in terms of the things it buys at home. A declining "price" for a dollar is what we call "inflation"—and it does not stimulate increased demand for the stuff.

There are likely to be unpleasant consequences when two pieces of paper that can be swapped for each other buy very different quantities of real goods and services. The country with the undervalued currency (worth less abroad) can sell its products cheaply in the country with the overvalued currency, creating unemployment for its trading partner and eventually, if the exchange rate persists, tariffs or quota restraints to stop the dumping. The country with the overvalued currency (worth more abroad) can cheaply purchase farms and factories in the country with the undervalued currency, creating not only political resentments but eventual restrictions on who is permitted to buy what.

As the high purchasing power of the dollar in Europe through the years of the shortage demonstrates, a currency can for some time be priced to buy more abroad than it does at home—and during that time, obviously, the currency of the country on the other side of the transactions will purchase less abroad than it does at home. But there was a purpose to that in the 1950s, and even if most people did not comprehend the purpose, the cause— the war—was plain to all. In the absence of some clearly perceived purpose or cause, the political life of nations—their common sense—will act to prevent ludicrous results in the exchange markets.

For common-sense purposes, we can speak of a "glut" when at any given price there are more sellers than buyers; and by that definition, the American dollar in 1978 was in a state of glut. Two years of American trade deficits totalling more than $70 billion (in constant dollars, more than the entire aid program under the Marshall Plan) had left foreigners with much more American money than they wanted to hold. Only by "intervening" in the market—by purchasing for official accounts dollars which the governments themselves didn't want—were the European and Japanese central banks able to maintain significant purchasing power for American dollars outside the United States. By universal consent, the American economy is the strongest in the world. In purchasing power at home, the private incomes of Americans are still by a healthy margin the highest of any group—except maybe the Kuwaitis. But there was a glut of dollars.

In 1978, the world travelers cooing over their bargains were to be found on Fifth Avenue or Rodeo Road, not on the Faubourg St.-Honoreé or Bond Street. Americans abroad found not only that the prices were fearfully high in dollars but that storekeepers and restaurateurs were reluctant to take dollar traveler's checks, often asking whether the customer didn't perhaps have local currency he could use instead and normally giving an exchange rate far below what was printed in the newspapers. And this apparent rip-off of the American tourist was only partly greed: most European and Japanese proprietors had by then had the experience of finding that the market rate dropped between the time when they accepted dollars and the time their bank converted them.

The international rich are acquiring homes in La Jolla, Key Biscayne, and New York, rather than in Portofino and Paris. In mid-1978, Continental-Illinois announced a mutual fund to purchase Midwestern farm land, for the convenience of Germans looking to spend some marks for that purpose; only an uproar in Congress prevented its formation. Japanese television and camera makers, German automobile manufacturers, chemical and pharmaceutical companies are building factories in the United States; in part to get set in this market before an anticipated onslaught of trade restrictions, in part for the same reasons of perceived bargains that lured the American "multinationals" to Europe in the 1950s. A German chain has acquired control of A&P; a French company has bought Korvette's; the English have taken over Howard Johnson's. American Motors has been looking to France for financial help—and, to some extent, for know-how. It doesn't begin to dent the supply of dollars in foreign hands.

The permanent American trade surplus foreseen in the 1950s—the economist's best bet, because America's trade had been steadily in surplus since shortly after the Civil War—became a deficit in 1971 for the first time in almost a century. It will be noted that 1971 was two years before the Arabs imposed monopoly prices on oil.

As of June 1978, according to calculations by Triffin in a study for Boeing Computer Services, dollars held abroad totaled $373 billion, of which something less than $150 billion was in foreign government accounts, the rest out in the private market. That number was actually larger than the measured domestic money supply of the United States; it was clearly much more than needed for reserve purposes or for the financing of international trade. Except for the governments of the nations most closely linked to the United States by political ties (the Common Market countries, Japan, Australia, and perhaps Saudi Arabia), dollar-holders everywhere were scrambling to "diversify," to increase the proportion of their reserves and their bank accounts in currencies other than the dollar. The scramblers included American as well as other multinational corporations, seeking to avoid losses from "excessive" holdings of dollars.

Again, the economists found an explanation, and forecast a grim future. By the 1970s, they said, the patterns of trade had become such that increasing income in America led to imports disproportionately greater than exports. An energy-based society no longer self-sufficient in oil would find oil imports rising more rapidly than Gross National Product. An economy in which most of the population was engaged in the production of services rather than goods would import increasing proportions of the goods it demanded. Cultural changes, reflected in political attitudes, had made America less receptive to innovation, less willing to risk, and thus less likely to generate the new products that had buttressed its trade surplus in previous years.

FROM POWER AND GLORY TO GLUT

In 1975, C. Fred Bergsten, who would become Assistant Secretary of the Treasury for International Affairs in the Carter administration, reported as a matter of fact that "in the United States the income elasticity of demand for imports exceeded the income elasticity of the rest of the world for U.S. exports. . . . The United States could grow only about one-third as fast as the rest of the world if it were to avoid a serious deterioration of its trade balance." So the dollar glut would last forever—or, rather, would last as long as our trading partners were willing to accept our dollars.

All three of the cardinal points on the compass by which we had steered in 1949 have shifted. The trade surplus has become a trade deficit; the dollar is now "undervalued" rather than "overvalued" in international purchasing power. Because of the perceived glut of dollars, the farm machinery now buys fewer Swiss watches, the X-ray apparatus buys less champagne, than it did before. Instead of supplying capital to the outside world to balance the books on our trade surplus, we now absorb capital from the outside world by selling our lands and buildings, keeping interest rates high, collecting returns on our previous loans and investments. Exchange rates are now flexible rather than fixed, and may change by 10 percent in a month, fluctuating around unsteady parities. The justification for our balance of payments deficit is no longer that we are supporting the development of other people's economies but that we are supplying a market they need for their products. The dollar as a high-inflation currency gives its instability to the rest of the world. The only constant from the glory days of the dollar is that the deficit persists.

3

The history of how we got from there to here is the substance of this book, with some concluding thoughts on where we are likely to go next and what we can do about it. But before launching out on the consideration of what must be, from present perspectives, a sad story, it is worth taking a moment to look again from the perspective of the years when the journey began. For except in a handful of countries where truly abominable governments have worked destruction—Burma, Uganda, Guinea, Cambodia, Uruguay, Argentina, Nicaragua and Zaire—the fact is that ordinary people live considerably better today than they did a generation ago; spectacularly better in the European countries and Japan which the system was originally emplaced to assist.

During the 1960s, the real per capita income of the residents of the twenty-two most developed countries rose by 50 percent—an unprecedented gain for a single decade. And much of this improvement in the international standard of living can be credited directly to the expansion of foreign trade, which permits each nation to specialize more efficiently in what it does best. That expansion was made possible by American organization and military dominance, by the stability combined with thrusting confidence of an American society pushing forth in what Henry Luce had called "the American century." Underlying the beneficent exuberance of economic miracles in Europe and political self-determination in the emerging colonies were the monetary arrangements put in place under American leadership during the first five years after the war—and maintained at some American sacrifice in the 1950s and 1960s.

Despite all the changes on the periphery of the monetary system in the 1960s and toward its center in the 1970s, we are still living essentially with the monetary regime established to resurrect the European economies: the American dollar is still predominantly the source of international liquidity and reserves. "Hegemony," as the political scientists call it, remains the operating principle. Robert Triffin demonstrated as early as 1959 that this hegemony could not be permanent, even if America avoided the inflationary binge that is the proximate cause of the dollar's miseries. There was a paradox at the center, he wrote. If America stopped feeding out dollars through a payments deficit, the lack of financing would choke international trade; if it did continue to supply the required liquidity and reserves, America would ultimately create a glut that would destroy the dollar's acceptability as the reserve currency. One could not have "both persistent deficits ... and continued unquestioned confidence." Eventually there would be a run on Kindleberger's bank.

To say that the international monetary system based on the dollar was destroyed by its own success—employing the now fashionable argument with which my master Joseph Schumpeter predicted the decline of capitalism—would be facile and not quite true at the end of a decade when hegemony wasn't that much of a success. What can be said is that institutions were created, jobs were designed to serve them, and attitudes were developed to improve performance on those jobs—and that these institutions, jobs, and attitudes persisted beyond the time when the purposes they served were clear. On the most simpleminded level, and much that happens in the world is in fact determined on that level, the system was, after all, hitting its primary target—to increase world liquidity and reserves.

Economists, central bankers, even government leaders could see and complain that American political and economic leadership was faltering, that the reasons for that dollar outflow had changed, and that the composition of the American deficit was a question of great importance. In 1977–78, the outflow was excessive to the naked eye; the story was on all the front pages and the covers of the news magazines. Even so, through all the storms that afflicted the monetary system in the 1970s, there remained a human instinct to keep the known compass headings rather than to set out on uncharted seas.

The cooperation among national authorities that marked both the growth and the decay of the system has been one of the most encouraging aspects of the postwar world. It was broken occasionally—most notably by the French in the mid-1960s, when General de Gaulle was accumulating gold like an oversized Nibelungen dwarf, though good harvests had reduced Russian gold sales and world liquidity was declining. But at the crisis points everyone pulled together. One of the German old-timers told Scott Pardee, manager of foreign exchange trading for the Federal Reserve Bank of New York, that if there had been in 1930 the kind of joint efforts that were undertaken in the 1960s, "there would never have been a Hitler." It's a comment that acquires a special resonance when one recalls that central banker Hjalmar Schacht was one of the very few carryovers from the Weimar Republic to the Nazi government.

There have been moments since 1958 when Americans were angered by the arrogance of the Germans, the selfishness (or timidity) of the Japanese, the insularity of the Swiss. "They were content to stand back," says Henry H. Fowler of Goldman, Sachs, remembering his days as Lyndon Johnson's Secretary of the Treasury. "They said, '*You* have a deficit. *You* cure it. But don't hurt us in the process.'" Since 1977, Europeans have taken to reading enthusiastic lectures to Americans about their irresponsibility in monetary matters, a *Schadenfreude* proving that central bankers are human, too. But when needed for the short haul over the rocks, the Europeans (and the Japanese) have always been there. "Whenever they think the situation can stand it," says Robert Roosa, who was Kennedy's Under Secretary for Monetary Affairs and has been involved in these matters for twenty years, "they want to be anti-American. But when you get into a really difficult situation, their eagerness to be pro-American is almost pathetic."

Through the deepening crisis of the 1970s, nations continued to adjust their policies—and to make ad hoc revisions to the international monetary system—in ways that balanced without gross hardship the domestic and international obligations of modern governments. And the adjustments served the immediate purpose. Even those most skeptical of the American performance in the years after the oil shock must concede that the acceleration of dollar outflows did keep the less-developed nations afloat—for the time being. But over the long run, as the fate of New York City so vividly demonstrates, you do no man a favor by lending him money he cannot repay.

The argument of this book is that a knowledge of what happened in the international monetary system from 1957 to 1978 is indispensable for an understanding of recent history—but you could gather all the Americans who do have that knowledge into one ballroom, and leave plenty of space for dancing. The international economic problems of the United States, especially those involving the international role of the dollar, are the result of a chain of events, not one sudden decision somewhere. And economic events, unlike political events, are never once-for-all: the past and those perceptions of the past that appear to give guidance for the future will always influence the present. In dealing with monetary matters, of course, we are two steps from the real difficulties: the thermometer doesn't cause the fever, and the fever doesn't cause the disease. But the information itself is excellent, and the peril of ignoring it is great.

Our political institutions, the limited education and mission-centered focus of our bureaucracies, the porosity of our social class structures—all these impede the development of institutional memories in the United States. Our media of information are, probably correctly, belligerently ahistorical, concentrating exclusively on what happened yesterday (in the case of broadcast media, today). We keep trying to fix what happened yesterday. But when the problem presented derives from a long accumulation of short-term fixes, the hunt for another such will eventually be ruinous. As Walter Bagehot wrote more than a hundred years ago, "The characteristic danger of great nations ... which have a long history of continuous creation, is that they may at last fail from not comprehending the great institutions which they have created."

What happened to the dollar is not a logical deduction from theoretical premises; it is a tale of real decisions taken by real people in real places, in the context of events some of which were on the front pages. It is a complicated story, because the details are important and interrelated in significant ways. But the institutions involved are far less mysterious than, say, the organization of a city government. The only mystery—the source of disconcerting emotion—is money itself.

2 / Truth and Money

The money-quality of assets is something imposed by the business habits of people; it is attached in varying degrees to various assets; and the attachment can be and is varied over time in a completely unpredictable manner.

—R. S. Sayers, historian of the
Bank of England (1956)

* * *

Almost throughout the world, gold has been withdrawn from circulation. It no longer passes from hand to hand, and the touch of the metal has been taken away from men's greedy palms. The little household gods, who dwelt in purses and stockings and tin boxes, have been swallowed by a single golden image in each country, which lives underground and is not seen. Gold is out of sight—gone back again into the soil. But when gods are no longer seen in a yellow panoply walking the earth, we begin to rationalise them; and it is not long before there is nothing left.

—John Maynard Keynes (1930)

* * *

In 1979, the economic world marked the four hundredth anniversary of the death of Sir Thomas Gresham, founder of the Royal Exchange in London, who gave his name to what is probably the best-known "law" of economics—"Bad money drives out good." People remember Gresham's Law better than most of the things they are taught in school because it has the feel of a paradox: normally we expect a good product to displace a bad one. Gresham's Law works because existentially money lies on the other side of the ledger. It looks to you like an asset ("I *wish* I had money," sings Tom Rakewell in the Auden-Kallman-Stravinsky opera *The Rake's Progress,* and with those words he summons the

Devil to take his soul). But it starts out, in the blinding flash of creation, as a liability—other people's liability, useful to you as an asset because everybody else acknowledges it.

This will take a little work. Not much (I promise); but some.

1

Except for Pilate's "what is truth?" the question "what is money?" is probably the most variously answered of human queries. Money, like truth, has lots of different functions, exists to a degree only in the eye of the beholder, and comes in a large variety of partial guises. But we do need a definition. For the purposes of these pages, "money" is defined as "a claim on something of value, that will be instantly acceptable to everyone as a payment or in discharge of a debt."

The words "will be" are crucial, for they imply that money not spent now can be spent later—in economist's terms, that money is a "store of value" as well as a "medium of transactions." Gresham's Law applies to situations where two moneys circulate, and one of them is considered superior to the other as a store of value—as a *future* claim. Such situations were the norm when both gold and silver coins were used, and in the United States in the early nineteenth century when banknotes of different banks were in circulation.

When two different moneys will buy the same goods and services today—but one is considered likely to have greater purchasing power tomorrow—people will use promptly (if they can, exclusively) the money that seems likely to lose power as a claim. That's "bad" money; people try to spend it fast, and save the "good" money. In the marketplace, as a medium of current transactions, the "bad" replaces, drives out, the "good." Because we are dealing with expectations, which continually change, the problem of the relative values of two moneys cannot be solved once-and-for-all—no less a calculator than Isaac Newton tried it with gold and silver when he was Master of the Mint, and failed.

The words "acceptable to everyone" imply a custom of almost

mystical strength, a legal requirement—or both. A second implication is geographical division, for it is impossible to imagine a
world so One that from every culture, race and tradition there
would arise a single universally recognized instrument of claim.
Except in places like Liberia (where U.S. dollars circulate), at the
Canadian–U.S. border and in the sections of France, Italy, and
Germany adjacent to Switzerland, "foreign currencies" are not
money. The demand for foreign currencies in any country results
from a desire to make purchases or investments abroad; the supply is created by the desire of foreigners to make purchases or investments in that country, plus whatever stocks of "reserve
assets" may be available.

If business is to be done across international boundaries, there
must be some mechanism of "conversion" by which the money of
one country can be made "acceptable to everyone" in the other.
As soon as the currencies are easily convertible, people who do
business internationally (for whom both currencies are money)
will respond to Gresham's Law, spending what they consider the
weaker and stocking up on the stronger. "Leads and lags," the analysts say, meaning that businessmen whose domestic currency
looks weak will try to convert it and use it for payments as soon as
possible, while businessmen whose currency looks strong will
hold off their conversions and payments as long as they can.
("The Saudis weren't *selling* dollars," says Treasury Under Secretary Anthony Solomon, discussing one of the traumas of 1978.
"They were just using their dollar assets, as they matured, to pay
their bills.")

That sounds very unstable, and as the experience of the latter
1970s has demonstrated, it *is* unstable. But there are mitigating
factors, of which the most important is that people like to earn interest on any stores of value they may have. French farmers have
gold in the garden and American recluses keep greenbacks in
cookie jars, but almost everyone sophisticated enough to take an
interest in foreign exchange will keep his surplus cash in savings
accounts or Treasury paper or bonds—best regarded as *claims to
money* rather than as money itself. And claims to money are not

subject to Gresham's Law, because different interest rates paid on bank deposits and bonds denominated in the two different currencies can make up for expectations that one currency will subsequently lose value by comparison with the other.

When the dollar was overvalued in terms of what it could buy at home, because foreigners wanted to use it as a store of value, American interest rates were lower than those elsewhere; when the dollar became undervalued in the 1970s because the world had lost faith in its future, American interest rates had to be higher than those in the strong-currency countries. Moving to defend the dollar on November 1, 1978, the Carter administration gained more credit abroad for dramatically raising the "discount rate" (the interest the Federal Reserve charges its member banks) than for the elaborate package of external support measures that accompanied the announcement. Presumably, some people who were not willing to hold dollars rather than marks as a store of value when dollar deposits paid two-thirds more than mark deposits (10 percent against 6 percent) might be persuaded to stay put if dollar deposits paid five-sixths more than mark deposits (11 percent against 6 percent).

And in trade matters, remember, we are dealing with two ledgers of double-entry bookkeeping. Every asset must be matched by a liability in two currencies, both "nostro" and "vostro," in the Italian of the Medici which can still be seen on computer printouts in New York and Frankfurt. A "deficit" in the balance of payments cannot mean that unequal values are exchanged across the borders, because a balance is a balance is a balance. Unless some business or bank or government agency is willing and able to supply an American automobile importer with marks in return for his dollars, the importer can't buy the Mercedes.

What happens is that someone with marks (or with other assets that can be used to buy marks) "accommodates" the sale of the real Mercedes for marks by spending marks to acquire a paper asset, a bank deposit or Treasury bill, denominated in dollars. All reports of "deficits" and "surpluses" are monumentally and—as the economist Fritz Machlup once showed—inevitably screwed up by the difficulty of deciding which currency flows are "autonomous" (in accountant's lingo, "above the line," arising from transactions the participants would wish to make under any circumstances) and which are "accommodating" (balancing items, "below the line"). The task is not made easier by the fact that often in the modern world the real purchase may be an "accommodation" for the execution of a foreign-aid program or the repayment of an old loan.

All this theorizing presupposes a complicated concatenation of markets for "foreign exchange"—and also some kind of unifying supermoney in which the currencies of different countries can be measured, through which they are traded. Though concepts like balance of trade and balance of payments imply only two moneys (ours and that of the rest of the world), there are at least ten and maybe as many as twenty significant national currencies at large in the jungles of international trade. And countries normally earn with their exports foreign money which is not automatically useful to them in purchasing their imports.

The path by which the immediate postwar Sicilian oranges earned steel for north Italian bridges may well have gone through London (which bought the oranges and exported woolens) to Stockholm (which bought the woolens and exported newsprint) to Paris (which bought the newsprint and exported the steel to Italy). In the course of these transactions, the Italians would have acquired pounds; the British, kroner; the Swedes, francs; and the French, lire—and each may have had only a limited need for such foreign money. Yet the four-way trade balanced out. Clearly, there has to be some *place* where a netting process can be carried through, and some "vehicle" currency (supermoney, "reserve asset") in which all the relationships can be expressed.

2

Which brings us to gold and, in some cultures, silver. (British "sterling" was originally, as the name implies, a silver standard, set in the reign of Queen Anne. "Gold," Newton's successor at the Mint, John Conduitt, wrote in 1720, "is only looked on as a commodity, and so should rise or fall as occasion requires. An ounce of fine silver is, and always has been and ought to be the standing and invariable measure between nation and nation." Britain switched to a "gold standard" in 1816, but the word survived.) Scarce and immensely durable, yet easily refined and worked, gold has been through recorded history an acceptable physical expression of the present and future claims that constitute money. As Karl Marx put it with his special gift for certainty and his ineluctable journalistic shallowness in economic matters, "Money is by nature gold and silver." Until well into the nineteenth century, silver was more widely used, simply because there was more of it; among the demonstrations of Gresham's Law was the tendency of the gold coins to vanish into hoards while the silver coins circulated merrily.

But, as always, Marx had a point: metallic money was in principle a claim no one had created, a generalized liability of the society (or international community) as a whole rather than of a government or a bank. Paper money came into circulation as a surrogate (not a substitute) for precious metals, as a claim initially on gold or silver. People used paper in their transactions because they were confident that if necessary they could get "specie" at the bank or from the government on presentation of the paper. Until the administration of Lyndon Johnson, the American dollar bill carried the legend, "Payable in silver to the bearer on demand."

Exchange rates among currencies were necessarily "fixed" by the relationship of the individual nations' commitments to buy and mint metals at a specific price. The act of "devaluation" was a reduction in the precious metals content of a coin of a given value, an increase of the price in its own currency at which the issuing government would buy gold or silver. Thus, a British pound in 1913 and 1930 would buy about .23 troy ounce of gold. One notes in passing that by the late 1970s the British pound bought less than .01 troy ounce of gold.

To a far greater extent than people now realize, the monetary circulation of Europe in the half-century before World War I consisted of metal coins, minted and certified as to gold or silver content by the various governments. (Triffin estimates the proportion at 70 percent to 80 percent in 1885–1913.) Such coins could and did circulate in different countries (and it should be noted that in nineteenth-century Europe there were no passports or travel restrictions, no trade quotas and relatively low tariffs). At the Paris Monetary Conference of 1867, Samuel Ruggles, speaking for Secretary of State William H. Seward, proposed unification of the world's coinage—identical gold content for the British sovereign, the U.S. half-eagle and the new 25-franc coin the French had agreed to mint at American urging—to help expand world trade. He carried the Conference by 17–2, but one of the two negative votes was British (the other was Swedish), which killed the scheme.

Because payments for imports could be made in gold across international boundaries, a negative "balance of payments" might mean a country's loss of gold. Because paper money was a surrogate for gold, central bankers and private bankers observing a reduction in their "reserve assets" might reduce the volume of lending by which they created the money that wasn't gold. The result was to raise interest rates (drawing gold back—Bagehot said that "seven per cent will draw gold from the moon"), and to restrict domestic demand for *all* goods and services, thereby reducing demand for imports, too.

Meanwhile, in the country receiving the inflow of gold, lending and money supply would expand, interest rates would go down, and demand for all goods and services (including imports) would rise. The balances would right themselves; the system was, in theory, self-equilibrating. But from the point of view of the debtor countries that had to reduce their domestic production and income in order to stop the loss of gold, the system required what everyone calls "a harsh discipline."

And it was not inherently stable. New mines might open up, increasing money supplies; in times of trouble, coins might disappear into mattresses, reducing money supplies; some gold wound up in jewelry or industrial use rather than in money. Gold could be hoarded by governments as well as private citizens—especially by the French government: one of the threads of modern European history is the French love affair with gold. What made the system work reasonably well in the nineteenth century, despite the recurrent financial panics and a steady deflation that kept people feeling poor as they got richer, was systematic manipulation of interest rates by the Bank of England and the worldwide dominance of the London money market.

It is now much more visible than it was before the American 1960s and 1970s that the price of maintaining British currency at the center of world trade was a consistently if slightly overvalued pound. Imported food was cheap; British exports were expensive, but because Britain had led the way in the industrial revolution, many British products were simply unavailable from other countries. (There was also, of course, a considerable captive market in the colonies; it will be remembered that the American Revolution was stimulated in large part by the colonists' resistance to absorption in an all-British commercial system.) Interest rates were normally lower in London than elsewhere, encouraging the outflow of capital—and permitting the Bank to suction back gold when needed by flash increases of interest rates that briefly reversed the ratios.

Because the pound was not just as good as but slightly better than gold, Britain was able to acquire the worldwide investments—from Argentine railroads and American cattle ranches to Indian jute factories and Polynesian copra plantations—that later had to be sold off to finance the wars against Germany. The situation was not unlike that of the United States in the 1950s. British colonies, commonwealths, associated countries (and their businessmen) needed reserves for their own currencies (and their trade), as the Europeans and Japanese did after World War II. They were happy to hold these reserves in pounds rather than gold (a willingness much reinforced by the attitudes of imperial headquarters in London) because pounds paid interest and gold did not, and pounds could always be changed for gold. In essence, they paid for this "liquidity" through the sale of real assets, farms and factories and railroads.

The proprietors of the pound in the years before World War I, in other words, ran the same sort of bank Kindleberger discerned in America in the years after World War II—they had a collection of short-term liabilities, pounds held abroad, backed in essence by long-term assets in the form of real productive facilities, like today's American investments abroad. In this, as in all other comparisons between the Britain that was and the America that is, there are a whole bunch of warnings; for the British situation eventually collapsed into a true bankruptcy when the long-term assets were sold off for national purposes while the short-term liabilities remained undiminished.

3

What wrecked the gold-exchange system as it had operated in the years before World War I was the vastly increased issuance of public debt (much of it currency) to pay the costs of fighting. At war's end, it was blatantly obvious that there wasn't enough gold to cover the paper money in circulation; the pound, which had been pegged at $4.86 (roughly 85 shillings per ounce of fine gold) before the war, hit bottom at $3.40 (122 shillings per ounce of gold) in February 1920. The Bank of England at first attempted to right the monetary balance between the stronger American economy and that of Europe by encouraging gold flows to the United States, in the hopes that the resulting inflation in America would lead to a general devaluation of currencies, allowing the system to resume again at a higher level. But the Federal Reserve System was having none of that, and through its operations in the American banking system converted a 15 percent rise in the nation's monetary gold stock to a 10 percent *decline* in the nation's money as conventionally measured, provoking a rapid deflation and the deep, if brief, depression of 1921.

A year later, the British gave up on forcing American inflation and began a long, deflationary march back to the restoration of the prewar gold value of the pound. The first step was a convocation of an international monetary conference in 1922 in Genoa, where it was agreed that everyone should "conserve" gold—i.e., supplement the limited stock of monetary gold by including foreign currencies (especially pounds and dollars) in their reserves.

Currencies in the early 1920s were not "convertible" in the prewar sense—among the major trading nations, only the United States maintained its obligation to buy and sell gold, and there was no "vehicle" through which pounds and francs could be exchanged for each other at a set price. (It would never have occurred to anyone in the first thirty years of this century that a currency could be made "inconvertible" by law, with residents of the country that issued the currency prohibited from selling it to foreigners or purchasing foreign currencies or gold for themselves. The power of the state simply did not extend that far until Hitler, Stalin, and Roosevelt improved the machinery.) For the first half-dozen years after the war, currencies fluctuated on the market with relation to each other: a pound might be worth 85 francs today and 125 francs in six months. Because the dollar was the only fully convertible currency with a gold price, the League of Nations used it as the measuring rod for all international statistics, even though the United States was not a member.

Ultimately, with the continuous agreement between Montagu Norman of the Bank of England and Benjamin Strong at the Federal Reserve Bank of New York (far more powerful in those days than the Federal Reserve Board in Washington)—and with the consent of Winston Churchill as Chancellor of the Exchequer—the pound was pegged at its prewar price, a value that restored the "gold standard" at a price in dollars of $20.67 an ounce.

Britain paid heavily in unemployment, taxes, and unjust income distribution, as John Maynard Keynes angrily argued, for the exchange value of the pound. By revaluing the pound upward, a nation with already high unemployment made its exports more expensive (thereby reducing jobs in the export-oriented industries) and made its imports cheaper (thereby reducing jobs in industries where some of the competition came from imports). But there is a sense—very important these days, because it is in the minds of the leaders of the German Bundesbank, who feel they run similar risks to help the dollar—in which one can say that the United States bore the burden. For the low-interest-rate, easy-money climate of 1927, which many economists blame for the speculative frenzy and collapse of 1929, was dictated by Strong's perception of what was then needed to keep the pound strong, to keep gold from flowing from the sterling bloc to the dollar market, not by any analysis of what the American economy might require.*

Meanwhile, gold outflows to pay the Versailles reparations bill and industrial exhaustion following the war had given the Weimar Republic a choice between uncontrolled paper money and uncontrolled unemployment. The Germans ran the printing press flat out; hyperinflation destroyed the currency and the middle class together ("having been robbed," Thomas Mann noted in the classic comment on inflation, "the Germans became a nation of robbers"). In France, the government budget had been in heavy and continuous deficit since the war, all excused by the proposition that "the Germans will pay." As Schacht rebuilt the mark— aided by U.S. loans and a restructuring of German reparations payments under the Dawes Plan—the French franc came under attack, losing 60 percent of its exchange value between May 1925 and July 1926. But the internal purchasing power of the franc did not fall in proportion (Keynes speculated that it was because French peasants deprived of gold were hoarding banknotes), and when Poincaré, as Premier, deflated and stabilized the currency,

---

*This was, at any rate, the European perception, reinforced by the fact that the Fed moved to ease American monetary policy immediately after an unofficial conference of Strong, Norman of England, Schacht of Germany and Rist of France at the Long Island home of Treasury Secretary Ogden Mills. Kindleberger, however, argues persuasively that the decision was in response to the domestic recession brought on by Henry Ford's long closing of his factories to make the shift from the Model T to the Model A.

he left it undervalued in terms of the pounds and dollars it would buy in the foreign exchange markets.

The result was a surge of French exports, the heyday of tourism (Scott Fitzgerald et al.), and the accumulation of considerable foreign exchange balances at the Bank of France. The British used the leverage of their continuing claims on France from World War I loans to block, briefly, the conversion of these balances to gold; but from 1928 on, the French government began to drain gold from the rest of the world.

The growth of French monetary reserves reduced that nation's eagerness for German blood-money, and in early 1929 a League of Nations committee chaired by the American banker Owen D. Young (serving as a private citizen without any authorization from his government: those were the days) reached agreement on scaling down by 75 percent the surviving total of German reparations. The Young Plan was an early victim of the oncoming Depression, but it left a significant residue: a Bank for International Settlements in Basle, as a place where the European central bankers could sort out the cash and credit components of the German payments. We shall be spending time in Basle later in these pages. For the time being, let it be noted that the last of these Young Bonds will pay off in the early 1980s at the rate of about $5 (not, as usual in these foreign issues, 5¢) for every dollar originally loaned. Germany has prospered.

4

In 1929, the devastation of values in the American stock market put in doubt the asset structures of all financial institutions. In 1930, the Bank of France speeded up its switch from pound and dollar holdings to gold, preventing interest-rate declines in London and New York in a period of declining employment, production, and investment. Stupidly seeking to save jobs by reducing imports, the United States in 1930 did the economic world the great disservice of the Smoot-Hawley tariffs. The inability of foreigners to gain dollars by exporting to America of course crippled their ability to buy American exports. "The United States," Keynes commented, ". . . set the rest of us the problem of finding some way to do without her wheat, her cotton and her motor-cars."

The German economy, which was the world's most fragile (and still burdened by reparations payments from the war), had boomed ahead in the 1920s on the strength of a risky credit expansion based in large part on short-term foreign loans. As Germany and Austria fell into depression, it became clear that those loans were not going to be repaid on schedule, a grim expectation verified publicly in May 1931 by the bankruptcy of Creditanstalt, the largest Austrian bank.

Moving late and clumsily—and without consulting the French, who reacted initially with fury—President Hoover proposed a moratorium on intergovernmental debt payments, reparations from Germany to the European allies, and war-debt obligations from France to Britain and both to America. ("The President of the United States," Keynes wrote acidly, "turned in his sleep.") But most of the German debts were private. Confronted with the choice between an immense new loan to Germany or German exchange controls that would in effect make the mark inconvertible, the allies preferred to see the mark drop out of the international monetary system.

A flight from all paper money began. For a wonder, the French saw the danger, stopped converting official sterling balances to gold, and offered loans to the Bank of England. The Netherlands central bank, which had the highest proportion of its reserves in British pounds rather than gold, also stood fast. J.P. Morgan Co., having gained from Ramsay MacDonald's government a pledge to balance the domestic budget (which meant cutting unemployment benefits at a time of monstrous unemployment), raised $400 million to defend the pound. Interest rates were held high in England despite the Depression in a futile effort to persuade private creditors to hold paper rather than gold. The British government's policy, Keynes wrote savagely, "is to reduce the standard of life of as many people as are within their reach." Having kept unemployment at an average level of 10 percent of the workforce throughout the 1920s to preserve an overvalued pound, Britain was forced to confess failure. On September 20, 1931, the pound was cut loose from gold, and promptly devalued in the markets. Gresham's Law, of course, guaranteed that British gold coins would immediately become a medium of investment rather than a circulating money.

Now the attack moved to the dollar, and the European central banks that had lost heavily on the depreciation of the pound protected themselves by converting their dollar holdings to gold. The Federal Reserve twice raised its discount rate by 1 percent (something that was not to happen again until 1978), hoping to keep gold in America. No way: in three months, the Federal Reserve lost 10 percent of the gold cover for American currency. Britain abandoned a century-old tradition of free trade, adopted the Import Duties Act of 1932, and established, at a meeting in Ottawa, a system of imperial preferences that worked to keep American manufactured goods off the market in the commonwealth countries, American food products and raw materials out of England.

The United States refused to extend the moratorium on debt payments, partly because President Hoover felt that the "damn debts" (as Secretary of State Henry Stimson called them) were a moral as well as a legal obligation of the wartime allies, partly because Treasury Under Secretary Ogden Mills was counting on foreign debt repayments to balance the domestic budget. Relations between the United States and the British Commonwealth were poisoned for the better part of a decade by American rage at British actions that appeared to cost American jobs and British fury at "Uncle Shylock," who demanded his pound of flesh in the midst of worldwide disaster. Following one last painful payment by Britain (but not by France) in December 1932, the European debtors (saving only "gallant little Finland") necessarily defaulted; efforts to reduce the Smoot-Hawley tariffs were derailed by demands that the British first dismantle imperial preferences.

Franklin Roosevelt came to office pledged to expanded foreign trade, a balanced budget, and a sound dollar. Among his first discoveries was that the banking system could not be restored to health without stanching the gold drain, and in April 1933 the United States not only stopped conversions of dollars to gold but forbade American citizens to use *or hold* gold coins or bars.

Secretary of State Cordell Hull went off to London for an International Monetary and Economic Conference that would restore fixed relative values for the world's great currencies and start the movement toward free trade that Hull single-mindedly considered the path to peace and prosperity for the world. (He put his faith, Dean Acheson recalled, in what he called, thanks to an unfortunate speech impediment, "Wecipwocal twade agweement pwogwams to weduce tawiffs.") The British were prepared to stabilize at $4 a pound, a 17.7 percent devaluation from the 1931 standard, and Hull's group agreed. But Roosevelt—under pressure from adviser Raymond Moley—had opted for economic nationalism, a corporate state, and domestic inflation through unbalanced budgets to raise the price of commodities and bail the farmers and miners and homeowners out of their debt burdens. Without informing Hull that he intended to do so, Roosevelt pronounced the futility of the London conference.

That fall Roosevelt made a fireside chat explaining the decline of American exports in terms the public could understand; it was very nearly word for word what Richard Nixon told the next generation of Americans thirty-eight years later (and Treasury Secretary W. Michael Blumenthal suggested in an unfortunate Paris press conference in 1977). Our exports were down, he claimed, "Not because our own prices, in terms of dollars, had risen, nor because our products were of inferior quality, not because we did not have sufficient products to export. But because, in terms of foreign currencies, our products had become so much more expensive, we were not able to maintain our fair share of the world's trade. It was, therefore, necessary to take measures which would result in bringing the dollar back to the position where a fair amount of foreign currency could again buy our products."

American intervention in the exchange markets drove the pound as high as $5.50, despite British efforts to hold it down. Roosevelt also bought gold through the Reconstruction Finance Corp., following a crazy theory of Cornell agricultural economist George Warren that the price of grain and the price of gold were always directly correlated. This was done by means of daily early-morning telephone calls from the President's bedroom to the New York Fed, setting the price at which the R.F.C. would buy on this particular day. It was a lark to Roosevelt, but not to others, in the United States or abroad. The franc, still pegged to gold, became the world's most overvalued currency; the glory days of expatriation to Paris ended, and the Depression came to France.

On February 1, 1934, in a truly savage act of permanent devaluation, Roosevelt reestablished a gold value for the U.S. dollar, and set a price of $35 an ounce, 69 percent above its level a year before. As the government had enforced the return of all gold coins and bullion to the Treasury, virtually all the profits from the price increase adhered to the United States Government. The total ran $2,805,512,060.87, which Congress sterilized down to the eighty-seven cents, in an Exchange Stabilization Fund that would earn no interest and would be administered by the National Advisory Council on International Monetary and Financial Problems, chaired by the Secretary of the Treasury. They were empowered to sell these windfall dollars internationally to make sure the dollar did not become overvalued by comparison with foreign currencies, but no sales were necessary. At $35 an ounce, the purchasing power of foreign gold in the American economy was enormous; the United States maintained a substantial surplus of merchandise exports over imports, and the gold piled up in the vaults.

The French hung on for thirty months, reducing wages, production, and consumption in the effort to sustain the gold value of the franc. Britain and the United States began to recover (the years immediately following the abandonment of gold, in fact, saw the greatest expansion of British industrial growth since the nineteenth century). Germany, working under Schacht's panoply of exchange controls and import restrictions, with bilateral barter deals for most of its trade, created a prosperity that gave the Hitler regime great prestige in Eastern Europe and Italy. Eventually, in fall 1936, Léon Blum's Popular Front government devalued the franc; and the United States, Britain and France entered into a tripartite monetary agreement which put a stop to official devaluations and provided that the central banks of the three countries would to some extent hold each other's currencies and try to minimize gold flows.

This worked only fair: the American recession of 1937 reduced U.S. imports and provoked declines in the value of the pound and franc which the central banks were unwilling and perhaps unable to halt completely. But now political considerations were uppermost. Roosevelt's recognition that Britain and France had to rearm against Hitler overcame his and Treasury Secretary Morgenthau's continuing fear that by devaluing their currencies the British and French would gain competitive trade advantages against the United States; and Britain, conscious that its security against Germany could be assured only by American help, acted to retard the decline of the pound—and even to reduce imperial preferences—in what Neville Chamberlain considered an economic appeasement of America to be conducted in tandem with the political appeasement of Germany. "The reason why I have been prepared . . . to go a long way to get this treaty," he wrote a friend, "is precisely because I reckoned it would help to educate American opinion to act more and more with us, and because I felt sure it would frighten the totalitarians." Stimulated by government budget deficits and a resurgent armaments industry, all the world's economies began to reflate behind the barriers of tariffs and managed exchanges.

5

The past at any time is what the present says it was. As American academics have come to believe that their fellow citizens are ill-motivated toward the rest of the world because of their infatuation with a criminal capitalist ideology—and as international economic relations have deteriorated since 1971—revisionism has reached out to find good in the nationalist monetary mess of the 1930s. Sociologist Fred Block of the University of Pennsylvania, for example, has lamented the passage of the 1930s systems he calls "national capitalism" (history has accidentally deprived him of the phrase "national socialism," which is what he really means: his "national capitalism . . . would have required a progressive narrowing of the private ownership of the means of production"). Germany's "domestic program," Block writes rather lyrically, "was more far-reaching and more successful than those pursued elsewhere; between 1933 and 1938, six to seven million unemployed German workers went back to work . . ."

No doubt an autarkic economy had worked well for Germany in the Hitler years. But there is some reason to believe that it was coming unstuck toward the end of the decade, and that Hitler needed his war for economic reasons. And for Britain, almost anything would have been better than the 1920s. But at the end of the 1930s, per capita income in the United States, France and Benelux was still below what it had been at the end of the 1920s. As with Soviet economic performance, which was always measured from the depths of War Communism in 1921 rather than from 1913, the autarkic economic systems of the 1930s seem successful only if it is believed that without them the world economy would have remained leaden at the bottom of the business cycle.

Every what-if argument is irrefutable, but some are more unlikely than others. By 1932, the governments of the world had done their worst. A cooperative resolution of the London Conference in 1933, symbolized by a return to the use of foreign moneys as well as gold in central bank reserves and confirmed by the reduction of tariffs and imperial preferences, would surely have produced results as good as those actually achieved by nationalism—and might even, as Cordell Hull believed, have led the world away from war. At the Bretton Woods Conference in 1944, Arthur de Souza Costa of Brazil expressed the prevailing view of the period just past: a "drama of all sorts of international blocked currencies, of economic isolationism, of competition instead of cooperation among central banks, and of general unemployment. The civilized world must not permit a repetition of this tragic situation."

Looking toward the postwar world, the United States was not prepared to see the reconstitution of the economic jungle of the 1930s. Hull insisted in summer 1941 that the lend-lease contracts between America and Britain provide for a guarantee of fewer trade restrictions when peace returned. Keynes, serving as adviser to the British Treasury, rebelled against what seemed to him an unwarranted and dangerous nostalgia for the gold standard, but on his return to England he reconsidered and began working on a plan for a new monetary regime that would permit both the benefits of the nationally managed economy and the values of expanded international trade. The beggar-thy-neighbor tariffs and competitive devaluations of the 1930s had not, after all, contributed much to the welfare of peoples. Instead of viewing domestic difficulties as a reflection of international economic warfare, one could regard the international problem as a product of incompetent domestic policy. "If active employment and ample purchasing power can be sustained in the major centres of world trade," Keynes wrote in his final prospectus for an International Clearing Union in 1943, "the problem of surpluses and unwanted exports will largely disappear."

What Keynes proposed was in essence a world central bank that would generate a reserve asset all countries could use in support of the international value of their own currencies. All nations would agree to make their currencies convertible to this asset (and thus, through this asset, to each other), to pay for goods and services in international trade. Exchange rates would be pegged, and governments would pledge themselves to intervene in the markets, buying or selling their own currency from or to foreigners, to keep them pegged. Rates could be changed only if experience demonstrated that they were wrong—that is, that they produced a continuing, "fundamental" imbalance of trade.

Because the central bank would generate deposits in the course of making loans—and all nations would agree in advance to accept payment in the form of these deposits—market intervention would not mean the destabilizing gold flows that had forced nations with a trade deficit to raise their interest rates and depress their domestic economies. Keynes gave these bank-generated deposits the name "bancor," which proved unfortunate, because it sounded to monolingual Americans like something from a Monopoly game. In the late 1960s, when international agreement created new Special Drawing Rights not unlike bancor, publicists called them "paper gold." But nobody pointed out Keynes's elegant little French pun that gave the deposits of his Clearing Union the name "gold of the bank."

One aspect of Keynes's worldwide central bank was different from anything anyone had ever proposed before. The great problem of the early 1930s had not been the country that tried to import more than it could afford because its own economy was unable to meet its people's needs or desires. The problem had been the country with unemployed workers and unused productive capacity seeking to export more than its customers could pay for as a way to resolve a domestic crisis. The country that piled up gold or foreign exchange through keeping its currency undervalued (France in the 1920s, the United States in the 1930s) was for Britain the true rogue elephant of the international jungle. Thus Keynes's central bank would charge interest not only to the borrowers drawing bancor to pay for a deficit in their trade, but also to lenders accumulating credits in bancor. There would be a "symmetry" of pressures that would push both on debtors to adjust by restraining inflation and on creditors to increase domestic demand even at the price of inflation. A generation before Jimmy Carter went to London for an economic summit to persuade the Europeans that their willingness to reflate was what the world economy needed, Keynes was trying to set up a *system* that would equilibrate the forces available for repairing a trade imbalance.

None of this pleased the American Treasury, which could see

only that Keynes was planning to bail Britain out of a postwar economic prison at no cost to the English. The limits on the generation of bancor were too wide—in Keynes's plan, more than $24 billion worth could have been created, the equivalent of more than $100 billion today. The currency that would be drawn, obviously, was dollars; the Federal Reserve would lose all control over the generation of U.S. money, at precisely the immediate postwar period when inflationary pressures would be greatest even without this foreign privilege of printing "bank gold" Americans would have to accept. Adding insult to injury, the United States would then have to pay interest on its contribution to the restoration of the world's economies. Besides, what would happen to *real* gold, of which the United States, by 1943, had so satisfyingly large a collection?

The American negotiator was Harry Dexter White, Assistant Secretary of the Treasury, an opinionated, rude, brilliant economist trained at Harvard (where he wrote a dissertation on French monetary policy), possibly a Communist (memoranda in his handwriting were among Whittaker Chambers's Pumpkin Papers) and certainly a fellow traveler—which did not, considering Marx's monetary beliefs, inhibit his faith in real gold. It was a matter of great emotional satisfaction to him to win arguments against the languidly aristocratic Keynes, symbol of the British Empire, probably the world's greatest living economist (*probably:* Irving Fisher was still alive, though very old; and Schumpeter was teaching at Harvard). And he argued with the backing of what was by some orders of magnitude the world's most powerful and invulnerable economy.

White's internal Treasury memoranda on postwar planning had originally proposed an ambitious world bank modeled on the American Reconstruction Finance Corporation, to finance state-sponsored foreign enterprise in the postwar years. By the time he came to negotiate with Keynes, however, he was suggesting a much more modest plan. This was an International Monetary Fund to which all nations would make a contribution, from which countries in deficit on their foreign trade could draw loans to tide them over an adjustment process that would restore balance. As in Keynes's plan, exchange rates would be pegged, and governments would pledge themselves to maintain the pegs unless their trade deficits proved intractable. The total resources available to the Fund, however, would be only $5 billion, contributed by all the United Nations according to "quotas" that expressed their economic importance to world trade. Some part of that contribution would be in gold, the rest in the domestic currency of the member nation.

The new Fund would not be able to create reserve assets. All it could do was assign to a member, up to a limit set by the exchange value of that member's own contribution, the foreign currency it needed for its current payments. A nation whose currency was drawn by foreigners from the Fund would gain an additional quota for its own future use up to the value of the drawing. Once other nations had taken all of a nation's initial contribution, its "quota," the Fund would no longer be able to supply that currency, and trade involving the nation that printed that currency would fall back upon bilateral loans as in the past.

By spring 1943 the parameters of a deal between the British and American Treasuries were emerging, and working papers were cleared through Parliament and the Congressional committees concerned with banking and monetary matters. That fall delegates from nineteen countries began meeting in Washington as a committee of Technical Experts to hammer out agreements. They signed a document in April 1944, and in May the U.S. State Department issued an invitation to more than forty governments for a meeting to be held in July at a resort hotel in Bretton Woods, New Hampshire, which had been closed for the war but would be reactivated for the purpose. Seven hundred thirty people attended, grievously overloading the facilities. The resulting "Bretton Woods" system of international finance controlled the development of the world's monetary arrangements from the end of the war until 1971.

As the United States and Britain were to put up almost half the resources of the Fund (after the Russians pulled out, the Anglo-

American contribution became more than half), the deal between Keynes and White controlled the conference. White had won most of the arguments. There would be no bank empowered to create bancor, no deficit country could draw from the Fund beyond the exchange-rate equivalent of the quota it had deposited, and a quarter of that quota would have to be paid in gold. No surplus country's currency could be drawn from the fund beyond its contributed quota.

The total of all quotas in the Fund would be about $8.8 billion, a figure arrived at not by any estimate of the future reserve needs of the international currency system but by Roosevelt's political assessment that Congress would not stand still for an American contribution greater than 30 percent and would balk at actually appropriating money for the Fund. But there were more than $2.7 billion of profits from the gold revaluation of 1934 still being held in the Exchange Stabilization Fund without a line on any domestic budget Congress had to pass.

Several concessions were made to Keynes's concerns, however. The restriction of the International Monetary Fund to the quota principle meant that it could not possibly be used to help finance the recovery of the war-torn economies (which could have been done with Keynes's bancor); thus, the conferees agreed to set up an entirely separate institution, the International Bank for Reconstruction and Development (colloquially, always, ever since, the World Bank), which could make long-term loans.

The likelihood that few nations would be able to sustain free convertibility of their currencies to dollars soon after the war was recognized by an escape hatch in the treaty—Article XIV—which permitted nations to join the Fund while maintaining exchange restrictions, until their economies were in shape to permit full obeisance to the IMF rules. European countries did not, in fact, accept the full rigors of current convertibility until 1961; the Japanese did not leave the shelter of Article XIV until 1964; most developing nations are still under it.

Finally, while the conference eliminated the Keynesian prescription for "negative interest" to be paid by countries accumulating surpluses, the treaty did recognize somewhat ambiguously that surplus as well as deficit countries had obligations to "adjust" domestic policies that might be creating unbalanced trade flows. To bring pressure on a country whose currency was so heavily demanded that its quota was nearing exhaustion, the IMF was empowered to declare a currency "scarce," at which point members would be permitted to impose exchange restrictions and tariffs discriminating against that country, its money, and its trade.

That this was a real concession by the United States is somewhat starkly demonstrated by the requirement, in the Bretton Woods Agreement Act which established American participation, that the United States-appointed representative on the IMF board *must* vote against any declaration of scarcity unless specifically instructed otherwise by the National Advisory Council. "Countries may get into a position where there is a scarcity of foreign currency," Harry White told a Senate committee, ". . . due to their own extravagant policies. . . . We could accept . . . no . . . assumption that if dollars became scarce in the Fund, that the fault was necessarily ours." Nevertheless, the United States agreed that such a report could be published with only a majority vote (weighted by quotas), though the declaration that a deficit country had misbehaved would require a two-thirds vote. And the United States joined in rejecting a Russian demand that no statement about any country's policies be published without that country's consent.

On Keynes's basic concern, that the international monetary system must not force a country to deflate its currency and impose reduced income and employment on its people to remedy a trade deficit, he was a clear winner. Exchange rates were pegged, but the peg was set in beaverboard rather than in concrete or gold, and could be moved at will on a showing of necessity. (A country *did* have to inform and "consult" IMF before devaluing, and the French spent part of the 1950s in the doghouse, denied the right to use their quota, for a failure to consult.) And the "scarce currency" clause did preserve a fig leaf's worth of concealment of the all but inescapable fact that the obligations of deficit and surplus countries are *not* symmetrical. Borrowers who want to borrow more have bargaining power only when their debts are so large that a repudiation will shake the system; lenders who want to lend more are always welcome.

Among the dissenters from the Keynes-White deal was the Federal Reserve Bank of New York, which thought the Fund idea visionary and unworkable; the President of the New York Fed was among the few invitees who refused to attend the Conference. And when the Bretton Woods treaties came before the Congress, they were opposed by the American Bankers Association as a giveaway to foreigners.

6

There was a good deal of sentiment at Bretton Woods that currency conversions should be accomplished on a government-to-government basis. Treasury Secretary Morgenthau proclaimed an ambition to "drive . . . the usurious moneylenders from the temple of international finance," and the delegates voted to ask the European central bankers to dissolve their Bank for International Settlements. But if trade was to be in the hands of private importers and exporters, a private market in currencies was all but inevitable. And for such a market to work, there had to be a "spread," a band of permissible fluctuation around the fixed exchange rate, within which the banks and currency brokers could work.

The Articles approved two mechanisms for conversion. Under one of them, a country could promise to hold its currency to a certain value in gold, buying or selling at the fixed price per ounce in its own currency, with the market open to all foreign official customers. Maintaining this sort of "convertibility" permitted a nation's monetary authorities to be entirely passive, taking action only when the monetary authorities of other countries offered or demanded gold. Under the other mechanism, a country would guarantee to supply its own currency for foreign currencies, or purchase foreign currencies with its currency, at a price within 1 percent of an established exchange rate. But a peg that held all the exchange rates for all currencies with stable reference to all other currencies would involve something like 5,000 separate ratios, several of which might be affected by a single transaction. Given the relatively limited trade between Italy and the Netherlands, for example, a Dutch importer of Fiats who wished to buy lire with guilders might set off a whole chain of needless reverberations in the exchange rates of both the guilder and the lira with all other currencies. We are back to the problem at the beginning of the chapter: the need for a supermoney—a single reference point, a "vehicle"—permitting the Dutch and Italian authorities to stabilize their currencies in ratio to a single standard.

The standard under the original Articles of the IMF was gold. But among IMF members (the Swiss have never joined) only the United States had opted to establish convertibility through the gold route, pledging to buy gold from or sell gold to any government at a price within ¼ of 1 percent of $35 per ounce. For convenience, the IMF valued the currencies contributed by its members in their quotas by comparison against a "gold dollar," which would buy 888.6706 milligrams of fine gold.

At the time that the Netherlands and Italy accepted full convertibility obligations under the IMF Article VIII (February 1961), the guilder was set at 3.62 to the dollar, the Italian lira at 620.6 to the dollar. Thus the "cross rate"—the exchange rate between these two currencies—was 171.436 lire to the guilder, .583 guilder to the hundred lire. But it must be remembered that each nation had agreed only to keep its currency fixed within 1 percent of the dollar "parity," up or down. Thus the range of assured support by the national central banks for the cross rates between the two currencies was from 168.042 lire to the guilder (or .595 guilder per hundred lire) all the way to 174.89 lire to the guilder (or .572 guilder per hundred lire). Within these margins, there was plenty of room for private banks to employ dollar holdings profitably as a vehicle for the easy conversion of guilders to lire or vice versa.

In later years, that permissible 1 percent fluctuation from the pegged exchange rate came to be regarded as a meaningless flexibility—but in 1944 it was significant. Keeping the costs low on their national debt, the allies were holding interest rates at 2½ percent or less. Thus a 1 percent discount or premium on a currency ate up almost five months' worth of interest that could be earned by lending in the more highly valued currency, which was a plausible brake on the operations of Gresham's Law. When the Smithsonian Agreements of 1971 sought to reestablish the Bretton Woods system without a dollar convertible to gold, the world's assembled finance ministers accepted a fluctuation of 2.25 percent in either direction as the margin within which an exchange rate for a currency could move without obliging the nation that prints this currency to intervene in the markets. But in the interest rate climate of 1971, a permissible fluctuation of 2.25 percent actually gave less leeway than the permissible 1 percent in the interest rate climate of 1944.

The question of how to defeat Gresham's Law was not prominent in anyone's mind in 1944, however, because at the heart of the Bretton Woods agreement lay an assumption that the world could separate currency movements called into being for purposes of international trade—required to balance the "current account"—from currency movements for purposes of short- or long-term investment (or speculation) in a foreign country. The IMF dealt with money to spend, which somehow was going to be kept separate from money to store.

Governments had defeated Gresham's Law domestically by imposing legal-tender rules on their peoples; now they would defeat it internationally by acquiring complete control over foreign exchange trading for any purposes other than the current financing of international trade. Of course, the same "fundamentals" that provoked capital flows were important elements in trade flows: the inflation that might create a flight of capital would show up also—perhaps first—in trade deficits. "Capital controls" would not enable governments to continue internationally destabilizing policies at an unreal fixed exchange rate; they could only give the governments time to make corrections and decisions that might otherwise be brutally forced upon them by the frenzies of speculation.

7

The omission of capital flows from the Bretton Woods reckonings reduced the system's viability over a period of time.

First, simply, because money is fungible—no piece of it is specially marked as destined for trade rather than for speculation or investment. As Gilbert Verbit of the Columbia Law School writes, "attempts to control capital flight quickly expand to systems regulating all outflows of foreign exchange. . . . [T]he almost immediate reaction of those wishing to remove their capital to a safe haven is to evade the controls through the vehicle of unregulated foreign payments. The most important avenue is to utilize payments for imports as a means of 'disguised' capital flight."

Either all foreign-exchange trading is conducted through the government's central bank (as was true in Europe during the days of the dollar shortage, and of course continues true today in the East Bloc), or there will be a leakage of domestic moneys out to foreign moneys that appear to offer a better store of value. Private markets and effective capital controls are incompatible. "There are no exchange regulations that anybody can put into effect," says chairman Walter Wriston of Citicorp, "that somebody brought up in Brazil or the Argentine cannot find a way to get around."

Second, because in the absence of capital flows a devaluation necessarily impoverishes the country that reduces the exchange value of its currency—which reinforces the natural inertia of government authorities, their desire to "defend" an exchange rate as a matter of national prestige. The problem is especially severe in what the British economist James Meade called "dilemma" situations, where a country has a serious inflation, a bad balance of trade—and high unemployment. Here a reasoned fear of the "adjustments" that would otherwise be required to reduce the inflation and the trade deficit argue strongly (as the Carter administration's economic advisers dangerously did argue in 1977) for a devaluation of the currency. But the devaluation by increasing the cost of imported goods and reducing the receipts from exports will lower the national standard of living, at least over the short run, unless it also draws capital investment from abroad, permitting an expansion of production and the absorption of the unemployed.

Finally, because in the world, as we have it, capital *should* flow from mature economies where the return on further investment is relatively low to developing countries where the benefits of investment are greater. But if capital flows are entirely controlled by governments, political considerations are certain to overwhelm economic logic—and corruption, often enough, given the real as against the textbook nature of government, will overwhelm both. When international capital flows really became central to the continued economic viability of nations, in the aftermath of the oil-price increases of 1973–74, private transfers in the form of bank loans took over from government aid and loan programs. At the moment of need, few governments will be competent or stable—let alone wise, efficient, farsighted or charitable.

None of this seemed important to Americans in the first dozen years after World War II. A Gresham's Law preference for the American dollar over any other currency made exchange control problems for the rest of the world, but not for the United States. With less than 5 percent of its production destined for export and 4 percent of its consumption provided by imports, the United States was a relatively "closed" economy, where developments abroad had little impact on income or employment at home. Under the Bretton Woods option of settlements in gold, America facing outwards could take a purely passive stand in monetary

51

matters, allowing foreigners to determine whether the United States would have a surplus or a deficit in its payments. Anxious to replace depleted reserves, foreigners were happy to see American payments in deficit. With the future value of the dollar in gold guaranteed, they preferred reserves consisting of dollars (which could earn interest in wholly liquid U.S. Treasury obligations traded on a market broad and deep enough to absorb virtually any quantity a holder wished to sell) to reserves consisting of gold (which earned nothing, and indeed cost something to store).

To both Americans and foreigners through most of the 1950s, this structure was the Rock of Gibraltar. Robert Triffin demonstrated in plenty of time that it was really a sand castle. But passivity in international monetary matters had become for American policy-makers and economists the institutional norm for the United States, from which any deviations were by definition temporary. Watching the erosion of the dollar, the United States began by trying to dam the tide, and concluded by damning the elements. It is that story which we picked up with Paul Volcker's visit to George Champion's office, and we are now prepared to follow it.

3 / Eisenhower's Conservatives

We are watching it closely. We are wondering just what has happened.

—anonymous Treasury spokesman, commenting to The New York Times on the jump of gold prices to $40 an ounce on the London market, October 20, 1960

*   *   *

For the Eisenhower administration, the crisis came in the gold market when frozen prices and limited supplies began to drain off the monetary gold that served as a "reserve" for the dollar both as a domestic currency and as the fundament of international trade.

Through the 1950s, foreign economic policy for Americans had been a matter of grants and loans and favors; perceiving a monetary problem toward the end of the decade, the administration sought to solve it by changing the terms of grants and expenditures and by modifying domestic policies to reduce the nation's deficit in international transactions.

But future events were being foreshadowed in the markets; the narrow measures taken by the administration merely shook the world's confidence in the dollar, beginning a retreat from American dominance that has still not found a defensible redoubt.

1

Dwight Eisenhower came to office in 1952 with the only Republican Congress to serve a Republican President over a period of (at least) fifty years. Though he had defeated the nationalist segment of his party in a difficult struggle with Robert Taft, most of his supporters in Congress had campaigned for office against the "global giveaways" of the Truman administration, that had "poured American taxpayers' money down a rathole." The Trade Agreements Act was up for renewal and might be in trouble; the maintenance of foreign assistance programs was among the most difficult struggles of Eisenhower's early months. With the thought that he wouldn't wish to go through *that* again, the President appointed a Commission on Foreign Economic Policy to advise him and the Congress on American trade, aid and monetary goals. Clarence Randall of Inland Steel, a certified conservative, was named chairman.

The first task of the Commission was to convince Congress and the public of the overwhelming strength of the American economy on the international scene. The Staff Papers (published a month after the Report—Eisenhower was in a hurry) stressed that with only 5 percent of the world's population, the United States had 40 percent of its total industrial output. More than half the world's entire production of petroleum was American, and half its production of motor vehicles. Exports were only 5 percent and imports only 4 percent of national income, and there were only a handful of products in which foreign demand accounted for any substantial proportion of the sales of American farms or factories—cotton, wheat, tobacco, textile machinery, sewing machines, tractors. But 20 percent of all world exports and 15 percent of all world imports were American. Of American exports in the years since the war, roughly a quarter had been financed by transfers through gifts and loans.

In 1953, the Commission found, the European civilian economies had earned their way for the first time since the war: nearly the entire American trade surplus was accounted for by U.S. military goods, which were financed through American aid. But the appearances were deceptive: Europeans were still doing without the consumption and investment goods they wanted and could even be said to need, because they didn't have the money to pay. The Staff Papers shrewdly noted that the American trade surplus—the "dollar gap," as seen from the European side—was a function of the quantity of aid and loans given by the United States: "Had we given less aid," the staff argued, "the 'dollar gap' would have been smaller; had we given more aid, it would have been larger." The Commission picked this up and added a warning: it found "a concealed dollar gap of some $2 billion to $3 billion annually, which would be increased if there were a change in the economic situation, such as a recession here or a deterioration in Europe's terms of trade." And, in fact, the 1954 recession in America did produce a $600 million drop in American imports and an increase back to $2 billion in the trade surplus, an increase financed mostly by private lending.

The recommendations of the Commission were that certain impediments to foreign sales in the United States should be reduced (especially the Buy American Act, which required the government itself to buy from American producers unless foreign prices were at least 50 percent lower). Greater European exports to the United States would be the best way to reduce the dollar gap— and would ultimately create greater American exports to Europe, for mutual benefit. It was too soon, however, to expect anything like free trade ("not possible under the conditions facing the United States today") or free convertibility of currencies to each other ("presents the danger of a vicious circle of inflation, and would require larger reserves than may be available to prevent currency depreciations from getting out of hand"). The best chance to close the gap was an increase in American investment abroad, which the United States should foster through changes in the tax laws. Additional help in that direction could be expected from changes in the European exchange-control laws which would permit easier convertibility by *nonresident* holders of a currency, allowing repatriation of the earnings from such investments.

A minority of the Commission wanted to go considerably further, especially in the direction of currency convertibility. Its report quoted testimony to the Commission by Bernard Baruch: "As long as currencies continue to be manipulated, all trade is made more difficult. What trade does take place tends to be forced through government channels. . . . Nothing stimulates trade more than the knowledge that currencies are freely interchangeable. Nothing does more to block the flow of trade, apart from war, than the fact that a nation's currency loses value beyond its own borders." Another statement, even closer to Republican concerns, was submitted by Per Jacobsson, then senior economic consultant to the Bank for International Settlements, later to be the Managing Director who made the International Monetary Fund a ponderable force in the world economy. "It is my honest belief," Jacobsson testified, "that the only way to stop aid safely is to see that the countries apply monetary discipline, and I know of no other way to get them to do it than to have convertible currency."

Everyone agreed, however, that the European economies (all of which were now producing considerably more than they had before the war) had strengthened sufficiently that American *grant* assistance was no longer necessary: public and private loans and investments should do the trick in the future. This recommendation was carried through: aid to Europe dropped from 63 percent of the U.S. assistance program in 1953 to 20 percent in 1957.

The Commission also earnestly recommended greater use of the International Monetary Fund, which had lain virtually dormant after its initial half-billion dollars of advances in 1947 (in 1950 it had made no loans at all), partly because the European problem was so much larger than the Fund's resources, partly because the United States as the dominating member had demanded high standards of banking prudence before the Fund would permit its members to "draw" any part of their quotas. (Officially, the Fund did not "lend" money to its members; the form was that the Fund "bought" the borrower's currency with a designated convertible currency from another member's quota—in practice at that time, dollars from the American quota.)

The IMF in the immediate postwar period had looked like a caricature of the old gag about bankers who will lend money only to people who don't need it; the Commission thought that if the rules were eased, some of the pressure for official American lending to Europe would be removed. (Old-timers at the IMF, by the way, deny the charge. They say their failure to lend resulted from the fears of the likely borrowers that if they were seen to be visiting the IMF window, their already shaky standing with other creditors would be demolished; only after the British came to the IMF in 1957 was it considered entirely respectable to "draw" from the Fund.)

Several themes that were to recur frequently and prominently were woven through the Commission's documents. One was a concern for sterling. The British currency still financed 40 percent of world trade in 1953, and was the medium through which the Europeans bought from and sold to not only the Commonwealth and the continuing colonies in Africa and Asia but also to the oil producers of the Persian Gulf. The heavy sterling balances accumulated in London during the war by the former subjects of the King-Emperor were still in large part there, unspent. (According to a later analysis by Triffin, 48 percent of the foreign exchange held as national monetary reserves in 1953 was in the form of sterling, but Britain held only 5 percent of the gold.) The worldwide preference for dollars over sterling had wrecked the first British effort to restore convertibility in 1947 and had forced an indefinite postponement of a new "dash for convertibility" previously scheduled for 1953. The existence of "blocked" sterling accounts in London was a barrier to more open trading patterns that would benefit everyone. Britain seemed to be pro-

57

gressing less well than its Continental neighbors; something special but unspecified would have to be done for Britain.

Another concern that would grow with the years was the danger of American job losses when American manufacturers had to compete against the products of low-wage foreigners. David McDonald, president of the United Steel Workers and a member of the Commission, was prepared not only to modify but to repeal the Buy American Act. In return, he wanted a Community Adjustment Assistance Act, which would help companies, workers, and towns that lost income from foreign competition. The majority disagreed with him, but printed his suggestion in the Report as a sort of Thought for This Week. Several members grumbled—this was a quarter of a century ago—that the essence of life is change, that companies and their workers are forever being placed in jeopardy by the development of new technologies and new industrial centers, and there was no reason to give special consideration to those whose bad news came from abroad. But the welfare state was in being; the Commission could not brush McDonald's caveats completely out of sight.

One significant comment in the Staff Papers, made in passing and ignored in the Report, would never again appear in an official document sponsored by the executive branch. The economists on the staff noted that the price of gold was too low. Nineteen years after Roosevelt had fixed gold at $35 an ounce, everything else cost about twice as much as it had in 1934—but gold was still $35. Thus there was little incentive to explore for gold, and only the most efficient mines were producing.

The staff left it at that; even then, the price of gold was a touchy subject. But the seeds of the Triffin dilemma were planted here, in the stony soil of the rigid gold price. In a time of expanding international trade, a gold-exchange system requires either an increase in the quantity or value of gold or an increase in the use of key currencies for reserve purposes. Sterling had remained a key currency for the British Commonwealth and the remains of the Empire, and also for assorted sheikhdoms and kingdoms east of Suez—but its status was strictly *faute de mieux* for many who used it. In the absence of additional gold, growth in the world's reserves would necessarily mean an expansion of dollar holdings outside the United States. And in one sense this was a false growth, because the United States had agreed to convert official dollar holdings to gold on demand, so that each dollar held in another country's reserve account was a claim on U.S. gold and was likely to be exchanged for gold, and thus extinguished as a reserve, if the system ran into trouble. The use of foreign exchange in national monetary reserves had been the first casualty of the Depression.

From the beginning, of course, there were strong arguments against increasing the price of gold. The gainers would be the United States, which then held 64 percent of the world's monetary gold and didn't need the profits; South Africa, already a pariah state under a racist government; and the Soviet Union. Keynes had denounced the monetary use of gold as a "barbarous relic," and economists almost without exception considered it irrational for people to prefer gold (which earned no interest) to other forms of wealth. Though James Madison had listed "a rage for paper money" as one "improper or wicked project" that could be avoided by assembling the good sense of the nation into a federal republic, the leaders of the American as of most other governments had come to see popular belief in gold as a statement of disbelief in *them*.

By the end of the Eisenhower administration, the continuing stream of American deficits would leave more than $10 billion in dollar holdings as reserves on the books of foreign monetary authorities—and there would be almost as much again in private hands abroad. Most of those dollars had been held in faith that they would continue to be convertible to gold on official demand at the established price.

Triffin would warn in 1960 that an increase in gold prices or the abandonment of free convertibility to gold "would be an act of sheer folly and a wanton crime against the people of this country, and against the friendly nations who have long accepted our financial leadership and placed their trust in the U.S. dollar and the integrity and intelligence of our monetary management." Breaking faith in 1960, quite apart from the political damage, would have meant a real risk of a run on the bank and the collapse of the international monetary system.

But in 1953, when the Randall Commission met, American gold holdings were still twice as large as total foreign claims against them—and many of those dollars abroad were used not only as reserves, but also as grease for day-to-day financing work, for which gold would not be suitable. (About two-thirds of foreign official dollar holdings in 1953 were in the form of demand deposits—non-interest-bearing checking accounts—at the Federal Reserve Bank of New York.) A policy to increase world liquidity by treating gold as an interest-earning asset—appreciating at a rate of, say, two-thirds of the actual market rate on 90-day U.S. Treasury bills, to leave some incentive for holding dollars rather than gold—would not have triggered a Gresham's Law flight from dollars to metal.

No doubt international agreement would have been required to establish a program of steady mild appreciation of gold in terms of all currencies (and the appreciation would have had to be steady through the year, at a rate of 2¢ or so a week, to make sure there were no notch effects on days when gold was about to be increased in price). No doubt, too, Triffin's Keynes-like plan for the deliberate creation of new reserve assets through agreement within the International Monetary Fund would have been a more rational way to manage the increasing need for liquidity to finance world trade. But it was not until 1967 that the first Triffin-type agreement could be reached, and not until 1970 that the first modest allocation of "Special Drawing Rights" (SDRs) began to increase world liquidity by systematic international action. Too little and too late: by then the Bretton Woods system was doomed. It is hard not to believe that intelligent gradual inflation of the gold price by government agreement starting in the 1950s would have made all the monetary problems of the 1960s and 1970s less hot to handle.

The only economists of any standing who had a good word for

gold in the 1950s were the Frenchman Jacques Rueff (who was defending a "gold standard" theory that bore no relation to the reality of any period in history)—and Roy Harrod, the biographer of Keynes, who in 1953 began what would be a long series of cries in the wilderness that the world's need for liquidity could never be satisfied by gold at $35 an ounce. For the others, giving gold increased utility as a reserve asset would have gone against deeply felt personal beliefs.

Triffin, at the end of his seminal book *Gold and the Dollar Crisis* in 1960, happily reprinted a fantasy from *The Economist* in which the price of gold, demonetized by all countries, had dropped to the $2.50 an ounce that dentists would pay for the raw material of their fillings. The conservative economist Fritz Machlup suggested in 1960 that the United States could stanch the outflow of gold by announcing a program of price *reductions*— nobody would want to hold gold if its market price steadily dropped, which the United States could easily arrange by selling off its stock.

"Nobody ever thought," says Federal Reserve Governor Henry Wallich, " 'What would happen if we went off gold and the price went sky-high?' " But it did; the economists had been wrong.

Janos Fekete, the stout, amusing, professedly Marxist deputy president of the Hungarian National Bank, stated the problem precisely at a meeting of the Per Jacobsson Foundation in Basle in 1973. "There are," he said, "about three hundred economists in the world who are against gold, and they think that gold is a barbarous relic—and they might be right. Unfortunately, there are three billion inhabitants of the world who believe in gold. Now the problem is how can we three hundred convince the other three billion of the correctness of our ideas. I think we could if we had time. But we need a lot of time."

Even the economists are not quite unanimous. Charles Coombs, who ran the currency market intervention programs of the Federal Reserve Bank of New York through the 1960s, said recently that "the biggest mistake at Bretton Woods was the illusion that you could establish by fiat a fixed price for gold." Milton

Gilbert, an energetic and sarcastic American who came from the Marshall Plan group in Paris to succeed Per Jacobsson as senior economic consultant to the Bank for International Settlements, recalled in 1978, shortly after his retirement, that among the assistants he found *in situ* on his arrival was "a very intelligent young Italian. Once a month, he took part of his pay and bought gold coins for his wife. I remonstrated with him about it once, and he said, 'Look, don't you Americans come over here and try to tell us how to live. I go home and I give that coin to my wife, and I tell her, If something happens to me, and to the Bank and all the governments, you can go out into the countryside and give it to a farmer, and with that coin you can eat for a week.' I came around to the opinion that he knew something I didn't know."

Gold, presumably, is a conservative's darling (though neither Gilbert nor, certainly, Fekete could be accurately described as a conservative). Discussions of the subject suffer from the separate neuroses of the conservative and liberal postures. Conservatives are by definition closer to the instinctive, inherited common sense of the population, but feel an emotional need to present their arguments in reasoned form. Liberals are more attuned to the dominant rationality of their time and seek to impose it on the body politic, but must mask their beliefs in popular appeals. The rational arguments against gold are and always have been almost overpoweringly strong, which leaves conservatives uncomfortable defending it. And in 1954 Americans had lived through more than twenty years in which possession of monetary gold was not only useless but illegal: there was no popular instinct to assuage. As Milton Gilbert puts it, "I used to say that in the United States there wasn't ten thousand votes in the price of gold."

Having noted that the price of gold was low, then, the Staff of the Commission passed on to other things, and the Commission itself never considered what would, after all, have been described as a "devaluation" of the dollar. (Assuming worldwide agreement to change the price of gold—and the position of the United States in 1954 was such that it could have forced such agreement easily enough—there would of course have been no "devaluation" of the dollar vis-à-vis other currencies, which is where it counts; but the press would certainly have got it wrong.) What may have been the last chance for maintaining the historic check against the tendencies of governments to buy out of trouble by inflating their currencies was allowed to pass without consideration. Eisenhower's people were conservatives: converting gold to a managed monetary asset would have been a radical proposal.

2

Britain moved gradually toward greater convertibility for sterling, paying a price at every step. In 1954, the many different categories of sterling—held by residents, colonials, foreigners, on current account or in investments, acquired through recent conversions from dollars or other foreign currencies, through recent or wartime sales in England—were consolidated into just two descriptions: "transferable" (which could be used only inside the sterling bloc) and "American account." The recognition of convertible "American account" sterling allowed the reopening of the London gold market because traders who purchased in a currency other than pounds were assured that they could sell for a currency other than pounds.

"Transferable" sterling as an inferior currency sold at a discount in world markets, encouraging British and Commonwealth commodity traders to "shunt" goods bought with these ersatz pounds into markets where they could be sold for dollars. The result was to cut Britain's officially reported dollar earnings, and in February 1955 the British Treasury announced that "transferable" sterling would be supported in the Zurich and New York markets within 1 percent of the rate on "American account" sterling. "These steps," the Radcliffe Committee reported to Parliament in 1959, "went a long way to establish *de facto* convertibility." They also cost Britain almost a quarter of her reserves—a fifth of her gold and a quarter of her dollar holdings.

The American economy rebounded strongly in 1955, with the

best peacetime year in increased Gross National Product (7.6 percent) since the recovery from the Depression. (This was accomplished, by the way, with a *reduction* in federal expenditures, a very modest increase in the budget deficit, an equally modest increase in the money supply, and a virtually stable price index; unemployment shrank by 20 percent. So much for all conventional explanations of macroeconomic phenomena.) It was a boom year in Europe, too: American imports rose by 10 percent, but exports rose even faster, and the "dollar gap" widened. Unevenly: the Germans, with relative price stability, saw their book of industrial orders from foreigners rise more than 25 percent, while the French and the British, caught in an inflationary consumer-based prosperity, became increasingly uncompetitive. By 1956, the Germans, en route to what would become a $4.6 billion credit in the European Payments Union before it was dissolved in 1958, removed all controls on capital exports and began encouraging Germans to invest elsewhere.

But 1956 would be the year when (perhaps for the last time, economically) the new world would have to be called in to redress the balance of the old. That summer Nasser nationalized the Suez Canal, expropriating the Anglo-French company that had owned and operated the waterway; that fall a clumsy Anglo-French-Israeli conspiracy arranged a war on Egypt that resulted in the closing of the canal and the disruption of oil shipments through the pipelines across Syria. Europe as a whole was left short of gasoline, and Britain and France were in serious monetary trouble.

The United States had the excess oil-producing capacity to make up the shortfall from the Persian Gulf in those days, but the monetary problem was more difficult. Capital flowed into Germany, linked with France and Britain through the European Payments Union, and the Germans in what would be the first of many desperation maneuvers forbade the payment of interest on bank deposits held by foreigners. (Presumably, people who couldn't earn anything on money they shipped to Germany would think twice about shipping it.) Gold flowed to the United

States, producing a billion-dollar increase in the American monetary gold stock.

Britain and France drew opposite lessons from American opposition to the Suez adventure. For Britain, the failure at Suez was a lesson that nothing could be done without prior coordination with America: the famous "special relationship" was that of servant and master. Britain came to America for money, from private lenders and from the U.S.–dominated International Monetary Fund, now under the leadership of Per Jacobsson, who wanted to see it become an active force for world monetary stability. The British payments deficit occasioned by Suez was precisely the sort of temporary disequilibrium the Fund had been established to smooth over: Jacobsson and colleagues cheerfully granted a combination of credits and standby credits totalling Britain's entire IMF quota. In return, Britain pledged to take whatever domestic steps were necessary to reduce the level of inflation—and in fact aborted its burgeoning recovery in summer 1957, raising interest rates dramatically, to preserve the exchange value of the pound.

The French drew the lesson that the Americans were not to be trusted, and that a united Europe had become a military-political as well as an economic necessity. The French eased their bargaining posture with their European trading partners in what had become a tediously unrewarding negotiation toward a customs union—and in March 1957 achieved the Treaty of Rome, establishing what came to be called the Common Market (officially, the European Economic Community, or EEC). Some wag commented that when the buildings to house the institutions of the EEC were erected, the statue in front should be of Nasser. But Britain, never enthusiastic about merging its destiny with that of the Continent, was now looking the other way; and a negotiation that had begun with the assumption that the customs union would cover all Western Europe wound up with only six signatories.

Saddled with an increasingly costly war in Algeria, and with insecure governments, France could not impose credible inflation-control measures (and deeply resented the IMF demand that it do so if it wished to make large-scale drawings from the Fund). In the spirit of the new treaty, France was not willing to add its voice to those who were calling on the Germans to correct the world's monetary imbalance by revaluing the D-mark to higher parity against gold and the dollar. In August 1957 the franc was devalued by 20 percent.

As the United States entered the third year of its recovery from the 1954 recession, inflationary pressures began to build. Seeing the cost-of-living index rising at a 4 percent rate, then considered intolerable, the Eisenhower administration reined in the economy. The federal budget had been in surplus in fiscal 1956 and was kept in surplus; the Federal Reserve kept the narrowly measured monetary supply virtually static, and raised the discount rate to the banks to 3 percent, the highest it had been since 1929. The United States slipped into a renewed recession and, as had happened through the postwar period, Europe followed.

But this time the results in the American balance of payments were very different. By contrast with 1949 and 1954, American imports dropped scarcely at all in 1958—and exports, automatically reduced when normal oil shipments were resumed from the Gulf to Europe, fell 16 percent. Meanwhile, the impending installation of the Common Market tempted increasing numbers of American companies to get investments in place in the new customs union before European customers shifted their business from the United States to neighbors whose goods could be imported with lower—and steadily diminishing—tariff charges. The United States payments position, which had been $0.5 billion in surplus in 1957, swung by $4 billion. Through the 1950s, foreigners had been willing to take dollars, hold them, use them as reserves, to finance American payments deficits. In 1958, they decided they had enough dollars. Gold with a value amounting to two-thirds of the United States deficit—10 percent of the existing American monetary gold stock—was transferred to foreign ownership. The run on Kindleberger's bank had begun.

Federal Reserve Chairman William McChesney Martin returned from the International Monetary Fund conclave in New Delhi with, he told a friend, "a notebook full of the conversations I had with people who expressed concern about the dollar. I was so distressed, I spoke to the President about it." Treasury Secretary Robert Anderson was even more upset. ("The central bankers scared the hell out of him," says Charls E. Walker, a Texas economist who had been summoned to Washington to be Anderson's executive assistant.) He spoke separately to Eisenhower, and told him the cause of the problem was the budget deficit; the President had better get the budget back in balance. The budget for fiscal 1960 (which had to be presented to Congress in January 1959) was prepared under conditions of unprecedented secrecy and forcefully presented. It showed a surplus—the last such until 1969. Arthur Burns, who had been Chairman of the Council of Economic Advisers in Eisenhower's first term, warned that so soon after 1958, this budget could abort the recovery, increase unemployment, and cost the Republican candidate (presumably Richard Nixon) the 1960 election. Nixon remembered that and brought Burns back to government when he got to the top of the greasy pole ten years later.

The French were still in trouble: even at the new exchange rate, deficits persisted. Early in 1958, Jean Monnet put together a package of $600 million of IMF and private loans. (Two amusingly different descriptions of this venture were later published. "A difficult and extremely complex assignment, and I put a great deal into it," Monnet himself recalled. ". . . It led to the unhoped-for loan." DeGaulle noted sourly that when he took office in June 1958, "Nothing remained of the last line of credit we had been able to raise—some five hundred million dollars—which had been reluctantly granted to Jean Monnet's begging. . . .") With the Common Market scheduled to come into effect in early 1959, DeGaulle and his adviser Jacques Rueff demanded an end to inflation, ordered reduced prices in the stores, denied both government employees and farmers increases to which they were entitled under the primitive indexing system which had helped the French accept a shrinking franc throughout the 1950s. And to make certain that France would enter the brave new world of low intra-European tariffs with an undervalued currency—once again—the franc was devalued one last time at the end of 1958.

Part of the brave new world was the end of the European Payments Union and most currency controls. The giant American deficit had left Europe fully liquid for the first time since the end of the war, and a 50 percent increase in IMF quotas, by international agreement, had made that safety net plausible. As a Christmas present at the end of 1958, all the major European currencies were made convertible to dollars with diminished restrictions, most of which did not apply at all to nonresidents. But instead of provoking a flight of European capital to America, as many economists (including Triffin) still feared, convertibility reinforced the tendency of American money to seek both merchandise and investment opportunity in Europe. As the American economy recovered from 1958—greatly stimulated by an almost $13 billion deficit in the fiscal 1959 federal budget, a source of monumental embarrassment to Eisenhower—U.S. exports remained steady, and imports (enlarged by a long, disruptive steel strike) rose by 20 percent. The favorable balance of trade almost disappeared; payments fell $3.7 billion in the hole, and another billion dollars melted off the American gold stock.

Washington began to get nervous. Right after the war, American aid had been given to foreigners with the thought that they would spend it to help each other—like the $350 million capital donated to the European Payments Union. Recipients were urged, where possible, to spend American largess away from the United States. As the years passed, the American government grew first neutral and then a little patriotic about where the aid dollars were spent.

In fall 1959, the Eisenhower administration dropped the first shoe, ordering that in the future Development Loan Fund dollars in the foreign aid program were to be spent to the greatest extent feasible for American products. "We got some pretty violent attacks for that," Treasury Secretary Anderson recalled recently.

"Newspaper editorials. We were abandoning free trade, returning to protectionist policies. One of the most famous American economists wrote me a letter that began, 'You should resign immediately.' A few years later he asked me to give him back that letter if I still had it, which I do, and I said I wouldn't; but I'd do him a favor and never give his name."

Presently Anderson arranged with the Germans to prepay about half a billion dollars borrowed in Marshall Plan days, to ease the strain on American reserves. In fall 1960, the other shoe dropped with a crash, when Eisenhower ordered home all dependents of American forces in Europe and demanded that procurement for the Army abroad was to be all but exclusively in the United States—even fresh vegetables were to be bought at home and shipped to the commissaries. Charls Walker had been sent to Paris from Treasury for an OECD meeting that started the morning the newspapers headlined Eisenhower's program. "They had been flagellating us for doing nothing," Walker remembers. "Now they complained bitterly that we were going to wreck their economies . . ."

3

In a book he wrote with his former assistant Kenneth Dam not long after leaving office, Nixon's Treasury Secretary George Shultz complained that "the distinction between trade and money makes little economic sense. Barter being rare, every sale of goods is simultaneously a trade matter and a money matter. An export (or import) involves a payment. Money and trade are closely linked in policy, not just in actual transactions." Arguing against Britain's dogged defense of the pound in 1930, Keynes had stressed that a currency devaluation was a far more effective way to remedy a trade deficit than any collection of tariffs—like tariffs, it raised the effective price of imports, thus presumably diminishing them; but it also lowered the effective price of exports, increasing domestic employment. From that argument, theoretically impeccable, had grown the competitive devaluations that disfigured the international monetary scene, and deepened the Depression, in the 1930s.

The Bretton Woods conference had dealt with trade and tariff questions as well as with monetary matters, and the delegates departed in the belief that their work had produced the groundwork for a new International Trade Organization as well as the treaties for the International Monetary Fund and the World Bank. But decisions about tariffs are something the Congress likes to keep for itself; from the Presidency of James Madison to the present, the extent of a President's authority to negotiate tariff changes has been a source of conflict between legislature and executive. In the days of Smoot-Hawley, each tariff schedule for each kind of import had to be separately approved by Congress, leading to logrolling that raised duties to preposterous levels. It had been hell getting Congress in 1934 to give Franklin Roosevelt margins of discretion in the determination of tariff rates; there was no way Congress was going to allocate such powers to an international organization. American delegations to international conferences were tightly restricted in what they could offer, and in 1947 President Truman abandoned the idea of a treaty.

What was substituted was a sort of floating crap game, a peripatetic series of multilateral negotiations for commercial codes of conduct and tariff schedules, conducted under the heading of General Agreement on Trade and Tariffs, or GATT. There have been seven "Rounds" of negotiations—Geneva in 1947, Annecy in 1949, Torquay in 1951, Geneva in 1956, Geneva again in 1960–61, the "Kennedy Round" at Geneva in 1964–67, and most recently the "Tokyo Round," which proceeded under the administrations of three American presidents to a treaty in spring 1979. Despite the name, most of the Tokyo Round negotiations occurred in Geneva, where GATT now has a large building in a park by the lake and a bureaucracy, to which (but only since 1968) the United States makes an annual contribution. Though a good part of the actual work of the GATT bureaucracy and the ministers accredited to it goes toward finding internationally acceptable ways to restrain the export of labor-intensive goods from low-wage countries to high-wage countries (especially textiles), the agreements themselves all purport to increase the volume and value of international trade, and convey to as many people as possible the advantages of an international specialization of labor.

The basic principle of GATT, as of all multilateral trade agreements, is the Most Favored Nation clause, which requires that whenever a nation reduces its tariffs on an import from one trading partner, it must give the same reduction on that import to all other members of the treaty group. But the agreements always left room for regional customs unions within which nations that traded heavily with each other could eliminate the tariff barriers between them without demolishing their protection against the outside world. The theory of the Treaty of Rome, establishing the Common Market, was that the Six as a group, reducing trade barriers among themselves, would impose against the outside world a tariff schedule that for each product would be an average of what the individual nations had charged before the Community came into being. This would keep everything kosher with GATT. The French, having been the most protectionist of the group, would have to reduce their tariffs and quota barriers the most (this justified, more or less, the 1958 devaluation of the franc); the Germans, having been the most open, would raise their tariffs against America and England to bring the schedule up to the average.

What the American attitude toward all this should have been, as a matter of self-interest, is one of those questions that has no easy answer. As it happens, the Eisenhower government was enthusiastic. The European Economic Community was obviously an outgrowth of the Organization for European Economic Cooperation, which had been established by the Marshall Plan and guided in large part by American economists and lawyers. Most economists believed that a good part of the explanation for the higher standard of living in the United States was the existence of a unified market across a continent, permitting economies of scale in production, marketing, and finance. In the most vulgar sense, anything that made Europe more like the United States had to be desirable (and Jean Monnet, architect of the Common Market, was leading a further thrust toward what he called the United States of Europe).

Those who were concerned about the tariff increases against American exports were reminded that other exporters were gaining—and that, after all, Common Market tariffs would come down as the Europeans prospered and grew more secure. (This did, in fact, happen—though not across the board, as we shall see.) The Benelux confederation, now absorbed in the EEC, had been good citizens of GATT at every negotiation. Moreover, if the Common Market worked—there were a lot of skeptics—the resulting increases in consumers' income would produce expansion of American exports to Europe even over the barriers of higher tariffs. This certainly turned out to be true: from 1958 to 1960, American exports to the Common Market countries rose 41 percent, while American imports from the Common Market rose only 26 percent. The improvement in the trade surplus was almost half a billion dollars.

But the existence of a huge market with decreasing internal tariff barriers and considerably higher external tariffs drew the investment interest of American companies that had previously exported their products from the United States to Europe. Wage rates were lower and profit levels higher in Europe, anyway—and the dollar was overvalued, which meant that existing businesses could be purchased, or new factories built, for much less than equivalent productive capacity would cost at home. Counting in capital flows, then, the creation of the Common Market created a large and growing deficit in the American payments ledger—until Yale economics professor James Tobin, speaking in 1965, could describe the EEC sourly as "a customs union which at the same time attracts American capital and excludes American exports."

As frosting on the cake, the American tax laws were still as they had been during the period of the dollar shortage, and gave tax advantages to corporations that invested abroad. For reasons of economic logic, tax savings and political desires to keep the host country happy, the American firms that expanded to Europe in the years after the Treaty of Rome tended to reinvest their earnings abroad rather than repatriate them to the United States. As the books were kept in international accounting, earnings overseas by American companies were not included on the black side of the ledger unless they were brought home. (In 1979, these rules were changed, and the Commerce Department began to include the unrepatriated foreign profits of American companies on the plus side of the balance-of-payments ledger.)

Worse lay ahead. Much of the growing American trade surplus was in machinery and know-how for the production of the packaged goods for the new European supermarkets, the consumer durables, refrigerators, washing machines, and dishwashers for the new European household, which the Common Market countries used to import from America. As Otmar Emminger of the Bundesbank wrote in 1977, "American industry ... invested in European industrial countries with lower labor costs and from these supplied not only its export markets but partly its own domestic markets as well." Like the United States of the economists' vision in the 1950s, European industry with American help was concentrating on import substitutes; and exporters to the Common Market, especially Americans, were going to face some hard times. In part, this was merely an ordinary example of the "product life cycle" initially described by the Harvard economist Raymond Vernon: a company that develops something new normally begins by exporting it, then builds abroad to satisfy foreign demand (and avoid foreign tariffs), finally imports to the country of origin from its manufacturing plants in foreign places. But in part it was something dangerously specific to the Common Market.

In 1960, when a new recession reduced American imports while rising incomes abroad stimulated American exports, the U.S. trade surplus expanded to the second-highest level since the war, surpassed only by the artificial oil-based export boom of 1957. But private capital outflows doubled—some long-term investments, some short-term loans drawn abroad by the gap between the high interest rates of prosperous Europe and the low interest rates of America in recession. The Germans, trying desperately to restrain an inflationary boom by restricting credit, found that they could indeed slow the growth of foreign-held deposits in German banks by imposing the "bardepot" (requiring German banks to keep high reserves against foreign-owned deposits), but they could not prevent German businesses squeezed at home from borrowing abroad and converting the proceeds of their borrowings to marks at fixed exchange rates. The German payments surplus grew; despite the improvement in the trade picture, the American payments deficit actually worsened, and foreigners took another $1.7 billion out of the American gold stock.

4

The April 1960 issue of *Foreign Affairs* contained a pair of articles on the American balance-of-payments problem and what could be done about it, by Treasury Secretary Robert B. Anderson and Richard W. Gardner, law professor and economist, recent author of a book on Bretton Woods and its aftermath (at this writing Jimmy Carter's ambassador to Italy). Gardner would later be critical of Anderson's failure even to suggest that a continuing deficit in the American balance of payments was necessary for world liquidity, but in fact the two men were almost equally disturbed by what was happening in the monetary world. Anderson wanted the payments deficit eliminated. Gardner thought it should greatly diminish, but that its persistence could be tolerated by foreign governments and central banks on political grounds: "Although it may not serve the interests of private holders to accumulate dollar balances at interest rates low enough to support our domestic expansion, the foreign governments and central banks which are the only holders in a position to demand gold and start a 'run on the dollar' must act on larger economic and political considerations. They have every reason to agree to small annual increases in their dollar balances . . ."

Gardner's list of steps to be taken was longer than Anderson's. He wanted foreigners "to speed the removal of . . . restrictions against American goods" and to ease their "restraints on capital outflows." The tax laws should be changed to "stop our encouragement of American investment in other than underdeveloped countries." European countries benefiting by the presence of American forces should pay for them; and there should be further acceleration in the prepayment of outstanding loans from the United States to Europe. The United States, which had a swollen credit position from previous drawings of dollars by foreigners at the International Monetary Fund, should use that position to acquire foreign currencies.

For foreign governments and central banks which could not suppress their concern about the future value of the dollar—and the memory of Dutch losses from sterling devaluation in 1931 was still greener than anyone not in touch with the bankers could realize—the United States could give a "gold guarantee" to official dollar holdings abroad, promising that these dollars would still be able to buy gold at $35 an ounce even if the price of gold was later allowed to rise. This would be safe because *we* knew that could never happen. . . . To make the guarantee credible, Congress should remove the "gold cover" from American currency, which then required the Federal Reserve to keep gold assets valued at 25 percent or more of the currency in circulation.

Both Anderson and Gardner saw the future exchange value of the dollar as a function of its domestic stability. Anderson called for sound fiscal policies "with a budget surplus in times of prosperity" and a monetary policy "keyed to the containment of the strong demand for capital which might otherwise break through into a major inflationary pressure." Gardner insisted that "we must check the creeping inflation of costs and prices. . . . Labor will have to show greater restraint. . . . Our balance of payments must not be subjected to the stress of another nationwide steel strike." There must be "much greater emphasis on advances in science and technology." Both insisted that neither American military expenditures nor aid abroad could be cut; both opposed restrictions on the free flow of capital ("an abdication," Anderson wrote, "of our role of leadership"); both demanded, as every American administration since has demanded, a "national export drive" to raise the trade surplus to a level where it would cover all the sources of dollar outflow.

Like every Secretary of the Treasury, Anderson wouldn't even talk about gold guarantees. They were unnecessary, because every dollar in official hands abroad carried a full guarantee automatically: he would "leave no one at home or abroad with any doubt concerning our intent or capacity to maintain the dollar as a freely convertible currency at the existing official price for gold." His mission was to decrease nervousness in general ("I do not feel we are confronted with an emergency"). But he was unable to suppress his annoyance that the United States was being called upon to settle its payments deficits with reserve assets when the source of the deficit was a capital flow: "It does not seem that the proper function of our gold reserve is to be heavily drawn down on a large scale over a period of years to transfer capital to the rest of the world."

The logic of this position was clearly correct. If private American investments abroad were sound—and one could assume continued convertibility of the currencies of the countries where those investments were made—then the debt in dollars incurred by the investors was really a solid security backed by the profitability of the investment—and surely not a claim on the reserve assets of the United States. And the reason the debt was denominated in dollars and looked like an American deficit (though Anderson was too polite to say so) was the failure of the Europeans to develop their capital markets as well as their industrial facilities—the American investors abroad would have been happy to borrow marks or francs or guilders for their needs (instead of borrowing dollars and converting them to marks or francs or guilders) if the Germans and French had created the institutions through which that borrowing could be efficiently and cheaply done.

But from the point of view of the German or French or Dutch central bank that acquired the dollars in the course of converting them to local currency, there was no visible difference between the U.S. currency that came abroad "on current account" and the U.S. currency that came abroad for investments. What they knew for sure was that they had more dollars at the end of the year than at the beginning, and by the rules of the game they were entitled to convert those excess dollars to gold. Statements like Anderson's, with their slight undertone of petulance, did little to reassure foreign holders of dollars, official or unofficial. The gold flow accelerated slightly through the summer.

Then Senator Kennedy made the loss of gold a campaign issue against Vice-President Nixon, arguing more that it should not be happening than that he knew how to stop it. In America, this was nothing more than campaign rhetoric, and a minor-league example of it at that. (Few voters knew or cared about gold outflows.) In Europe, the monetary authorities were deeply conscious of the fact that the easy way for the United States to stem the outflow of gold was to devalue the dollar. Kennedy was cloaking himself in the mantle of Franklin Roosevelt, and that was what Roosevelt had done. Moreover, it was the orthodox Keynesian solution. European bankers knew that among the economists around the candidate were several doctrinaire Keynesian academics whose irresponsibility could be excused by their lack of market experience, but could not be entirely ignored.

Though foreign monetary authorities could buy their gold directly from the United States Treasury, most of them picked it up on the London market, where supplies from South Africa and the Soviet Union were available—for dollars. The Bank of England acted as agent for the suppliers, prepared to acquire gold for its own account if the metal fell below the U.S. Treasury price ($35.04, including 12¢ for shipping and handling), or to sell gold from its own stock if the metal rose above the U.S. Treasury ceiling ($35.20, again with 12¢ for shipping). If the demand at that price began to deplete the Bank's own stocks, it could go to the Treasury for replenishment, which happened increasingly often as 1960 rolled on.

In September 1960, the Treasury approached the European central banks with the suggestion that if they wanted gold, they should acquire officially from the Federal Reserve Bank of New York, the Treasury's agent, rather than jostling with private customers in London. But even with the larger central banks out of the market, the demand for gold in London exceeded the supply of newly mined metal. Some of this demand came from Americans, who were allowed to own monetary gold abroad, though not at home. (Gold ownership abroad by Americans was finally prohibited by executive order that December; probably without much effect, as there was no way to police it.) In total, $638 million of gold dropped from the American reserve in the third quarter alone.

The U.S. Treasury had protested the opening of the London gold market in 1954. Before then, there had been small unofficial markets in Tangiers and Hong Kong, neither linked in any way to the American gold stock. Now there would be an official market managed by the Bank of England, which had access to the gold window. Under the Bretton Woods agreement, all signatories had pledged themselves to exert their influence to channel gold to monetary uses—that is, to prevent private hoarding that would reduce world reserves. "The British breached that," Anderson says. "When I complained, they said they had Commonwealth obligations to create markets for the principal products of the Commonwealth nations—and the principal product of South Africa was gold. That obligation superseded the pledge to IMF, which was merely 'to use influence.' "

As a normal matter, gold sold to a foreign government or central bank was merely moved from the assay office to a vault at the Federal Reserve Bank of New York, and "earmarked" for that foreign account. In October 1960, with its stocks of metal depleted, the Bank of England asked for a purchase to be shipped to London. Anderson got on the telephone to the Chancellor of the

Exchequer to inquire why physical shipment was necessary, given the costs and the risks of handling the stuff. He was told that with gold leaving the country through the market the quantity in the vaults at Threadneedle Street was down, which worried some politicians. The Chancellor wanted to be able to say in Commons that the physical object was in England.

At the International Monetary Fund meeting in Washington a few weeks before, someone from the United States had indicated to someone from the Bank of England that the Treasury did not consider the replenishment of stocks sold on the market to be a suitable reason for the Bank of England to profit by its privileges at the U.S. gold window. Coupled with Anderson's phone call, this message seems to have produced some rather informal guidance to the operating level at the Bank of England, that it would be desirable to minimize gold sales. Instead of running down its own stocks to meet demand for gold at $35.08 per ounce f.o.b. New York, the Bank of England in mid-October let the price edge up. On October 20, 1960, gold shot suddenly to $40 an ounce. The first reaction from the U.S. Treasury when the news came over the wire was scarcely such as to encourage foreign monetary authorities. "We are watching it closely," a spokesman said. "We are wondering just what has happened."

Under the heaviest kind of pressure, then, the United States had to make an immediate and fateful decision: did the $35 peg apply to private as well as official trading in gold? Among the complexities to be considered was the fact that gold was as fungible as money and could be sold through any intermediary. If the private price ran above the official price, any central bank or foreign government could turn a neat little profit by selling in London and then converting its dollars in Washington. America's friends wouldn't do that, of course, but not every government in the IMF was necessarily that friendly. To separate the private and official market would require a good deal of preliminary spadework followed by potentially complicated negotiations. The Bank of England was authorized to draw upon American monetary reserve to sell gold in the London market, and the price was pushed back down to $36. But now the world had changed: there was a direct link between privately held dollars abroad and the American gold reserve.

The breakout in the gold market led to a drain of almost a billion dollars in gold from the Treasury in two months, much of it to a demanding array of twenty-five foreign governments and central banks: so much for America's friends. Some years later, Milton Gilbert would write in an Annual Report of the Bank for International Settlements that "Although by early 1961 conditions in the gold market were temporarily back to normal, the former absolute confidence in the dollar was never again restored." There was some rumbling from the Republicans that loose talk by Jack Kennedy had produced the disaster.

The Democratic candidate responded vigorously a week before election in a speech at Philadelphia. He would maintain the dollar at its par value of $35 an ounce—nobody need have any fear about that. The proper procedure for stabilizing the balance of payments was an economic policy that would put an end to "the steady inflation which has priced us out of many foreign markets. For example," the next President added, "industrial prices alone have risen thirty percent in the last ten years." The dollar would be sound abroad because it would be sound at home. That was what Secretary Anderson had been saying, too.

Shortly after the election, Eisenhower announced his drastic steps to reduce the foreign exchange cost of American armed forces stationed abroad, and sent Anderson and Under Secretary of State Douglas Dillon to negotiate with the Germans about a much larger contribution from Bonn. "The indirect costs of our presence in Germany," Anderson recalls, "were greater than our payments deficit. They were an affluent nation. We didn't owe them anything for providing a common defense from which they benefited more than we did. I saw Adenauer, and he said, 'From the standpoint of economics, you're right. But you fellows are not going to be in office that long. And it could mean I'd have to impose additional taxes on my people.' I said, 'Well, it all depends on how much you value those dollar reserves you're holding on to in the Bundesbank.'

"When I got back to Washington I had a call from that handsome fellow at *The New York Times*—Arthur Krock. He told me, 'You were no more than airborne when I was called to the State Department and told they thought it was the most foolish thing in the world, to impair our political relations with Germany that way. They said, "Why does he think he has any power left?" ' My staff wanted me to tell the press, but I said, 'It wouldn't be good for the country; the State Department stays in power after we're gone.' "

Kennedy had refused to send an emissary with Anderson and Dillon—that was one of the reasons Adenauer was unhelpful. (Another reason was the fact that in 1960 the dependents of American soldiers in Germany were still living higher on the hog than the wives and children of German workers, who were thus more likely to resent being taxed for their support. By 1978—*sic transit*—German charities were raising funds to help alleviate real hardship among American servicemen's families.) But the President-elect met with Anderson on his return, and then spent several afternoons with him during the succeeding weeks.

An accountant, Anderson had been elected Collector of Taxes for the State of Texas in the 1930s, and as the youngest statewide elected official had been chosen by Franklin Roosevelt as chairman of the Texas branch of the National Youth Administration (in which capacity he had supervised the work of the state NYA director, a gangling ex-schoolteacher named Lyndon Johnson). In 1951, he had been Harry Truman's mediator in the great war between the Treasury and the Federal Reserve over the Fed's refusal to keep pumping up the money supply to hold down the Treasury's financing costs, and he had helped negotiate the famous Accord that gradually returned control of American monetary policy to the Fed. He had also recommended as part of the deal that Assistant Treasury Secretary William McChesney Martin, then forty-four years old, be made chairman of the Fed.

Anderson had come into Eisenhower's administration as the house Democrat, and while he had changed registration while in office on grounds of loyalty, he hadn't made any noise about it. Kennedy was looking for one holdover appointment from the Eisenhower cabinet, and asked Anderson to stay on. "I told him I wouldn't," Anderson said recently in his Rockefeller Center office in New York—a splendid old man now with silky white hair, still active as an international consultant, traveling half the year, at work every day before eight in the morning, wearing a pin-striped charcoal vested suit with a gold lapel pin that reads TRY GOD. "I'd been in Washington seven years, and I didn't have Potomac Fever. But for six months, he sent me advanced copies of every message he gave about financial matters."

Kennedy, as President-elect, also saw William McChesney Martin, who had been troubled by some of the candidate's speeches. "Frankly," Martin said recently, "I wasn't sure I could work with him. But we talked for hours, and I found he was really a very conservative fella." Kennedy and Martin agreed that the time had come to tighten relations between the Fed and the foreign central banks. Charles Coombs, manager of the foreign department at the Federal Reserve Bank of New York (and a former classmate of Kennedy's at Harvard), was sent to Basle for the monthly meeting of the Bank for International Settlements, where the United States had never been officially represented— not to occupy the empty American chair at the table, exactly, but to be an "observer" and stress to the assembled central bankers the sincerity of Kennedy's pre-election gold pledge.

Though much junior to the representatives of the European banks, Coombs was courteously and encouragingly received (by men who, as he later wrote, "collectively held more than $6 billion, all convertible to gold at the U.S. Treasury window"). Coombs came home and reported that if ways could be found to handle the legal and technical problems, the Europeans were more willing to be helpful than Anderson had thought.

John F. Kennedy had been in the home stretch of a rapidly tightening campaign when his advisers persuaded him that he had to take some part of the final, precious week to speak on gold and the dollar. When he went to the White House for his first briefing on his new job, Eisenhower (to quote Charls Walker) "pummeled him for two hours about the dollar." Such experiences concentrate the mind. Kennedy asked Douglas Dillon to be Secretary of the Treasury because, Dillon says, "it would give public credence to his determination to stabilize the dollar. The shock in the gold market was the only reason I came in. He had some trouble within his party—there were lots of deserving Democrats who wanted the job. When he first spoke to me he said, 'I don't know if I can do it.' But if he'd appointed Albert Gore, who wanted the job, the results would have been terrible as far as the dollar was concerned. Everything I had from the very first was this deep emotional attachment Kennedy had to the price of gold."

4 / Kennedy's Improvisers

This nation will maintain the dollar as good as gold, freely interchangeable with gold at $35 an ounce, the foundation stone of the free
world's trade and payments system.

— John F. Kennedy, Message to
Congress, July 1963

*   *   *

Kennedy . . . used to tell his advisers that the two things which scared
him the most were nuclear war and the payments deficit. Once he
half-humorously derided the notion that nuclear weapons were essential to international strength. "What really matters," he said, "is the
strength of the currency."

— Arthur M. Schlesinger, Jr.

*   *   *

Committed to activism, the Kennedy administration abandoned the previously "passive" stance of the United States
in the international monetary struggle.

The Kennedy team established close relations between the
Treasury and the Federal Reserve and developed a wide range of
ingenious and temporarily effective expedients for preserving the
fixed exchange rate. ·

These expedients reduced the pressure on the American gold
stock and maintained the dollar as the keystone of the world's
monetary arch.

At the Treasury, in the Congress and in the Oval Office, academics (mostly) and politicians strove to find new definitions that might make old problems less disturbing and disruptive.

Meanwhile, the management of the exchange markets themselves was entrusted to the Federal Reserve Bank of New York and the foreign central bankers' club that met monthly in Basle.

But when steady improvement in American economic fundamentals did not resolve the American monetary dilemma, Kennedy moved to impose controls on the outflow of dollars for the first time since the war.

1

The presidency, Theodore Roosevelt observed, is a bully pulpit. It is also a splendid classroom seat: everybody wants to teach the President. Kennedy soon after his election commissioned a mass of studies and reports for his personal consideration. His monetary "task force" was chaired by George Ball, a Wall Street lawyer and friend of Adlai Stevenson's, and included such luminaries as Otto Eckstein of Harvard and Paul Samuelson of MIT, Robert Triffin and Richard Gardner, Joseph Pechman of the Brookings Institution and Edward M. Bernstein, who had been Harry White's deputy at Bretton Woods. The dominant figure in the group, however, turned out to be Robert Roosa of the Federal Reserve Bank of New York, a research economist, Rhodes Scholar, who had (rather against his own wishes) been put to work supervising the Fed's day-to-day operations in the money markets and thus, quite simply, knew things the others didn't know.

The members of the task force disagreed on both analysis and recommendations, but they all finally signed a report calling for "a program to resolve the deficit and reserve problems" as "a matter of the highest priority." The age of passivity would have to end: the United States could no longer live with an international monetary policy based entirely on the willingness to sell gold on demand or buy it on offer from foreign official agencies. The program urged upon the new President instead was aggressively different both domestically and internationally.

On the domestic side, the task force called for legislation that would hold down the prices of American exports. There should be "systematic machinery to restrain cost-price spirals," and an agricultural support program that would stabilize farmers' incomes rather than prices, permitting price reductions that would make American food products more competitive on the world market. Seeking to smooth the business cycle, the government should rely more on fiscal measures (budget deficits and surpluses) and less on monetary measures that might put interest rates in America out of line with those elsewhere.

To remedy the balance-of-payments deficit, Kennedy should seek much greater liberalization of foreign trade, elimination of quotas and restrictions everywhere and tariff reductions of 50 percent on trade around the globe. Some American industries might be hurt and some American jobs might be lost in the process, but other industries would gain and more jobs would be created. The Europeans should abandon their restrictions on capital outflows to the United States—but the United States should establish "close surveillance over private capital outflows."

In the more narrowly monetary focus, the International Monetary Fund should encourage borrowers to draw the currencies of the surplus countries (D-marks, guilders, lire, Belgian francs) rather than dollars—and the United States should draw from the Fund for its own needs. The Treasury should "undertake a study of desirability of continuing free gold markets." And negotiations should be started to explore the chances for creating (à la Triffin) a reserve asset that would be neither a national currency nor a precious metal, to be generated through the IMF.

Kennedy showed this report to Douglas Dillon. As Republican and banker, as confident yet cautious aristocrat, Dillon was unattractive to those members of the Kennedy entourage who later wrote books about Camelot, and his appointment as Treasury Secretary has been treated as a sop to the moneyed interests. Robert Solomon, senior economic consultant to the Fed, has noted with splendid condescension that Dillon "showed an ability to grasp difficult problems, was briskly efficient, and was given to dogged hard work." Much the same could be said about Kennedy, and the two men shared much more: both were the sons of parvenu Wall Street pirates who had made enough money to buy their children New England prep schools, Harvard, and social cachet. (Dillon's father, as virtually nobody remembers, was born a Rumanian Jew whose name was not Dillon.) Both men had been naval officers during the war.

Dillon may have seemed an aloof figure to the White House staff, but there is no reason to believe that Kennedy shared their perception, or disagreed with Dillon's views on financial matters. Moreover, Dillon had a great ally in the background: "We always winced when Jack went up to Hyannisport for a weekend," says a man who was in the White House, "because we knew his father would chew his ear off about the balance of payments and he'd come back all upset."

Dillon found the Ball task force recommendations extreme: "There were," he recalls, "some task force things that weren't very practical." Kennedy quickly established a new committee, chaired by Allan Sproul, retired president of the Federal Reserve Bank of New York, which produced more conventional—even pious—proposals. ("First, as a government and as a nation we need to give more explicit attention to the subject of improving productivity. . . .") But Ball had convinced the President about Roosa, who was one of only two names Kennedy suggested Dillon consider as Under Secretary (the other was Coombs), and presently Roosa was the number-two man at Treasury.

A week after his inauguration, Kennedy met at the White House with the members of the Sproul Committee, Dillon, Roosa and Walter Heller, the Chairman of his Council of Economic Advisers, to plan a fast message to Congress on gold and the balance of payments. He had pledged "to get the country moving again," and though the recession had in fact bottomed out in the last quarter of 1960, nobody knew that in early 1961. Almost any stimulative efforts undertaken by Washington in 1961, however, would raise suspicions abroad, and it was important to reassure the foreigners that the United States did not regard the dollar with what would later be called "benign neglect."

On February 6, then, Kennedy submitted a message renewing the commitment to a dollar pegged to gold at $35 an ounce and conceding that "the United States must in the decades ahead, much more than at any time in the past, take its balance of payments into account when formulating its economic policies and conducting its economic affairs." We would not adopt protectionist policies or capital controls, and we would carry forward our military and aid programs. We would rely mostly on export expansion (to be helped by cost and price stability at home, and financed by additional loans and guarantees through the Export-Import Bank). We would encourage travel and investment by foreigners in the United States, and reduce the duty-free allowance of returning American travelers from $500 to $100.

On reform of the international monetary system, Kennedy threw the disappointed Triffin a bone, ordering the Secretary of the Treasury to begin exploring with other countries ways to strengthen the IMF and lessen the world's reliance on dollars as the source of additional reserves and liquidity. There was no rush about that. "The United States could safely continue to be the principal banker of the free world." Dillon and Roosa both believed, to Triffin's disgust, that foreigners in 1961 would see an American drive toward a Keynes-type IMF the way Americans in 1944 had regarded the initial Keynes proposal—as a means for a debtor to escape paying his debts. No less than Eisenhower or Nixon, Kennedy and Johnson believed that the United States should negotiate only from strength, and in 1961 the dollar was not strong. All in all, as the Treasury said in a report in 1968, the Kennedy program "was in accord with the general objectives of the Eisenhower Administration."

But there were changes, ultimately far-reaching if not immediately striking. Throughout the Kennedy statement ran the unspoken theme that the United States could no longer be passive in the foreign exchange markets, simply responding to developments elsewhere by reflex sales and purchases of gold. We announced a readiness to borrow from the IMF to acquire foreign currencies, reducing the need for foreign central banks to acquire dollars (and thus the temptation to convert excess dollars to gold) when the United States had a payments deficit. Moreover, we were prepared to make special arrangements to borrow dollars from foreign holders. If the interest rates on normal U.S. Treasury issues weren't high enough to make up for the Gresham's Law disadvantage of the dollar versus gold, we would sell special nonmarketable U.S. government securities at a higher interest rate to foreign monetary authorities and central banks.

More. American law forbade the payment of interest on bank deposits of thirty days or less, and set ceilings on the interest rates American banks could pay on longer time deposits. Those laws were to be waived for deposits made by foreign governments and central banks, and the interest paid on such deposits was to be exempted from American taxes.

Meanwhile, Kennedy sent another message—a confidential aide-mémoire to the government of West Germany—urging Bonn to participate in an "equitable distribution of international burdens." The German payments surplus was "splitting up the international community," and its growth should be stopped. This was not a recommendation for a mark revaluation—as a market man, Roosa knew that a change in the par value of any currency would roil the relations of all the others. (The task force had specifically rejected the idea of urging German revaluation.) Instead, the American government was recommending that the Germans dispose of their surplus through a greatly enlarged foreign aid program: "exports of long-term capital, especially to developing countries, should equal, or even exceed, the export surplus of the surplus country toward the whole world."

By 1961, the Germans themselves were not at all happy with their surplus, which was pumping money into an overheated domestic economy on the brink of dangerous inflation.* In June 1960 the Bundesbank had squeezed the German banks to wring out excess liquidity, imposing the highest discount rate since the war—only to see capital rush to the mark when, only one week later ("a tragic coincidence") the Fed eased conditions in the American money market and reduced the discount rate to help the American economy out of its gathering slump. The inflow of short-term capital increased the German surplus and inflationary peril, and worsened the American payments deficit. Back to the drawing boards.

In July 1960, the EEC Monetary Committee recommended to the Council of Ministers—with the concurrence of the German delegate, Otmar Emminger, later president of the Bundesbank—that the mark be revalued. Decision was put off until after the IMF annual meeting in September, at which nobody in the conference hall or the corridors pushed on the Germans, leaving them with the feeling that the problem did not seem urgent to the rest of the world.

The German government had, in fact, explored Kennedy's suggestion of relieving inflationary pressures by exporting marks, but every time the analysts looked at the problem, they came back with the conclusion that giving foreigners more marks to spend would increase their expenditures in Germany itself, exacerbating the inflation and keeping the surplus high. Moreover, there was some question at the Finance Ministry whether it was safe for Germany to put out long-term investment funds as a way to neutralize an inflow of short-term money drawn by higher interest rates. The United States might be happy to serve as the world's banker; it was no job for Germans. Nevertheless, almost

---

*In 1978, a confused Carter administration kept telling Congress and the press that a trade deficit was inflationary. In fact, a trade deficit is *deflationary* (goods arrive from abroad to sop up money), and a surplus is inflationary (people are paid to produce goods that they can't buy with the money). If exchange rates are flexible, the country with the deficit suffers a depreciating currency, which is inflationary; but in the 1960s the exchange rates were fixed.

$1 billion worth of marks were put out in foreign investment, mostly in other Common Market countries, during 1960.

In October, the Bundesbank again recommended a revaluation of the mark, and Chancellor Adenauer personally turned down the proposal. Germany had just begun to acquire gold reserves, and revaluation would mean a loss on the gold; moreover, it would penalize, through reducing the mark value of their external loans and investments, the German banks and companies which had accepted the government's invitation to export capital. The central bank's council then decided that the tight-money policy had proved counterproductive to the balance of payments, and that the external situation had to take precedence over the needs of the domestic economy. Despite the mounting inflationary pressure, the Bundesbank lowered its discount rate and eased reserve requirements for the German banks. Perhaps for the first time in the history of relations between a government and a quasi-independent central bank, the government complained that the bank had made money too easy.

Into this atmosphere came the Kennedy aide-mémoire. It produced a quick decision for revaluation. On Friday, March 3, deputy president Emminger flew to Washington to inform the U.S. Treasury and the IMF. On Saturday, March 4, the value of the D-Mark in dollars was raised from 23.81¢ (4.2 marks to the dollar) to 25¢ (4 exactly). The Dutch, closely tied to the German economy, quickly copied; everyone else stood fast. The size of the revaluation, Emminger comments dryly, "was a compromise between those in favor of the measure and those against it." It was universally considered insufficient, and further money flooded into Germany in the belief that a second revaluation would occur. Speculation dominated the exchange: after all, the man who had bought $1,000,000 worth of D-marks on March 3, could swap them for $1,050,000 on March 6. If the mark were now to be forced up to 26.32¢ (or 3.8 to the dollar), which many observers expected, the man who put $1,000,000 into marks could hope to take out a profit of more than $52,000. Quickly.

In choosing the currency to sell while purchasing marks, the speculators went first to the British pound; for whatever happened, it was clear that the pound would not rise in value. But the British still had some exchange controls in place, and pounds in enormous quantities were not that easy to come by. For the first time, speculators began to borrow dollars for the purpose of purchasing another currency. Prior to 1961, the decision about how to manage a world currency problem had always devolved upon Washington; now the power to act lay elsewhere.

2

In December 1946, twenty-nine months after Resolution V of the Bretton Woods conference had called for the liquidation of the institution, the governors of the European central banks met for the first time since the war in the converted old Basle hotel which then housed the Bank for International Settlements. (It now has a gleaming tower, the very lobby of which cannot be entered except by appointment; the largest building in Basle.) The European central bankers were not bound by Bretton Woods, they had enormous problems in common, and they needed a place to meet where they would be free of the otherwise ubiquitous presence of the United States.

Formed as part of the Young Plan that would permit Germany to finance its World War I reparation payments through private loans, the Bank for International Settlements was and is an original bird in the aviary of international organizations. Though it was established by a treaty among the Belgian, British, French, German, Italian, Japanese and Swiss governments—though its members are all governmental or quasi-governmental bodies—though it can accept deposits only from official bodies—BIS is a private company, with shares traded on the Paris Bourse and profits that recently have run $100 million a year. It can buy and sell gold, commercial paper, and corporate bonds, but it cannot lend money to treasuries or hold treasury paper from any member country. Its directors (one of whom serves as president) were to be the governors of the central banks of Belgium, France, Germany, Great Britain, Italy, and the United States, plus seven individuals from private business and nine representatives of central banks in other countries.

But the United States never joined (the shares of stock assigned to the Federal Reserve in the prospectus were bought, and later sold to the public, by J. P. Morgan & Co., and the First National Banks of New York and Chicago; an odd result of the American abstention was that the BIS can and does invest in U.S. Treasury paper because the United States is not a member). During the war, the private business representatives fell off the board; and when the institution struggled back to life, the only other countries supplying directors from their central banks were Sweden, Switzerland, and the Netherlands.

Even at the time the BIS was established with a capitalization of half a billion Swiss francs, the relationship between central banks and governments was formal and close; but most of the central banks then maintained at least a legal fiction of private ownership. (In the United States, the Federal Reserve Banks—though not the Federal Reserve Board—are to this day supposedly owned by their member-bank shareholders, who receive an annual 6 percent dividend on the subscription price.) So the BIS charter, while specifying that directors are to be the governors of central banks, also says that directors cannot be government officials. Quaint.

BIS had maintained some of its functions through the war. Most of the belligerents had to make occasional payments in Switzerland, and BIS was in place to act as agent for anonymous member central banks. It was the fiscal agent for the International Red Cross and the Universal Postal Union, both of which continued active in 1939–45. But its main function—to serve as a central bankers' club, where they could learn, as the 1935 Report had it, "how to avoid doing harm to one another"—had necessarily been in abeyance. The December 1946 meeting was a reconstitution of the club.

The United States considered itself bound by the Bretton

Woods resolution, and the Fed had never participated in BIS, anyway. The institution Americans liked was the IMF, which was in Washington, official, subject to control by governments, and dominated by the United States. For three years, the Truman administration tried to persuade its allies to order their central banks out of BIS (the Japanese were made to renounce their membership as part of the peace treaty, and did not return until 1970)—and failed. When the European Payments Union was formed with American help in 1950, BIS took over the intricate task of receiving funds, netting out balances, and allocating surpluses between convertible and inconvertible currencies—and the U.S. Treasury threw in the sponge. An official statement noted the diplomatic efforts to dismantle BIS, reported that "the response of other governments was virtually negative" (a fine complaining phrase) and concluded that "the United States Government regards this issue as closed."

The key provision of the BIS charter was that the directors were to meet once a month, ten times a year. (Nothing much was supposed to happen in the money markets in the summer.) To guarantee the attendance of the governors in person, these monthly meetings were held over weekends. It helped that Basle has excellent restaurants; even so, the willingness to cap an always busy work week with Friday-night-to-Sunday-evening sessions argues a seriousness of purpose among central bankers not always found in lesser policy-makers.

On March 10, 1961, in any event, there was no difficulty securing full attendance at the BIS meeting. Since the German announcement, money had been flowing to the mark in unprecedented quantities, swamping the foreign exchange facilities of all the central banks and endangering the international monetary system itself. Other than closing the market for a few days of cooling off—an expedient that would in fact be tried in later years—there was no obvious way to avoid the worldwide highly inflationary monetary expansion that would result if central banks, to keep their own economies on an even keel, expanded their own money supply to compensate for the draining off of their currencies to Germany. (This was a major source of the desperate inflation of 1979: American insistence on expanding domestic money supply in 1977–78 to frustrate the automatic correctives that would have followed the outflows of dollars caused by the trade deficit.)

In the middle of the week, the Germans had figured it out: the Bundesbank would lend marks to the central banks of countries with currencies under attack. Instead of foreign currencies moving into marks through market channels and appearing at the Bundesbank for conversion according to IMF rules and parities, they would be sopped up in their countries of origin by the local central bank. The marks sold abroad by local central banks would not flow to Germany in any great quantity, because the "bardepot" forbade the payment of interest to foreigners by or through German banks (and, to ice the cake, forbade German banks to lend out most of any increase in foreign deposits). The foreign currency converted to marks would never leave its country of origin. The fixed exchange rate could be sustained.

In the nature of foreign-exchange transactions, the upward pressure on the mark was being exerted through "forward" purchases (i.e., marks to be delivered to the buyer and paid for at some future time) rather than "spot" purchases (for immediate payment and delivery). In normal times, the great bulk of the business done in the foreign-exchange markets finances international trade. Foreign trade is not accomplished by impulse buying: exporters and importers sign contracts for future delivery and payment. Thus a trade surplus shows up as a demand in the "forward market" for the domestic currency, which foreign importers will need to make their purchases; a trade deficit shows up as a demand in the "forward market" for foreign currencies to finance the domestic imports.

Banks make it possible for manufacturers, distributors, and retailers in domestic or foreign trade to acquire their inventory by borrowing its cost, and for suppliers to be paid in cash as they ship their goods. Lending dollars to an automobile dealer to permit him to pay an American automobile manufacturer for the cars in the showroom, a bank sets its interest rate at a margin over what the bank must pay to the depositors who are in effect lending their money to the bank. Lending marks to a dealer to permit him to buy BMWs, which requires marks, his bank must borrow (solicit deposits in) marks. After, say, ninety days, when the BMW dealer pays back his loan (in dollars), the bank will pay back its foreign depositor in marks. For safety's sake, then, the bank must know not only how many marks it can get for its dollars now (which determines the size of its dollar loan to the dealer) but also how many marks it will be able to get for its dollars when the automobile dealer repays. Banks—good banks, at least—make their profits from the spread between the interest rates they pay to get money and the interest rates they charge to lend it, not from speculating on foreign exchange.

To facilitate lending across borders, then, the banks need contracts which guarantee the exchange rate on the day when their borrowers repay them and they then repay their foreign depositors. If currency flows are unrestricted and cost-free, this forward market must present rates that are in a sense a mirror image of differences in the interest rate in the two countries. When the annual interest rates are 7 percent in Germany and 5 percent in the United States (which is about where they were in 1961), a German banker can get the use of $1 million now by promising $1,012,500 in ninety days, and with the mark at 4-to-1 can convert that $1 million to D-M 4 million—which he can then lend for ninety days to return D-M 4,070,000. Unless forward dollars are at a ½ percent "premium"—that is, unless the dollar will buy 4.02 marks or more in the ninety-day forward market—it will be profitable for the German bank to fund its loans with dollar deposits instead of mark deposits—and it will do so. The dollar was definitely not at a premium against the mark in the forward market. That was the source of the short-term capital outflows that were bedeviling the U.S. Treasury in 1960.

(Two points about this example are highly significant and widely ignored. One is that a relatively small "premium" or "discount" in the forward exchange rate will compensate for a rather large difference in interest rates for short-term loans to finance trade because a ninety-day loan requires payment of only one-quarter of the annual interest. The other is that what normally counts in the day-to-day operations of an international monetary system is *not* the currency in which holders choose to keep their assets or reserves—which is what all the talk in both the newspapers and the textbooks is about—but the currency in which debtors, banks or nonbanks, choose to borrow. High interest rates work to protect a currency partly because they draw deposits in that currency, but also because they persuade borrowers to borrow elsewhere. We shall have occasion to revisit this territory later.)

Fortunately, the machinery—even today—is not so well greased that currency flows are unrestricted and cost-free, which gives nations some margin for moving their domestic interest rates to meet domestic needs. In 1961, currency convertibility was still to some extent restricted (e.g., the "bardepot") and banks were still unaccustomed to soliciting large deposits from or lending large sums to customers in other countries. Nevertheless, in a healthy international money market, the currency of the country with the higher interest rate should always be selling at a discount in the forward market. If the high-interest-rate currency actually sells at a *premium* in the forward market, debtors will find ways to borrow like crazy in the low-interest-rate currency.

The week after the German revaluation in March 1961, the mark actually sold for a few hours at a 4 percent premium over the dollar in the ninety-day market. In other words, people were willing to promise to pay $1,000,000 for D-M 3,840,000 in ninety days, even though that same million dollars would buy D-M 4 million today. For if the D-mark were revalued another 10 percent, to a rate of 3.6 to the dollar (which was where some put it), the 3,840,000 marks could then be converted to $1,066,667. Meanwhile, people with marks to lend got more interest on their money than people with dollars. An intermediary borrowing dollars and lending marks, and covering his risks back to dollars in the forward market at a premium of 4 percent, a man could guarantee himself a return of 5.9 percent in ninety days, a rate of 23.6 percent a year, absolutely safe. Left alone, this would produce a hemorrhage of dollars. The Bretton Woods system had gone blooey.

The Friday of the week after the revaluation, the manager of the foreign department of the Bundesbank called Charles Coombs at the Federal Reserve Bank of New York and made him a tentative offer he couldn't refuse. Subject to confirmation after both sides had checked with their governments, the Bundesbank was prepared to supply the Fed with $250 million worth of D-marks, to be sold by the Fed in the forward markets to drive down the premium. These transactions would, of course, leave the Fed with a debt in D-marks that would have to be repaid at a higher exchange rate if the mark revalued again. The Bundesbank would guarantee any such losses, selling the Fed D-marks at the rate of 4-to-1 whatever the actual rate might be on the day the forward contracts had to be fulfilled. If there were profits, on the other hand—if the D-mark were *not* revalued and our speculator's D-M 3,840,000 could be bought back for only $960,000—the Bundesbank would be happy to split them 50-50 with the Fed. Coombs called Roosa in Washington, told him the kraut mob had invited him to shoot craps with their money, and had an okay to proceed on that basis in less than an hour. All transactions were to be for the Treasury's account: the Federal Reserve Board was not yet ready to enter the foreign exchange markets, even on a risk-free basis.

Meanwhile, the Germans and the Swiss had put their heads together on the problem of shoring up the pound. For Britain to accept help from Germany, only sixteen years after the defeat of Hitler, would be hard; but the British had nothing against the Swiss. At breakfast in Basle on Saturday morning, the manager of foreign exchange for the Swiss National Bank offered his counterpart at the Bank of England a $310 million credit for intervention in the exchange markets. In private bilateral meetings later that day, the other central banks individually chipped in, raising the kitty to over $900 million—and on Sunday BIS calmly announced to the world that the central banks of Europe were "cooperating on the exchange market." What had been done was too new to describe—its very novelty would have unsettled the market.

Quite a lot of money was committed to maintaining these approved exchange rates (at its peak, the Bundesbank forward credit to the New York Fed as agent for the Treasury ran to $340 million worth of marks) but eventually the speculators ran for cover. The rates established in this exercise would endure for six years; and the central banks—a matter that may not seem important to you but did to them, for they must all report one way or another to a legislature—showed a handsome profit on the operation. But the experience may have been misleading; what returned the mark to its new parity had nothing to do with Coombs's interventions. The forward premium on the mark actually rose to its peak in June, when the ninety-day contracts from March expired and the technical condition of the market (all those people who had to sell the marks they had bought forward) should have been pushing the mark back down. But that summer Khrushchev rattled the saber over Berlin, and his bully-boys built the Wall. The political risks of holding marks overcame the market's economic judgment.

3

The direct involvement of the Federal Reserve Bank of New York in the 1961 crisis opened a buried fissure in the institutional structure of American government. During the 1920s, the New York Fed had been by far the most important policy center for American monetary policy. New York was the commanding height of American finance and the point of contact between American and European markets; Ben Strong, the president of that bank, was both J. P. Morgan's son-in-law and a good friend of Montagu Norman at the Bank of England. The system of influencing interest rates by central bank purchases and sales of securities, acceptances and gold ("open market operations") had been developed ad hoc by the New York Fed, which considered itself not merely the operator but the proprietor of this increasingly important tool.

When financial collapse precipitated the Great Depression, much of the opprobrium attached to the New York Fed—and, indeed, to central bankers everywhere. (Central bankers, of course, always carry the can: Nicholas Biddle in the United States in the 1830s and the Bank of England in the 1870s experienced similar episodes.) The revisions of the banking laws put in place by the New Deal were specifically directed to bringing New York under the close supervision of the Federal Reserve Board in Washington. When the dollar was formally devalued in 1934, the Exchange Stabilization Fund established to pocket the profits on gold was specifically established in the Treasury, with only a minimal role for the Fed as a whole and none at all for New York. Communications networks were such that New York could not be completely eliminated, but in both open market operations and foreign operations it was labeled nothing more than a fiscal agent for controlling bodies in Washington. Allan Sproul, by character and intelligence, had pushed the tide back a bit, but it was always pressing in.

As long as the United States maintained a passive posture in the foreign exchange markets, selling gold on demand and buying it on offer at an established price, there was no need for expertise or decision making in the foreign area at the New York Fed. Now the Treasury was trying to conserve gold, and needed help—and big trouble had revealed the weakness of the International Monetary Fund, where decisions could be taken only by vote of twenty "executive directors" who had to check back with their governments before they could move. The central bankers' club in Basle had taken command, no doubt with the consent of the governments but without close control by the finance ministries.

The United States was not even a member of the Bank for International Settlements. Prior to December 1960, it had never sent anyone to the monthly governors' meetings; and the man finally sent as an "observer" was Coombs, then a relatively junior officer of the New York Fed (though his status in both Basle and Washington was doubtless enhanced by the knowledge that Kennedy thought well of him). Day-to-day operations in the management of that forward-mark fund would have to be conducted by New York on a long leash, and they might have profound influence on the future course of American international monetary policy.

Though everyone was grateful for the sturdiness of the central bankers in March, there was some question about whether that was really the way to go. Testifying eighteen months later before Congressman Henry Reuss's subcommittee on international payments, the Canadian economist Harry Johnson, a brilliant neo-Keynesian gut fighter who held his own in the neo-classical atmosphere of the University of Chicago, commented that "It seems to me undesirable from the standpoint of either a liberal economic system or a democratic system of government that a matter as important as this should be left to arrangements by agreement of a secret or delayed-publication kind between individuals who are not representative of elected governments and who are inevitably concerned with national ahead of international objectives.... Past ... efforts to keep the international economy running by agreement between central bankers ... could be described as successful in the short run but not in the long run. Their effect was to accumulate disequilibriums."

Moreover, the Basle club was a very exclusive group. The Kennedy administration was developing its Alliance for Progress, and Latin America was not represented in Basle. An effort was afoot to woo India, which had a large quota and some influence at the International Monetary Fund, but nobody at the Bank for International Settlements. The 1960s had been labeled by the United Nations as The Development Decade and new African countries were springing up like dandelions. They all dealt in dollars, and they had no input at Basle.

Per Jacobsson had come from Basle to the International Monetary Fund, and was conscious of the elements of competition between the two organizations. In 1960, he had sold gold to the United States from the IMF stocks to help ease the pain of the break-out on the London market. But in seeking to help the United States over the next stile, the IMF was limited by a financial structure geared to help other people get dollars. Nearly $6 billion in dollars was available at the Fund to be drawn from the U.S. quota and other people's repayments of past drawings—but the total amount of possibly usable European currencies was the equivalent of only $1.6 billion. Jacobsson produced a plan by which European financial strength could be linked to the near-universality of the International Monetary Fund—a special arrangement by the governments of the large countries to make their currencies available on special call through the IMF.

These negotiations produced an institution of some importance—the Group of 10, consisting of Belgium, Britain, Canada, France, Germany, Italy, Japan, the Netherlands, Sweden, and the United States—and a public relations ploy called the General Arrangement to Borrow, under which these nations agreed to commit an additional $6 billion to the IMF if necessary to shore up the fixed exchange-rate system. Of this total, the United States pledged $2 billion and Britain pledged $1 billion, so the net extra available to the key currency countries was only $3 billion—but that doubled what was already there. This money would not be provided automatically, however: the case would have to be proved to the satisfaction of the lenders as well as the IMF. Lending through the GAB would require what the Arrangement called (the demand for it was French; the wording, Canadian) "multilateral surveillance." Roosa remembers calling from Paris to Washington to clear the phrase with Dillon: "He gave a kind of whistle, and then said, 'Well, if we have to.'"

The GAB turned out to have uses for Britain during its long struggle to maintain the exchange rate of the pound despite deteriorating productivity of the workforce, and for France to cushion the shock of May 1968. The restrictions hedging the

Arrangement, however, made it from the American point of view rather like the famous case of spoiled sardines that circulated in hyperinflationary China as acceptable "money" until some damn fool opened one of the cans. GAB was *trading* sardines, not *eating* sardines—useful as an announcement but not for consumption. In any event, the Arrangement did not come into effect until October 1962 because Congress took its sweet time approving the contingent appropriation.

There were many balls in the air, but Roosa had his eye really on only one: the preservation of the American gold stock, the avoidance of "asset settlement" of the American payments deficit. The demand for gold from Europe reflected a return by European central banks to historical preferences for gold as the major component of currency reserves. The United States, with a law requiring 25 percent "gold cover" for Federal Reserve currency, could scarcely be too critical of such attitudes. But the inevitable result was that these countries, acquiring dollars, would spend them for gold rather than hold them as reserves. And it was a one-way ratchet: when their payments swung to deficit, the Europeans ran down the remaining dollar component of their reserves rather than sell back the gold. What was important, then, was to keep dollars from piling up at the European central banks. As long as the deficits persisted, the risk would be there—but there were what Roosa called "perimeter defenses" that could be reinforced.

The Bundesbank had provided a credit in marks to the Fed. Roosa now supplemented that credit by requesting the Germans to denominate in marks a little less than one-fifth of a $587 million advance repayment of Marshall Plan loans in May 1961. In the summer, the Swiss central bank was being inundated with dollars from British repayments of the advances made during the March crisis; Roosa sopped them up with a special issue of U.S. Treasury securities denominated in Swiss francs rather than dollars, and carrying a low Swiss interest rate of 1½ percent. Such issues were called "Roosa bonds" until late 1978, when the idea came around again as part of the last-ditch defense of the dollar, and appropriately larger sales of U.S. obligations denominated in other currencies (but sold to the public rather than to foreign central banks) were called "Carter bonds." The legal basis for such issues, fortuitously remembered by William Heffelfinger, a 40-year Treasury veteran, was the Second Liberty Bond Act of World War I days, under which the United States had once sold an issue in pesetas to Spanish bankers to finance the purchase of war materiel in neutral Spain. Roosa presented this background to Congressional questioners as though rather surprised that they didn't know about it themselves.

Italy was another country with a payments surplus and a strong currency and a tradition of holding reserves in gold. With the Italians, Roosa arranged a "swap line"—i.e., a standby agreement by which the Italians would on request temporarily trade lire for dollars, permitting the United States rather than Italy to intervene in the exchange markets and supply lire to people who wanted them. On a smaller scale, a similar deal was made with the Dutch and (actually the first to be announced) with the French.

What characterized the arrangements with all these countries except Germany was that the United States in effect was guaranteeing the exchange rate on the dollars in the deal. If the dollar was devalued while a swap was outstanding, the borrowed currency would have to be returned, though buying it back from the market under the new rates would cost the United States many more dollars. (When devaluation finally did come in 1971, the loss to the United States on swap lines ran "close to $400 million." The loss on Swiss-franc-denominated Roosa bonds has been more than a billion dollars, and is still climbing.) By the same token, the countries on the other side of the swap received an assurance of continued value for this part of the dollars in their reserves, and were thus content to refrain from trips to the gold window. (And, of course, the United States in recent years has sold the gold conserved by Roosa bonds at profits much greater than the losses on the bonds.)*

But negotiations between governments were time-consuming and clumsy, subject to cabinet discussions where extraneous issues were likely to arise, never entirely free from political pressures. Roosa was trying to keep the outflowing dollars from threatening the gold stock, partly by absorbing some of them into American debt denominated in other currencies, partly by structuring the private markets to persuade individuals and businesses to keep the dollars in their private reserves. For both these purposes, he needed market intervention and market expertise, and that meant heavy use of the facilities of the New York Fed. Even as the staffs at the International Monetary Fund and the U.S. Treasury labored to keep the world's governments front-and-center of the monetary system, the central banks were elbowing them aside.

Truman's and Eisenhower's Secretaries of the Treasury had been Midwesterners and Southwesterners; Kennedy's was a New Yorker. Roosa had been a vice-president of the New York Fed and was if anything a Trojan horse at the Treasury; he not only lacked fear of the New York Fed, he liked it. In its generation-old dispute with the Federal Reserve System, and especially the New York Fed, the Treasury gave ground. In February 1962, with Treasury approval, the Open Market Committee gave Charles Coombs an okay to intervene in the foreign exchange markets with the Fed's own funds, and to arrange swap lines directly with the foreign central banks. For the next nine and a half years, though ultimate authority never left the Treasury, the command post for the defense of the dollar would be in New York.

So it was Coombs, a solid, worried-looking Harvard-trained economist, now a vice-president of the New York Fed and after March 1961 a regular participant in the Basle meetings, who handled the organization and operation of the gold pool.

---

*It was only American actions that could trigger American losses, however: if the foreign country revalued its currency upward, the United States could under Roosa's agreements buy the foreign currency at the old rates and extinguish the swap just before the action took effect.

(Coombs's boss, Alfred Hayes, president of the New York Fed, also attended some of the meetings and took over where necessary; Federal Reserve Board Chairman Martin went to Basle two or three times a year.) Not without difficulty, Coombs sold the BIS members on the proposition that everybody had a stake in holding down the London prices, and that everybody should put some gold into the account being managed by the Bank of England. This took until November, but produced a deal—never put in writing, as Coombs admiringly reports. ("The personal word of each governor was as binding as any written contract.")

Some $270 million of gold was committed, half of it by the United States, 11 percent by the Germans, 9.25 percent each by the British, French and Italians, the rest by lesser folk. The non-American participants did not, in fact, agree to hold the dollars they might receive from the sales, and remained free to replenish their gold at the Treasury's window—but they did agree not to enter any gold market as buyers and to increase their national gold holdings, if at all, only via Washington.

The pool weathered the shock of the American stock market break in spring 1962 and the greater shock of the Cuban missile crisis (during which, oddly enough, the Russians took advantage of the fact that gold was at its maximum permissible price to sell some $60 million out of their stock). In 1963, the combination of a South African trade deficit and the collapse of Khrushchev's "virgin lands" schemes brought floods of newly mined gold to the market, and the pool became a large-scale purchaser of gold, which was divvied up among the participants according to their shares. By September 1964, Coombs reports, the activities of the pool had increased the central banks' store of gold by $1.3 billion worth. But the United States did not get to keep its share, for the central banks of the lesser countries and—especially—the French kept buying at the window.

Nevertheless, Roosa's policies had created an atmosphere: it was now understood that good friends of the United States would hold back from converting to gold the dollars that came in to them from the continuing American payments deficit. It was even more firmly understood that the use of the dollar as a conduit for the conversion of sterling from British deficits to gold at the American window would provoke high and reasonable displeasure. As the British economist Roy Harrod put it, the United States had "institutionalized the inconvertibility of the reserve currencies through gentlemen's agreements."

But Roosa did not for a moment believe that this psychological barrier at the gold window would be an answer to the dollar's problems. "We must," he said in 1962, "sell abroad, on commercial terms, enough to pay for all of our imports, for all of the governmental programs which prudence commands, and at the same time support the unrestricted flows of capital that our national interest requires. . . . That is the only fundamental solution."

The question remained: how do you do that?

Worse yet: how do you do *what?* "You can no more define equilibrium in international trade than you can define a pretty girl," Per Jacobsson once said, "but you can recognize one if you meet one." In the great balance-of-payments anxiety that afflicted the Kennedy administration, with its presidential announcements, Congressional hearings, international confabs— what were people worrying about?

4

Let us distinguish five measurements:

(1) *The trade balance.* This one looks relatively straightforward. It measures the value of exports against the value of imports. Even here there are complexities: The American trade surplus of 1962, for example, included some $2.2 billion of food shipped abroad under the terms of Public Law 480, under which the United States accumulated nonconvertible currencies in poor countries where people might otherwise go hungry, plus machinery exports financed under the aid programs or by the outflow of private American capital.

Customs figures, which provide the basic import data, may well be misleading: those who must pay a duty ad valorem are tempted to understate the value. Where subsidiaries abroad ship to parent companies at home, tax considerations may dictate the declared price: the Bernstein Committee on Balance of Payments Statistics found that in the early 1960s United Fruit was charging itself 2¢–2.5¢ a pound for bananas sent to New York when the wholesale price in the banana republics was 3¢–4¢ a pound.

Accounting procedures influenced the numbers, too: we credited our exports f.a.s. (free alongside ship—that is, at the border) while foreign importers reported the prices they paid c.i.f. (including cost of the merchandise, insurance and freight charges). This meant that our trade surplus was always reported as smaller than our partners' trade deficits. In 1962, the United States had a $4.5 billion trade surplus.

(2) *The current account.* This figure includes the trade balance plus receipts and expenditures on services and "invisibles"—tourism, interest payments and repatriated dividends on investments, earnings from fees, patents, and copyrights, insurance, shipping, etc. Arms sales, for reasons never satisfactorily explained, were included under "services." It was characteristic of the American current account that invisibles were a plus; characteristic of the German current account that they were a minus. In 1962, the American current account was in surplus by $5.1 billion.

(3) *Liquidity.* This figure was the "balance of payments" reported by the Commerce Department after 1958. It was, simply, the net change in liquid claims held by foreigners against the United States before "settlement" of any of those claims through transfers of reserve assets (i.e., gold sales, or during the Roosa days changes in the Treasury's stock of foreign exchange). Strangely enough, the Eisenhower administration never included foreigners' drawings of dollars from the IMF as offsets to the liquidity deficit, or the increasing American credit at the IMF as part of the nation's reserve assets—but in 1958–60, when the turn against the dollar began, foreigners' repayments of those dollars to the IMF absorbed $1.3 billion of the payments deficit.

From the foreign point of view—forced on the United States

through its vulnerability at the gold window—the liquidity balance was the number that counted. But this measurement could be grossly misleading for "the world's banker"; one does not criticize a bank for its growing deposit liabilities if they are matched by growing assets in the loan portfolio. The American liquidity balance could look bad even if the American economy was really in surplus; for a foreign country in deficit, borrowing in the American market to carry that deficit, could push the United States into the red. In 1958, for example, the French carried their deficit with Germany by borrowing dollars in America. From the German point of view, the Bundesbank was deluged not with francs but with dollars—simply because Jean Monnet knew some bankers in New York.

As long as world trade was financed with dollars, its expansion *required* an increasing collection of dollars, claims against America, in the outside world. And if Quebec Hydro raised the money to build a dam by selling bonds in New York—because the Toronto market was too thin to absorb so large an issue—the result on the liquidity balance was a minus for the United States because the bonds purchased by Americans were not counted as "liquid" assets, while the dollars received by Canadians were nothing but.

The anti-American bias of the liquidity balance was made worse by a peculiar accounting quirk at the Commerce Department. If an American bank made a ninety-day loan to a British cigarette manufacturer to finance his purchase of tobacco, that was a "short-term capital outflow" because it established, however briefly, a dollar deposit in the name of a foreign entity. (And because American banks require borrowers to keep some of their loan on deposit as a "compensating balance," part of the money would stay on the books for the entire ninety days as a foreigner's "liquid" deposit.) But if a British bank made a ninety-day loan to an American liquor importer to finance the purchase of Scotch, that was not for the Commerce Department a "short-term capital inflow." In fact, in the lunatic system employed in Washington, it was counted as *another* "outflow," because it gave the British bank a liquid claim for dollars from the importer. The Bernstein Committee sternly described the liquidity balance concept as "unsatisfactory in principle and difficult to apply in practice."

In one way, the liquidity balance figures as published are a refreshing rarity among government statistics, for they are *admittedly* inaccurate. After tracking everything they know how to track, the Commerce Department balance mavens make the books come out right at the end by throwing in a final line labeled "Errors and Omissions." In the late 1970s, that line, now renamed "Statistical Discrepancies," would grow to awesome size ($7 billion in the second quarter of 1978, an incredible $20 billion in the first quarter of 1979); but even in the early 1960s it was typically large enough to account in most years for more than a third of the deficit. In 1962, the liquidity deficit totaled $2 billion; "errors and omissions" were $1.2 billion of it. And even that was to a large extent guesswork. How should the government count fund transfers between subsidiaries of a multinational corporation? How, indeed, could the government find out about them?

(4) *The basic balance.* This one was the economists' favorite. Developed at the Commerce Department in 1943 but abandoned in the official figures after 1950, the basic balance measured the current account plus long-term capital flows. The logic here was compelling: the American dollars that traveled to Canada to build a General Motors factory in Windsor would be a long time returning, and their outflow was indeed part of the American payments problem. But the American dollars that helped finance trade—quite possibly between two foreign countries, for the dollar was the "vehicle currency"—were quickly recoverable at worst and automatically recovered if one of the parties to the trade was American. The basic balance consistently showed American deficits far smaller than the publicized figures. For 1961 and part of 1962, in fact, the American basic balance was in surplus. Unfortunately, the distinction between long-term and short-term capital flows was artificial; some "long-term" investments in foreign securities might come back fast when the securities were sold, and some short-term lending might be part of a

pattern of rollover financing that left growing stocks of dollars at work abroad for many years.

(5) *Official settlements.* This measurement looks like the most accurate of all, and in the early 1960s it was plausibly the most important. It simply totaled the American loss of gold and the increase in the stock of dollars held by foreign central banks and governments—the dollars that were recognized claims against the American gold stock. Any dollars remaining in private hands were disregarded: presumably, private individuals, banks and businesses abroad held onto dollars because they wanted them. Supplying dollars to people who wanted them abroad was part of the banking function and not part of the balance problem for American government policy. In 1962, the deficit in the official settlements ledger was about $1.5 billion.

This way of measuring the balance of payments was recommended to the American government in 1965 by the Bernstein Committee, a study team named for Edward M. Bernstein, who had been Assistant Secretary of the Treasury and chief economist-statistician for the IMF. Unfortunately, there were two things wrong with it. One was that foreign central banks, under pressure from the United States not to cash in their dollars at the gold window, could push them back into the private markets—specifically, into the Eurodollar market, which we shall examine in the next chapter—because the earnings on dollars in those markets were greater than they were on Treasury bills in the United States. Moreover, the stock of dollars in official hands was useful to foreign monetary authorities for open market operations to manipulate the quantity of domestic money. Thus the change in "official" dollars might on occasion reflect the domestic monetary policies of foreign countries rather than any payments balance.

The second thing wrong with the official settlements balance was more serious. The liquidity concept, the Bernstein Committee complained, "implies that all foreign holdings represent an equal threat to the reserves, whereas in fact only foreign monetary authorities can draw down reserves." After November 1960, this theoretical truth was a practical error. In deciding to fix the price of gold on the London market—a decision specifically and bluntly confirmed by Treasury Secretary Dillon in Vienna at the annual IMF meeting in fall 1961—the United States had formed a direct link between gold and dollars in private hands. Should a crisis occur, foreign dollar holdings by official agencies would be if anything *less* of a threat than foreign dollar holdings in private hands. The officials would be constrained by political considerations and a sense of responsibility for the international monetary system, while the private holders would follow the dictates of Gresham's Law and the rule of *sauve qui peut*. Misleading and wrongheaded as it was, the liquidity balance was what the Kennedy administration could not ignore.

5

Given the persistence of the liquidity deficit, the question was whether the United States was faced with what the Articles of the IMF called a "fundamental disequilibrium" or whether the balance could be righted by "adjustments" and should be financed until those adjustments took effect. Kennedy, Dillon, and Roosa had no doubt that the situation could be adjusted, and that Coombs's operations at the perimeter defenses would guarantee the financing for as long as necessary. "Our efforts to safeguard the dollar are progressing," Kennedy proclaimed in his State of the Union message for 1962. " . . . Speculative fever against the dollar is ending—and confidence in the dollar has been restored."

The problem, after all, was not that the American economy was uncompetitive with the rest of the world—the balance of trade was in surplus—but that the United States had made political and economic commitments not only in its own interest but in the interest of the "free world." As Kennedy said to the IMF annual meeting in 1962, "The United States could bring its international payments into balance overnight. . . . We could withdraw our forces, reduce our aid, tie it wholly to purchases in this country,

raise high tariff barriers and restrict the foreign investment or
other use of American dollars." Fortunately, he added, "the basic
strength of the dollar makes such actions as unnecessary as they
are unwise."

To help the *trade balance,* Kennedy launched the already traditional export drive, backed with new lending authority to the
Export-Import Bank and an expansion of government-backed
programs (already commonplace in Europe) to guarantee the receipts of exporters through insuring that foreign importers would
pay for the goods. Under the Trade Expansion Act of 1962, the
United States also launched a new round of multilateral trade
negotiations under the GATT umbrella. In these negotiations,
the United States would seek greater tariff concessions than it
would give, partly on the argument (which may have been true)
that American tariffs were already lower than those abroad,
partly on the grounds that we had deficits and our European
trading partners had surpluses.

General restriction of American demand through government
action—tight money, budget surpluses—could not even be considered. The Europeans were running full speed ahead, with
shortages of workers to fill jobs, while the United States had an
unemployment problem that would not go away even as Gross
National Product increased at a better than 4 percent annual rate
in 1961–62. Imports ran to only 4 percent of GNP, and certainly
to less than 10 percent of what Americans bought with additions
to (or would stop buying with subtractions from) their total income. "To propose paying $30 or $40 billion per year in reduced
income to American workers and investors to obtain a $2 billion
to $3 billion reduction in the payments deficit," Henry Reuss
grumbled in the Report of his International Payments Subcommittee in 1962, "is to reduce economic calculus to absurdity."

To help the *current account,* Kennedy sought to reduce American expenditures for services (especially the employment of
foreigners at American military bases and diplomatic and aid
missions abroad), and to promote tourism by foreigners in
America.

But the fire was concentrated on the capital flows that dominated the *liquidity* balance. Part of the problem was the fact that short-term interest rates were higher in Europe than in the United States—partly a natural result of a situation where Europe was booming and America was not, partly the result of differences in economic theories about how governments should manage national economies. In Europe, the prevailing school looked for tight money and high interest rates to limit inflation, while government budgets expanded as necessary to provide stimulus in downturns. This was much easier for the Europeans to do because they had cabinet systems of government that could move budget changes through a legislature in a week and because the national governments controlled the financing of local authorities.

To raise interest rates across the board might restrict American demand and domestic investment, which was precisely what the Kennedy administration refused to do. The solution, which Roosa had proposed while still at the New York Fed, was what later came to be called "Operation Twist," an effort to keep long-term rates low while pushing short-term rates higher. This was accomplished—and it *was* accomplished, for a while, until the markets adjusted—by having the Federal Reserve System and the Treasury trust funds put money into the banking system with purchases of long-term Treasury bonds (increasing the demand for, and thus holding down the interest rate on, long-term debt instruments) while refraining from its traditional purchases of short-term Treasury bills (increasing the supply of short-term instruments left in the market, and thus raising the rates short-term borrowers would have to pay). By late 1962, American short-term interest rates were level with or higher than those in the markets of most of the surplus countries—but long-term rates, which are what influence investment, stayed low.

Long-term capital flows presented the administration with two different problems. By far the more serious was direct investment by American firms abroad, building factories behind the tariff walls of the Common Market or elsewhere in Europe. The Department of Commerce estimated that from 1957 to 1961, American exports of manufactured goods rose by only $500 million—while production at American-owned factories in Europe rose by $4.4 billion. Roy Blough, one of the members of the Sproul Committee that had advised Kennedy, told the House Ways and Means Committee that "if our investment programs abroad go on over a period of years, we will wind up with our best, most efficient manufacturing operations . . . operating abroad, giving few, if any jobs to American people and not contributing to our export surplus but draining [it]." One of the darkest moments of the Kennedy administration was the day that Henry Ford II announced that he was spending $350 million to buy out the minority interest in British Ford. The normally courteous Dillon called Ford personally, gave him unshirted hell, and saw that the press heard about it. This had no effect on Ford, but it may have discouraged others.

Here the Kennedy strategy was simple: increase profits on investment at home by lowering taxes, and decrease profits on investment abroad by raising them. The 7 percent investment tax credit introduced in 1962, and applicable only to investments made in the United States, in effect increased by 1 percent the rate of profit on new domestic investment. Meanwhile Kennedy requested that U.S. corporate income tax be collected on all foreign earnings of U.S. businesses, not just those that were brought home to headquarters—but Congress, heavily lobbied by the Canadians, Japanese, and Italians as well as constituents, imposed the taxes only on earnings in the more prominent "tax havens." Part of the problem was that European governments relied more on sales taxes and less on income taxes for their revenues, so that corporate profits were less heavily charged abroad. By 1963, Kennedy was urging reductions in the corporate income tax rate in the United States, to encourage both Americans and foreigners to spend their capital on these shores.

The more complicated long-term capital problem was the outflow on "portfolio investments"—American purchases of stocks and bonds in foreign—especially European—enterprises. Prior to the 1960s, the tight capital controls abroad had prevented foreign companies from selling dollar-denominated instruments. As the rules on convertibility eased, the temptation grew for Europeans to raise funds at lower interest rates in America.

But quite apart from interest rate questions, capital was *available* to enterprise in America, and not in Europe. Domestic capital markets in Europe were thin and narrow, controlled by greedy banks (or, what amounts to the same thing, by governments for the benefit of the greedy banks, many of them owned by the government). The American capital market was deep and broad, and drew not only American savings but foreign money, both licit and illicit. Thanks to the efficiency, honesty, and freedom of the American capital market, what was a lower interest rate to the European borrower might produce yields to the European investor higher than those available to him at home. As many as 70 percent of the sales of European paper on Wall Street were to European investors, and Europeans purchased American securities, too.

Nevertheless, the net effect was a drain of dollars, and a serious one. A study by Benjamin J. Cohen of the Federal Reserve Bank of New York put a number on it: $3.7 billion from 1957 to 1962. The cloud had a golden lining, of course—dividends and interest from these investments would be warming America eventually— but right now it was raining and cold. And in the first six months of 1963, with the European economies booming and the American economy in a state of pause after two years of rapid growth, money was much tighter and harder to come by in Europe than in the United States. The sale of foreign bonds became a hot activity on Wall Street. Dillon warned that "our balance of payments problem limits the amount of long-term capital which we can prudently supply to others." But the only suggestion he could suggest publicly, as late as July 1963, was more purchases of American stocks and bonds by European investors: "We need to export securities as well as goods."

6

Other observers, outside the administration, felt that more fundamental measures were required. A Harvard school of economists demanded a devaluation of the dollar, by about 15 percent, to make American exports cheaper and imports more expensive. "A choice will have to be made," Hendrik S. Houthakker said, "between maintaining exchange rates and reviving the economy." This was rejected out of hand: dollar devaluation would benefit the Russians, the South Africans, and the gold speculators, all of whom we disliked; it wouldn't work anyway, because our trading partners would simply devalue in tandem; and the long-term impact would be devastating. "Every holder of dollars before the devaluation," Roosa said, "would have been tricked into heavy losses. . . . The possibility that the dollar could again serve, in any meaningful volume, as a usable part of general monetary reserves, would disappear." According to Theodore Sorensen, Kennedy forbade even the discussion of the idea.

Inside and outside the administration, there were critics of Dillon and Roosa who insisted that undue attention was being paid to the balance of payments problem, and that Treasury policy was preventing the government from giving the economy the boosts necessary to restore full employment. What the United States needed was easier credit from the rest of the world, to ride out this temporary situation, and the best way to achieve this ease was a reform of the International Monetary Fund, preferably, Congressman Reuss thought, along the lines proposed by Robert Triffin.

Support for such reforms came sporadically from across the ocean, from the other key currency and debtor country, Great Britain. Averell Harriman reported back from a trip to London in early 1962 that Prime Minister Harold Macmillan was unhappy about the lack of liquidity in the international monetary system now that the United States trade surplus was increasing; he wanted to see IMF reorganized to provide international money for the use of those who needed it. But the day after Kennedy heard Harriman's report, the British Treasury attaché in Washington called the White House to murmur in a rather embarrassed way that in his conversation with Harriman, Macmillan had been off on a frolic of his own: he had not discussed the subject with the Cabinet, and the caller wanted the White House to know that Macmillan's view was not that of H. M. Treasury.

By fall 1962, Macmillan had brought his Treasury around. Chancellor of the Exchequer Reginald Maudling came to the IMF meeting in Washington with a prepared speech urging that IMF be made more like a bank, to which the lucky countries that had money could bring it (receiving in return a gold-guaranteed deposit) and from which the luckless countries could borrow in quantities limited only by the extent of the deposits.

Roosa had been warned that Maudling was coming with some such scheme, but was unable to find out what it was until just before the Chancellor spoke. He was used to hearing this sort of thing from academic economists, but not from people who were carrying the burdens of the real world. What was wrong with these proposals, he told the Reuss subcommittee in December 1962, was that they had no chance to be adopted by the people whose surpluses were to supply the deposits. "It is relatively easy," he said with visible annoyance, "to draw up a plan for a systematic monetary network of conduits, pools, and valves for the storage and release of international credit. It is a very different task to induce creditors and debtors to put into that network the credit itself—without which the whole mechanism remains on the drawing boards, or if it exists has little practical significance."

Seven months later, Roosa laid it on the line for Reuss: "In the present setting," he said, "the only way adequately to handle our present problem is to deal directly with those countries that have the surpluses, and to so arrange the handling of the deficit that we don't impair the prospects for the future.... There has been a great deal of comment on the part of people who just wish and hope, as urgently as we do, that there was some way of just opening a door on a new scheme and it would be over.... The creditors would not know what was happening to them and we could get financed and have freedom from adjustment without internal pain for a much longer period. . . .

"This is the sort of thing where it is not central bankers, it is treasuries, who are involved. I guess I probably negotiated every one of these transactions, or was involved in it, and I know pretty well what is consistent with their own thinking and their own sense of responsibility about the way the payments system should work. . . . There is no way of getting a large group of countries together to make additional automatic credits available on a large scale on the conscious premise that the United States just ought to have freedom from paying for three, four or five more years . . ."

So Roosa expanded his bag of tricks. Some $700 million of indebtedness to the United States was prepaid by Europeans in 1961–62. On January 1, 1962, the Germans paid in advance for some $450 million of military equipment to be delivered sometime that year. The total of Roosa bonds sold in foreign currencies (mostly Swiss francs and Italian lire) reached past $700 million. Coombs had a $1.5 billion swap facility available for emergencies. The United States paid $100 million of subscriptions to international organizations in the form of non-interest-bearing debt instruments which would not be cashed (and thus would not turn up on the balance of payments) until the money was actually needed. When repayments of past drawings by foreigners had stuffed the IMF so full of dollars that it could no longer accept dollars, the United States drew foreign currencies and sold them to the nations involved for them to use in their repayments, to prevent them from using the gold window.

The trade "fundamentals," to use a word that would become popular at the Treasury in 1978, were in fact turning rapidly in America's favor. If employment had expanded less rapidly than output in the United States in 1961–62, that meant "productivity" had improved. ("Productivity," though it sounds like something specific, is merely a residual ratio—output divided by the number of people working.) During the first two years of the Kennedy administration, the wholesale price index actually declined. Meanwhile, the Europeans were struggling with inflation. As American prices held steady and European prices rose, American sales to Europe—and also to all the world markets where Americans competed with Europeans—would rise. The trade surplus would increase enough to pay the bills.

But Roosa was playing in what was, if the pun is forgivable, a fixed game. Exchange rates had been set in concrete by the Basle group early in 1961, and their fixity became credible as it survived a Canadian crisis of 1962, an Italian crisis of 1963, and (this one was harder) a British crisis of 1964. Quite apart from governmental actions, the inflationary pressures in Europe were pushing up European interest rates—in inflationary times, borrowers were willing to pay more for the use of money that will be worth less when they pay it back, and lenders are likely to demand more.

In a normal situation, the money of an inflationary economy not only buys less at home, it also buys less foreign currency. Eventually, in the absence of fixed rates, inflation in Europe and price stability in America would push the dollar up and the European currencies down in the foreign exchange markets. Then the interest rate differentials would have no appeal to Americans, because any added income from loans to Europe would be lost when the money was converted back to dollars.

As long as the exchange rates were credibly fixed, however, Americans could cheerfully send their money abroad, where it brought a higher return. The European inflation that looked likely to improve the trade situation worked perversely to make the capital-flow situation worse. And because the books at the end of the year showed continuing American deficits, the inflating European currencies actually *looked* stronger on the "fundamentals" and sold toward the top of the range within which the IMF permitted fluctuations. Indeed, the few economists who were calling for flexible exchange rates thought they would produce a devaluation of the dollar.

With the slowdown of the American economy in the first half

of 1963 and the growing confidence of the market that exchange rates were truly locked in place, the outflow of long-term capital from the United States accelerated. Kennedy was working for a tax cut that would leave extra money in the hands of Americans; there was a serious risk that some fraction of that money would be used for investment abroad.

On July 18, 1963, one of the cornerstones of established American foreign economic policy was carted off for repairs. In his second statement to Congress on the American balance of payments, after affirming the sanctity of gold at $35 an ounce, Kennedy imposed—"temporarily"—an Interest Equalization Tax of 1 percent on all foreign securities sold in the United States by most of the countries that had been selling them. (Canada and Japan were exempted.) There was no great confidence in the administration in such capital-flow controls. Dillon had told the Reuss Subcommittee only ten days earlier that "a partial system of exchange controls would soon break down as funds flowed through uncontrolled channels—spurred by the fear of still further controls. In the end, a complete system of exchange controls would be required." But something had to give; and the principle of the free international movement of capital—which no other country in the world maintained—was the least painful sacrifice that could be offered.

Like everything else the Kennedy administration did in defense of the dollar, the IET was delicately calculated. "We hoped," Dillon remembers almost wistfully, "that it would stimulate foreigners to develop their own capital markets." The tax was accompanied by a rise from 3 percent to 3½ percent in the Federal Reserve discount rate, to help hold short-term money, and by a strong push for the tax cut to gain stimulus by fiscal means. In the light of our experiences since, Kennedy's delicacy—informed as it was by a sense of the realities and sensibilities of the rest of the world—seems hugely admirable. But within a few months the leadership of the United States was to pass into hands that, whatever their other qualities, were quite incapable of delicacy.

7

Robert Roosa—the name is Dutch in origin, pronounced with a short "o"—is still hard at work, a slightly pudgy man with thinning brown hair and unathletic posture, who speaks in long phrases and keeps his smile behind his horn-rimmed glasses. He is, as he has been since he left the Treasury in 1964, a partner at Brown Brothers, Harriman, a private Wall Street bank. It is widely and wistfully believed—quite without foundation, Roosa says—that he could have been Treasury Secretary or Chairman of the Federal Reserve Board for Jimmy Carter if he'd been willing to take the job. He is frequently consulted by the government—and was, even in the Nixon days—on international monetary questions.

Now as during his time at the Treasury, Roosa does not claim to have all the answers. Indeed, he is impressed with how much harder the questions have become. Sitting in his comfortable, dark, old-fashioned little room behind the banking floor at Brown Brothers the other day, Roosa shook his head in incredulous recollection. "When I think," he said, "of all the things we had to go through and all the worries we had—at a time when the United States had a big trade *surplus!*"

5 / Johnson's Warriors

Although many tasks remain ahead in the field of international monetary reform, one of my comforts as I left the White House was that the dollar was once again strong.

— Lyndon B. Johnson, 1971

* * *

Lyndon Johnson took an interest in international monetary affairs, as he did in everything that might affect public perception of his performance in the White House.

But American policy in this as in all other areas was made reckless by the hubris of this administration—the belief that for every problem there existed a solution, for every lock God had made a key, which could be found through the exercise of American ingenuity.

Because everything was sure to come out all right in the end— all the academics and advisers said so, if only because you lost your access to the President if you didn't say so—the need was for expedients that could bridge what was always seen as a temporal gap between appearance and reality.

Thus all the temporary measures Roosa had designed for Kennedy were carried forward—and supplemented, as the need arose, by blunter instruments.

In international monetary matters, as in the politico-military matters that dominated the headlines—and, for that matter, in the domestic matters that took most of Johnson's time—this most expansive of administrations was ill-adapted to deal with situations where the government's real freedom of motion was being steadily restricted by events.

The great accomplishment of the administration in international monetary affairs was the creation of the first nonnational, nonmetallic universal asset, the Special Drawing Right of the International Monetary Fund.

Presented at home as an example of American strength and leadership, the SDR was perceived in foreign finance ministries and central banks as an expression of American weakness dictated by the nation's shift from the status of creditor to the status of debtor in world transactions.

By the end of the Johnson administration, the foreign perception was accurate.

1

The entire Kennedy financial program for 1963 was still unfinished business when Lyndon Johnson became President in November. The tax cut initially flown as a trial balloon in August 1962 had been officially proposed that January—and still had not reached the stage of committee hearings in the Senate. The Interest Equalization Tax was bogged down in both houses. But the economy (especially the rate of investment) had begun to turn up. And because the bills to accomplish the IET had made the tax effective as of the day of their introduction, the financial markets had reacted to the proposed interest surcharge on foreign issues as though it had already happened. Sales of foreign securities subject to the tax had virtually stopped on Wall Street, and the week before the assassination, the Federal Reserve Bank of New York was able to report that for thirteen weeks there had been no reduction in the American gold stock, the first quarter without a loss in five years.

Though instant history labeled the tax cut passed in 1964 as the quietus to the simpleminded American faith in balanced budgets, Johnson got it through only by cutting $4 billion out of the proposed expenditure ledgers. Federal outlays actually dropped in fiscal 1965 (at least on paper) for the first time in ten years, and an 8 percent increase in personal income (the best since 1952) raised tax receipts more than the tax cut diminished them. The result was a reduction in the federal deficit to less than $2 billion in fiscal 1965, despite the steady buildup in Vietnam. Unemployment, which had been at 5.7 percent in 1963, dropped steadily to 4.2 percent in 1965.

In Europe, inflationary pressures rose through the year 1964. In Italy, burgeoning consumer demand outran the supply potential of the domestic economy, produced a huge trade deficit and also a political crisis, an "opening to the left" that provoked a flight of lire (much of it trucked across the border to Switzerland in the form of actual currency because government restrictions prevented banks from making foreign transfers). In Britain, a Conservative government that had put the gas pedal to the floor in stimulating domestic demand lost an election to Labour—which took office to find sterling reserves at a minimal level, half the nation's standby credits with foreign central banks already exhausted, and ever-increasing inflation threatening a rapid rise in an already staggering trade deficit. Afraid to begin his term of office with a devaluation, Prime Minister Harold Wilson proclaimed the sanctity of the pound at $2.80, jumped the Bank of England discount rate from 5 percent to 7 percent to discourage borrowers, and introduced a six-month "surcharge" of 15 percent on virtually all British imports. With this program, and with encouragement from America (which contributed a third of the rescue fund), Wilson was able to raise $3 billion in credits from foreign central banks, beat back the speculators, and maintain the exchange rate.

From the American point of view, 1964 should have been the best of years. With Europe's prosperity pulling in imports, the American trade surplus in 1964 passed $8.5 billion, the highest level since the crisis year of 1947. But the deficit on the liquidity basis rose because rising short-term interest rates in Europe tripled the outflow of short-term private capital from the United States. Dillon's warning had proved out: with the sale of their securities taxed on the American market, foreigners multiplied their borrowings from American banks.

By early 1965, less than a month after his inauguration as President in his own right (and almost four years to the day from Kennedy's first message on the same subject), Lyndon Johnson felt compelled to move on the balance of payments. His style was a little different from Kennedy's. "The state of the dollar in the world today is strong," he said in a message to Congress, "—far stronger than three or four years ago. . . . *Clearly, those who fear for the dollar are needlessly afraid. Those who hope for its weakness, hope in vain.* A country which exports far more than it imports and whose net asset position abroad is great and growing is not 'living beyond its means.' *The dollar is, and will remain, as good as gold, freely convertible at $35 an ounce. That pledge is backed by our firm determination to bring an end to our balance-of-payments deficit.*" [all italics in official transcript]

Johnson's program extended the Interest Equalization Tax (originally scheduled to expire in December 1965) through the end of 1969 (it would in fact endure until 1974), and broadened it to cover bank loans and all nonbank credit of more than one year in duration. Withholding taxes against foreigners' earnings on American investments were to be cut, the Export-Import Bank was to work harder to promote American exports, promotion of tourism in America was to be increased, and the duty-free allowance for returning American travelers was to be cut all the way back to $50. But the main thrust was for voluntary cooperation by business: "I am directing the Secretary of Commerce and the Secretary of the Treasury to enlist the leaders of American business in a national campaign to *limit their direct investments abroad, their deposits in foreign banks, and their holding of foreign financial assets* until their efforts—and those of all Americans—have restored balance in our country's international accounts."

The Secretary of the Treasury—still Dillon—turned the problem of keeping bank funds at home over to the Federal Reserve Board, which said thanks a lot and developed what was called Voluntary Foreign Credit Restraint. Under VFCR, banks "voluntarily" agreed to hold their loans and investments abroad below 105 percent of the total outstanding on December 31, 1964, a ceiling later raised to 109 percent in 1966. The limits did not apply to branches abroad. . . . The Commerce Department set up a parallel Voluntary Cooperation Program which ultimately got pledges from 708 companies to fight harder for exports, delay direct investment expenditures in developed countries (and use funds borrowed there rather than here if the investment couldn't be postponed), return foreign earnings posthaste, and repatriate "short-term funds which were held abroad merely to earn a small but differentially higher rate of interest."

These measures were Roosa's last official contribution. He had resigned to move to private banking at the end of 1964, but stayed in Washington to help design Johnson's package. Dillon continued in the cabinet till April, and then moved back to New York. Leadership of the Treasury devolved upon a new team—Henry H. (always "Joe") Fowler, a soft-spoken Southern lawyer and career civil servant who had been Dillon's other Under Secretary from 1961 to 1964, returned after a year away to be Secretary; and Roosa's job was taken by Frederick Deming, president of the Federal Reserve Bank of Minneapolis. They found themselves with new problems—problems so new that for a long time they remained below the surface of government consciousness in the United States.

2

Foreigners had been trafficking in dollars since the end of the war, mostly illicitly. The "errors and omissions" line in the Commerce Department reports had been a plus figure until the late 1950s, reflecting the success of Europeans and South Americans in smuggling their money out of their home countries and putting it into their personal accounts in the United States. Foreign central banks held dollar balances to help their banks finance trade through controlled exchange markets, and the Bank for International Settlements held a dollar fund as part of the European Payments Union. But all those dollars were kept on deposit in New York, some in the form of interest-bearing time deposits or Treasury bills, most in checking accounts because they were needed every day.

Soviet planning for foreign trade had contemplated the restoration of the 1930s nation-to-nation barter systems, with which Communist governments felt at home. As market economies expanded under the beneficent rays of the Marshall Plan, the Russians found themselves with a need for dollars. After 1954, they could get dollars easily enough by selling gold in London—but they did not want to leave their dollars on deposit in New York, where American courts could enforce various U.S. claims arising out of the wartime loan programs. So the Russians started their own bank in London, which made loans denominated in dollars to non-British firms participating in the London commodity markets. Eventually there would be a network of Soviet banks, including Zurich, Rome, and Paris (where the Russian bank finances the unpublicized activities of the French Communist party), and Singapore, where the Russians got conned and dropped a bundle.

After the 1956 Suez War, when the United States under surviving "neutrality" legislation blocked the American bank accounts of all the participants (and included briefly the accounts of the Arab oil producers who were presumed ready to come to the aid of Nasser), several of the Persian Gulf countries grew itchy about the idea that their reserves might be impounded at any time by the government of the United States. They wanted to switch at least some of their holdings from sterling to dollars, if only to punish the British, and they began to hold dollars in Paris and in Switzerland.

With the return of convertibility at the end of 1958, increasing numbers of Europeans were authorized to hold dollars for their own account instead of being compelled to turn over all dollars to their central banks. For foreign exchange dealings even inside Europe, as noted in Chapter 2, it was convenient to use the dollar as a "vehicle" currency, saving banks and dealers the expense of maintaining inventories of all the currencies their customers might want. As the quantities of dollars in private hands mounted with the continuing American deficit, central banks saw no reason why importers and exporters should not borrow their own dollars rather than convert and reconvert through official agencies, which could distort the reserves picture.

Gradually it came to be accepted in Europe that businesses might legitimately borrow dollars for almost any purpose, supplementing the typically inadequate resources of the local capital markets. As interest rates in Europe were generally higher than in the United States, American corporations abroad took to leaving their profits overseas after converting them to dollars, to earn higher returns in European banks before bringing them back home. The central banks themselves began depositing some of their reserve dollars with European private banks, sometimes in their own country, sometimes (through the BIS) in neighboring countries. By 1963, there was enough money around for foreign banks to be willing to make dollar-denominated loans on a somewhat longer term: the government of Belgium borrowed $20 million for three years at 5 percent from London banks. Later that year, S. G. Warburg in London underwrote the first "Eurodollar" bond, $15 million, for the Italian highway authority.

Since the middle of the nineteenth century, when the banking crises described in Bagehot's *Lombard Street* and the third volume of Marx's *Capital* had exposed the fragility of the joint-stock banking system, European governments have relied on central banks to keep order in the credit markets. (The United States had no such institution until 1913, and suffered as a result from recurrent money panics, which sometimes produced real economic crises.) Central banks originally established to issue paper currency on the foundation of the national debt (profit-making enterprises with public responsibilities) were expected when necessary to provide money to individual banks through "discounting" their loans—purchasing the paper at a "discount" price below what the borrower would eventually repay. The same principles were followed when the central banks became government-controlled institutions, and the "discount rate"—the penalty that banks needing funds would have to pay to get cash from the one assured source—became the more obvious tool of monetary policy. It was customary for banks to lend at interest rates high enough to cover the existing discount rate and leave a little over. Obviously, the lower the discount rate, the more money the banks would lend, and the lower the interest rate they would charge the borrowers.

The foundation stone of every national banking *system* was the capacity of the central bank to provide funds in time of trouble, to act as "the lender of last resort." One lesson pretty thoroughly learned in 1930–32 (Bagehot had begun teaching it in 1873) was that the losses from general collapse through insufficient "liquidity" (cash) were greater than the losses a central bank might suffer if questionable discounted paper failed to pay off. Depositors in and lenders to banks could rest assured in the postwar world that some official agency was guaranteeing that their money would be there when they needed it.

But if banks were to be protected against collapse, national economies had to be protected against overlending by the overly secure. We defined money as "a claim on something of value, that will be instantly acceptable to everyone in discharge of a debt." That's what a bank creates when it makes a loan to someone through the process of giving him an account on which he can draw checks. The European countries limited money-creation by banks through controls on what they could lend and to whom—

and by structuring the relations of the private banks with the central bank in such a way that the private banks were always in hock to their masters and could be penalized by an increase in the discount rate.

In America, the Federal Reserve System controls money-creation by limiting how much of what comes in to them the banks can lend out, requiring that banks keep some fraction of their deposits as reserves (which may not earn interest). Then the Fed buys and sells Treasury paper in the "open market" to increase or reduce the total reserves available to the system. (When the Fed buys, it puts money into bank reserves; when it sells, it takes money out.) In addition, the Fed until the 1970s kept banks (which create money) from competing too hard against nonbank lenders (which cannot create money) for any new funds offered in the marketplace. American banks were forbidden to pay interest on deposits that had not been on the books for more than thirty days, and through the notorious "Regulation Q" a ceiling was imposed on the interest rates banks could pay for "time deposits" of various duration.

Banks in other countries that accepted deposits in dollars and made loans in dollars had no such supervision. They were beyond the arm of the Fed, and the national authorities that closely supervised their lending in the local currency soon found that they could interfere with their dollar lending only at the price of watching the business go elsewhere. Anyway, the local central bank could (it was thought) impose its will at the moment when the dollars were converted to local currency, controlling the impact of Eurodollar lending on the local economy.

Quite apart from the fact that loans outside the United States tended to give the lender a higher interest rate, a bank in this permissive atmosphere could afford to pay more for dollar time deposits than a bank inside the United States. As Alan Greenspan, head of Gerald Ford's Council of Economic Advisers, likes to put it, "the Eurodollar market arose because it didn't have to carry the costs of regulation." Because a bank in America could lend out only about 94 percent of a time deposit, the effective costs of such a deposit to a Eurodollar bank was significantly less than it would be to an American bank. Presumably, in the absence of a lender of last resort to the market—a central bank that would supply dollars when needed—the Eurodollar banks would have to keep even larger reserves than American banks, but such reserves could be kept in interest-bearing short-term form. They could be kept, in fact, with other banks. There grew up a fantastic network of interbank lending, and the cost of funds in that interbank market—LIBOR, for London InterBank Offered Rate—ultimately became the base interest rate, the functional equivalent of a national "discount rate" for the Eurodollar market.

Meanwhile, all the numbers banks reported for their Eurodollar deposits and loans became meaningless, because one real dollar in the market could show up on the books of three or four banks as it sped around the interbank circuit. To this day, nobody knows the real size of the deposit base in Eurodollars; estimates in 1979 ranged from $125 billion to $800 billion.

Though the marketplace for Eurodollars settled in London, all the larger European banks borrowed and lent Eurodollars. Where once upon a time banks in Italy and the Netherlands would have had to exchange guilders and lire to service trade between their two countries, now they could settle their accounts with each other in dollars. The cost of currency conversion inside Europe was greatly diminished—from the banks' point of view, eliminated. "The Eurodollar," the economist Peter Kenen told a Congressional committee as early as 1962, "provides Western Europe with something quite close to a common currency."

Looked at as a Eurodollar bank would see it, the Interest Equalization Tax of 1963 was a piece of candy. Interest rates in a given currency range themselves along a relatively stable schedule: when you change one, you affect all. Though it applied only to stocks and bonds, IET tended to make all dollar borrowings by Europeans in New York a little more expensive—without in any way affecting dollar borrowings by Europeans in Europe. The Eurodollar banks now had larger margins to work with; so, of course, they drew more short-term capital out of the United States.

Lending in dollars was the business of American banks, and as the 1960s wore on they grew increasingly concerned about the loss of their natural market to foreigners. Slowly at first, then with a rush, larger American banks opened branches abroad. If the Fed had made them keep reserves at home against the dollar deposits on the books of foreign branches, or had held interest rates on deposits in these branches to Reg Q ceilings, they would have been unable to compete—so the Fed looked the other way. When Voluntary Foreign Credit Restraint came, it was not applied to foreign branches—most of which, in any event, were chartered under local banking laws, which did not permit control of their practices by U.S. regulators.

Now the Eurodollar interbank lending system had a certain source of dollars in a crunch, and the market ballooned. But now, too, Eurodollar lending became a two-way street, or highway.

In 1966, when the Fed tried to slow domestic lending by American banks, holding below the level of rates on the money market the Reg Q ceilings on the interest rates the banks were permitted to pay for deposits, the big international banks that had European branches where Reg Q ceilings did not apply pulled Eurodollars back home—more than $3 billion of them. On the U.S. books for that year, the trade surplus shrank, the payments deficit on the liquidity basis scarcely changed—but the balance on Official Settlements actually showed a surplus, as foreign central banks supplied dollars to the Eurodollar market, at attractive interest rates, for the branches of the U.S. banks to send back to the home office.

The American and European money markets had become indissolubly linked. So long as exchange rates were fixed, interest rates on the two sides of the Atlantic could not diverge too far too long without provoking major capital flows. The "Voluntary" programs were helpful at the margin, but everyone knew that a foreign branch with a borrower in tow would get a dollar deposit from an American customer somehow to fund the loan. In late 1965, when the "Voluntary" restraints were still new and presumably at their most effective, Congressman Reuss, normally a defender of low interest rates at all times for all purposes, proposed major changes in American domestic policy to make up for what seemed an inevitable upward pull of interest rates from Europe:

"What the Europeans usually do not take into account is the effect of higher rates on small business, homebuilding, local school construction, and other activities that are interest-sensitive. European governments often provide interest-rate subsidies for these activities, which shelter them from the depressing effects of general rate increases. If monetary policy is going to be more and more determined in the light of our external position, the question of whether or not we should provide such subsidies deserves careful consideration."

The most serious impact of the growth of the Eurodollar market, however, was not in America but in Europe; since the flow of Eurodollars changed European but not American reserves. And the long-range damage was done not in the marketplace itself, but in the institutional nexus. Credit creates money. If all the world's borrowing is concentrated in one currency, there will be too much of it. Through the years, virtually every American academic and political commentator on the balance-of-payments problem complained about the pressure on the exchange value of the dollar resulting from the inadequacy of the markets in which business—or governments, for that matter—can borrow currencies other than dollars. Even in 1978, when the total value of German trade passed the total value of American trade in the world's markets, borrowing in marks was a nuisance, subject to restrictions and interference by the German government, while borrowing in dollars was a cinch. But there was no reason for Europeans to develop their own deep and broad capital markets in their own currencies: through the unregulated Eurodollar market, whatever programs were designed in Washington, they had easy, inexpensive access to the biggest, most efficient and most honest capital market in the world. And one of the most potent political groups in America—the bankers—stood vigilant guard to assure that no government would seriously impair that access.

3

Though the preconditions for all the later worries had locked into place by 1965, neither the Treasury nor the Congress was troubled that year by the visions that had disturbed Kennedy, Dillon, and Roosa. A euphoric President had carried into office a Congress commited to his Great Society at home and to the defense of our friends in Southeast Asia. His February 10 message had told the foreign speculators where to get off. And the community of liberal economists whose advice Johnson sought had come up with theories and projections that not only released American domestic economic policy from consideration of foreign restraints, but actually proposed that expansion at home would cure rather than exacerbate the international payments problem. Indeed, the hearings of the International Economics Subcommittee of the Joint Economic Committee in 1965 focused upon the problem of providing adequate liquidity for the rest of the world after the American payments deficit stopped pumping out dollars.

The central document was a 1963 report from a Brookings Institution group headed by Walter S. Salant (and including, it is interesting to note, Alice Rivlin, who would later become chief of staff for the Congressional Budget Office). Entitled *The American Balance of Payments in 1968,* the Brookings Report projected trends in Europe and the United States and came up with the good news that the American trade surplus would keep growing ("the price competitive position has turned in favor of the U.S."); that outward capital flows would diminish and perhaps even reverse as interest and dividend payments grew ("the U.S. balance of payments has already felt the strain of adjustment to an increased level of capital outflows, and now is moving into a position where it will reap benefits from these outflows"); and American aid and defense programs abroad could be financed through our sales to foreigners. Just hang on a while.

The basic assumption in the Brookings study was that inflation in Europe, which already had full employment and overfull utilization of productive capacity, would push up the cost of European exports and increase European demand for imports; while expansion in the United States, which was suffering substantial unemployment and underuse of capacity, would lead to increased productivity and continue price stability as wasted resources were put in play. In the early phases of this process, the Brookings economists thought, the American trade surplus might shrink as the government stimulated increases in total American demand—but this would be more than offset by quick improvements in the capital account.

That was a new idea—indeed, a new theory. Citing a historical study by Jeffrey Williamson, the Brookings economists argued that the "U.S. balance of payments . . . improved during periods of rapid growth and deteriorated when growth was slow or absent, because rapid growth increased the rates of return on securities in the United States relative to the rates of return available elsewhere, increasing capital imports and decreasing capital exports by more than enough to offset deterioration in the trade balance. . . . The historical experience . . . would have led to the correct prediction that the recent retardation of U.S. economic growth would result in a deterioration of payments."

Even those who agreed with the Brookings policy recommendations were reluctant to put too much weight on the results of the study: "The underlying assumptions are so questionable and the uncertainties of forecasting international accounts so great," the Joint Economic Committee concluded, "that no substantial reliance should be placed on the quantitative results." But there was to hand another theory, reaching full flower in the mid-1960s, which argued that the American payments deficit made no difference, that it was always the responsibility of others to adjust their policies to what the United States did, never the other way around.

This theory of America as an "optimum-currency country" had been launched as far back as 1961, by the Canadian economist Robert Mundell. The initial thrust was mathematical, a demonstration that if n countries traded with each other, their internal monetary policies and exchange rates could reach a stable solution only when one of them served as a reference point and shock absorber for all the others. The United States as a relatively "closed" economy, with little dependence on foreign trade, should simply adopt whatever policies would maximize its internal "welfare" (full employment and utilization of productive capacity). Its balance of payments would then be a function of other countries' policies. If they wanted to increase their reserves they could depreciate their currencies, absorb foreign capital, or hold down inflation rates. If they wanted fewer reserves, they could revalue their currencies upward, permit inflation, or lend to the world. It was their problem. Yale professor James Tobin, formerly a member of Kennedy's Council of Economic Advisers, bluntly told the Reuss subcommittee that "the main thing that should be done about our payments imbalances should be done by somebody else, not us."

Having held federal outlays level in his first budget, Johnson now loosed the restraints. (In fact, the restraints had always been somewhat illusory: when someone admired Johnson's budget cutting for fiscal '65, House minority leader John Burns said, "Yeah. But just look at the obligational authority he's putting through for later.") Federal expenditures rose by almost 14 percent in fiscal 1966, and then by another 17.5 percent in 1967, when the federal deficit would reach $8.7 billion, the second largest since the war. The gamble seemed to work, though not exactly in the way the Brookings study had predicted (Brookings had thought the trade surplus would shrink in the early phase of domestic stimulus, but it rose). Partly thanks to the 7 percent investment tax credit, the American expansion was led by capital investment, which required few foreign inputs, rather than by private consumption, which was increasingly associated with imports. The payments deficit remained stable at a level well below the danger years of 1958–60.

The United States was no longer negotiating from a position of weakness: in July 1965 Treasury Secretary Henry Fowler officially proposed that the International Monetary Fund be empowered to create new reserve assets that would eliminate the need for new monetary gold or increased holdings of dollars around the world. Unbeknownst to Fowler, however, the tide had already turned against the dollar. The Brookings projections were not going to prove out, and the Mundell theory was not going to work.

4

Federal Reserve Board Chairman William McChesney Martin began to hear in spring 1965 from his friend Richard Russell, chairman of the Senate Armed Services Committee, that whatever Johnson and Defense Secretary Robert McNamara might be telling Joe Fowler, military expenditures were soaring above their budgeted limits. As early as March, Martin raised the possibility of tighter money at the monthly meeting of Johnson's "Quadriad"—himself, Fowler, budget bureau director Charles Schultze, and Gardner Ackley, chairman of the Council of Economic Advisers. "I was given a gentle hee-haw," Martin recalled recently in his office as consultant to the Riggs National Bank in Washington. (He has another office as president of the Tennis Foundation: lean and athletic in his seventies and a formidable antagonist on the tennis courts, the former "boy president" of the New York Stock Exchange in the 1930s is still a man of parts.)

"My argument," Martin said, "was that we would run into a period when confidence in the dollar would be shaken. Johnson gave me a fatherly talk—he would get a tax increase before that would happen, he wouldn't let the war profiteers take the money. But by May I was getting really worried, and I began trying to sell the idea on the Board. I got two members with me, one on the fence. In July and August it became perfectly obvious that military spending was *roaring,* even though the figures didn't show it. I kept waiting—I think I waited too long.

"In October, I was hauled over to the White House by Johnson, just when I was ready to go. He said, 'You know, Bill, I'm having my gallbladder out. You wouldn't do it while I'm having my gallbladder out, would you?' All I could say was, 'I've had my gallbladder out. It isn't so bad.' But I went home to my wife and I said, 'Well, suppose the President is in the hospital and I raise the discount rate and he dies . . .' " In early December, when Johnson was safely recuperating on his Texas ranch, Martin moved. Johnson reacted with an outraged statement to the press, and called Martin down to Texas for a chewing-out.

This is a discomfiting episode in American political history, for the fact is that the Defense Department, the budget bureau, and the President were lying to the Treasury, the Economic Advisers, and the Fed. The nation's bankers knew better, because the trick was to give letters of obligation, which had no budgetary status, to the arms purveyors—who then used the paper as collateral for loans. Roy Reierson of Bankers Trust in New York went public with estimates that the war was costing $5-$10 billion more than what the government said. At the American Bankers Association convention that fall, Treasury Secretary Fowler swore Reierson was wrong, saying that if the figures in the newspapers were true, he wouldn't be at the convention, he would be back at the Treasury working on a tax increase. "Joe was in a tough spot," Martin says. "He was a subordinate. I wasn't."

But by December everybody knew. A man who was at the first high-level planning meeting for the 1967 budget recalls that Gardner Ackley opened the session with a mock-humorous question to Charles Schultze, the budget director: "Are you going to tell us the truth this time, Charlie, or give us the same bullshit you gave us last year?" Since the President was unwilling to ask for a tax increase, the burden of reducing the inflationary threat would have to fall on monetary policy. Internationally, as noted, the first result was to pull Eurodollars to American banks from both the private European market and the official central bank reserves, but the long-term problem grew more serious.

Mundell's theory had failed because it required other nations to accept what monetary theorists called the "hegemony" of the dollar; the French publicly and everybody else privately were unwilling to go along. And they could push on American policy through the pressure point of the gold market.

A more sophisticated variant of the theory by Charles Kindleberger, resting on his bank analogy with the dollar as the universal currency of the American-managed worldwide bank, failed because it assumed the convergence of interest rates among countries with money markets linked by free convertibility. The Federal Reserve didn't believe in the theory, and all countries were to some degree restricting currency flows. ("I know of no reason," Governor Sherman Maisel wrote grandly, ignoring the long-standing U.S. policy of promoting free convertibility, "to expect that similar interest rates should prevail and be the proper ones for the major nations of the world.") In practice, Kindleberger's theory would mean that everyone would have to live with the rates the Fed decided were correct for the United States, because America was completely unwilling to let foreigners make or even participate in the making of such decisions for the domestic economy. And the foreigners had needs and views different from those of the Fed.

The Brookings projections had omitted some practical and theoretical factors of first importance. The Common Market countries could hold down the inflationary effects of a tight labor market by importing Spanish, Portuguese, Turkish, Algerian, Yugoslavian, and Greek "guest workers." And they firmly would *not* permit their inflation rate to worsen drastically: in April 1965, as Congress was debating Lyndon Johnson's 14 percent increase for the fiscal 1966 budget, the Council of Ministers of the Common Market committed themselves to hold the 1966 increase in their government budgets below 5 percent.

The Europeans had already decided to reduce agricultural imports from America by tariffs on the items their farmers produced, at levels which would be high enough to make the import no less expensive than the local product. This "variable levy" was outrageous from the international as well as the American point of view; its first severe effect was on the importation of chickens, then being produced by industrial process in the United States alone, with such spectacular results that American exports of chickens to the Common Market had risen from 10 million pounds in 1958 to 160 million in 1962. The resulting "chicken war" between America and the EEC lasted roughly until the Europeans had mastered the techniques themselves. Angry as he was about the Common Market tariffs, Congressman Reuss could not forbear his admiration for the cleverness of the language used. "You don't know," he asked a witness from the Agriculture Department, "the name of the man who thought of this word 'variable levy,' do you?" American fury at such behavior had to be muted a little, however, for the United States was guilty of a comparable sin, having established a small list of products (including chemicals, carpets, and glassware) on which duty was assessed not according to the price the importer had actually paid abroad but according to the "American Selling Price" at which domestic manufacturers marketed their wares. Everybody was cheating.

What was most disturbing was the way the Europeans kept down the prices of the manufactured goods they exported even as their other prices rose. Partly, these relatively lower prices on export goods were a benefit from the institution of the Common Market: most goods the Europeans sold to Americans were also goods they sold to each other, and increased competition from neighboring countries under the customs union had made European manufacturers (especially the French) rationalize their production systems and sharpen their pencils. High rates of investment in export industries kept yielding economies of scale that could be fully enjoyed only by keeping the plants going full-blast, even at reduced profits on export sales. Kindleberger points out that in Germany in 1962 a "slight recession at home led a number of industries, especially the electrical, to ask their export departments why they had gone to sleep. The resulting export push was remarkable."

It was easy—natural—for American commentators to see this activity as "dumping" (selling abroad below cost), and occasionally there probably were concealed "export subsidies," an absolute violation of GATT rules that the Geneva organization rarely did anything about. But the pejorative language neither helped nor explained, and the convenience of its use prevented the sort of analysis that might have prevented misunderstanding in later years, when both the Germans and the Japanese kept selling like crazy as their currencies appreciated against the dollar, driving up the price of their exports. Export markets do not fall from heaven: someone has worked to build them, investing his company's money and his own blood. Without subsidies or government encouragement, simply as a matter of business judgment, shaving profit margins for a while will seem a perfectly reasonable marketing expense to preserve a future presence in such markets. Trade in commodities will shift rapidly from supplier to supplier depending on relative prices (it is, in economists' terms, "price-elastic"); trade in manufactured goods, where the buyer is used to the seller and his individual product, will be much stickier. Brand loyalties create cherishable partial monopolies: that's why businesses advertise.

In any event, the experience of the mid-1960s was that European surpluses did not greatly diminish even when the "fundamentals" were turning against the Common Market countries. What would happen if the fundamentals turned back? If the products of the "optimum currency country" became uncompetitive against those of the rest of the world?

5

Britain had never been an optimum-currency country, in Mundell's terms, because its dependence on foreign trade could force adjustment of domestic interest rates. But it had been the world's banker on Kindleberger's terms: changes in British interest rates had affected interest rates in all other countries, often rather quickly. It had been able to play that role in the nineteenth century without balance-of-payments problems, a Chancellor of the Exchequer argued half-seriously in the 1960s, because in those days there were no balance-of-payments statistics.

Left over from the time before the wars was the fact that the British currency—backed in the 1960s by an economy smaller than that of either Germany or resurgent France—was used as a reserve by the monetary authorities of a number of former colonies and client states. They now wanted out—in the more polite language of 1978, they wanted "to diversify their reserves." But the bank was busted: Britain had nowhere near enough "reserve assets" to cash the checks.

To defeat the Gresham's Law rule that led members of the bloc to spend sterling and save dollars, Britain had to maintain interest rates higher than those of any plausible alternative currency, and to place the entire burden of stimulus of a decaying economy on government deficits. This produced a vicious circle. Business investment lagged because companies could not afford to pay the price for investment capital; consumer demand steadily stimulated by government deficits and unrequited by expansion in domestic production pulled in increasing imports Britain couldn't afford; and to seduce foreigners to make the loans to fill the trade gap, British interest rates had to rise yet again.

Experience after the German revaluation of March 1961 had persuaded the central bankers and finance ministries that any change in parities was risky for the whole system, and a change in British parities was especially perilous. The problem was that once the pound lost value, those countries still holding their reserves in sterling would fly the coop as fast as possible. Having been burnt once by holding their reserves in foreign exchange rather than in gold, they were unlikely to stop in their flight when they had acquired dollars, and their central banks were as good customers as any other central bank at the Treasury's gold window. Everyone would then have to face the fact that the United States, too, did not have anywhere near enough reserve assets—gold—to cash the checks.

As Britain sank deeper and deeper into trouble, the BIS, the IMF and the individual finance ministries rallied round with the loans. In November 1964, Coombs of the New York Fed had put together a $3 billion support package literally overnight. (He slept at the bank and began his telephoning at 4 A.M. New York time: he was "so accustomed... to the time differential," John Brooks reported, "that he was inclined to think in terms of the European day, referring casually to 8 A.M. in New York as 'lunchtime.' ") Thereafter, Coombs and his colleagues at the Bank of England did acrobatic turns on the high wire, punishing speculators with sudden overwhelming interventions in the market to ease their enthusiasm for gambles against a pound that by any economic logic had to be devalued. A deeply divided Labour government cooperated by cutting social services and support for housing, reducing overall stimulus to domestic demand, putting a lid on national income.

Fowler's efforts to create a new reserve asset in the International Monetary Fund were greeted with suspicion by the non-Anglo-Saxon community, which thought it might be designed to serve as what Triffin called a "garbage can" for pounds and—ultimately—dollars that could not be paid off in the normal course of business. When the IMF annual meeting in Rio in 1967 approved the creation of Fowler's "Special Drawing Rights," the Common Market countries let it be known that they would permit the SDR facility to be "activated" only after the payments deficits of the reserve currency countries had been substantially eliminated. And by now the United States was again part of the problem rather than part of the solution: the difference between the Johnson budgets and the Common Market budgets of 1966–67 had defeated the Brookings study assumptions and American trade surpluses were beginning to diminish. The United States sopped up some of the payments deficit deriving from the Vietnam War by selling long-term Treasury bonds to

Thailand, Taiwan, and Japan, all benefiting mightily by the war in Southeast Asia, but there was a lot left.

In this monetary climate, Nasser decided that the time had come for a final solution in Palestine. When his success in ordering out the United Nations peacekeeping forces resulted in the Six-Day War of June 1967, his allies in the Persian Gulf, who had looked forward joyously to a massacre of the Jews, lashed out in impotent fury. They couldn't reach the Americans then; they could reach the British. The Labour government had been discreet in the Middle East, but clearly thought Israel was right; De-Gaulle (though not the French population) was on the Arab side. Oil money moved in a lump from London and sterling to Paris (though mostly to dollars rather than to francs).

Despite the American payments deficits, international reserves had not been expanding. The repatriation of Eurodollars to gain the high domestic interest rates of 1966 had, as noted, reduced foreign official claims on the United States; and the Russians were enjoying grain harvests large enough to enable them to hoard rather than sell their newly mined gold. Industrial demand for gold on the London market was growing—and the French were converting an ever-increasing proportion of their dollar holdings to gold, partly as a return to historical French monetary patterns, partly as a Gaullist disapproval of American policies in Vietnam, partly as a defense against the takeover of French businesses by American multinational corporations.

DeGaulle had denounced the "exorbitant privilege" the Americans enjoyed because the reserve currency status of the dollar allowed them to pay for foreign factories with paper from their national printing press. Given the constipated condition of the French capital markets, France could not continue its spectacular economic expansion without investment by foreigners. But if Americans wanted to buy French assets, DeGaulle would, in effect, make them pay in gold. The transfer of gold from the United States to France reduced American reserves—but left French reserves unchanged because it merely substituted metal for dollars.

The flight from sterling diminished during summer 1967, more out of respect for vacation schedules than out of respect for the pound, but when the Rio meeting of the IMF failed to produce anything responsive to the British crisis the speculators and hedgers ("the gnomes of Zurich," as Foreign Minister George Brown had called them) struck hard. Britain began losing reserves—and they were borrowed reserves—at a rate of a quarter of a billion dollars a day. Foreigners who had debts in sterling delayed payment, expecting the pounds they owed would soon be cheaper; Britons with debts to pay in foreign currencies hastened to convert and settle. In Washington, the Federal Open Market Committee (with three of the seven Governors of the Federal Reserve Board dissenting) approved additional lines of credit for Britain; in New York, Charles Coombs planned one last big bear trap to punish the evil conspirators against the fixed exchange rate. The Federal Reserve Bank of New York made an overnight deposit of $250 million in the Bank of England on September 30 to allow "window-dressing" of the quarterly statement to show that British reserves were greater than they were.

Reporters and photographers mobbed the October meeting in Basle and the sessions of the Working Party on monetary affairs at the OECD in Paris as the British government made its last dignified presentation of what it would need to maintain the pound at $2.80. It was the wrong occasion for dignity: bungled timing of the devaluation announcement cost Britain more than a billion dollars of reserves, spent on Friday to permit the delay of the announcement until Saturday. On Monday, November 20, the pound was officially worth $2.40.

"Now the dollar is in the front line," said U.S. Treasury Secretary Henry Fowler. "I was criticized strongly for saying that," he remembered the other day; "but it was true."

6

Despite his fatuous proclamation to the British people that "the pound in your pocket is as good as it ever was," Prime Minister

Harold Wilson knew that the new rate would need defending. The devaluation brought $750 million of pounds back in short order—from speculators who had made a quick 14 percent and were content with that—but then the drain began again. Over the long run, the fact that imports would cost more and exports would sell for less would improve the trade balance—but in the first months, the devaluation meant only that Britain had to pay more for what it got and received less for what it sold. Devaluation is inflationary even in a country where imports are less than 10 percent of Gross National Product, as the United States would painfully (and a little slowly) learn in 1978; in Britain in 1967, imports were almost 20 percent of GNP. The immediate increase of their price in pounds would have to be counterbalanced by deflationary government action; the Bank of England discount rate jumped to 8 percent, consumer credit was cut back, and a tax increase was promised for 1968. New lines of credit were begged in Basle and New York, and the last of the British quota at the IMF was requested on a standby basis. Wilson even sold the family jewels—$800 million of U.S. corporate securities commandeered from private hands for public use early in World War II and held ever since as an emergency reserve.

To support sterling, Britain had to buy pounds—with dollars, for the dollar was the "intervention" currency. The dollars that flowed into the money markets—some from the reserves of the Basle group, most from the United States itself, including the $800 million from the securities sale—moved toward the gold market; the gold pool began to leak at an accelerating rate. France had backed out, and the United States was now responsible for supplying 56 percent of the gold to be sold in London. The European members were reluctant to part with the other 44 percent—and except for the Germans, who had explicitly and in writing agreed to keep their payments surplus in foreign exchange rather than metal, they were entitled to reconstitute any losses through the pool with purchases at the Treasury's gold window.

Confidence was not improved when the American monetary

authorities, near panic, proposed a harebrained scheme by which the United States would issue gold certificates to replace the gold lost through the market. As Kindleberger told a Senate Committee two months later, this "looked to outsiders like sleight of hand," because it would permit the United States to print not only dollars that served as reserve assets for foreigners but pieces of paper that America itself could count in its reserves.

On New Year's Day 1968, President Johnson delivered "to the American people" a far-reaching message on the balance of payments, concluding with the statement that "The dollar will remain convertible into gold at $35 an ounce, and our full gold stock will back that commitment." It slowed the flight to gold for a while, but not for long. Law still required a 25 percent "gold cover" for the Federal Reserve notes that are American currency, and while the Fed could suspend the requirement (and Fed Chairman Martin had said he would do so), the market believed that only the surplus over the legal cover was really available for sale. With the losses of late 1967, that had shrunk to little more than $2 billion worth—and the drain was approaching $250 million a week.

The Tet offensive in Vietnam did nothing to encourage the rest of the world to believe in America's mastery of its problems, or to persuade Lyndon Johnson that the time was ripe for reasoning together. Chairman Martin went personally to Basle for the March meeting of the BIS governors to persuade them to hold the line and continue the pool. Very reluctantly, they did so; at the ritual Sunday dinner, Jelle Zijlstra of the Netherlands, who was Chairman of the BIS, said to the table: "If we were commercial bankers, I wonder what advice we would give to our customers after reading the communiqué tomorrow. I suspect we would all urge them to go into the gold market and buy."

The next week the hemorrhage of monetary gold to private hands approached half a billion dollars a day. Except for the Germans, the members of the pool now informed the Fed of their intention to replace their losses at the Treasury's gold window. The jig was up.

Martin asked the Bank of England to close the gold market, and he summoned the BIS Governors to a meeting in Washington. While they were en route, the administration frantically lobbied the Senate to pass a bill removing the gold cover requirement—and got it through by a two-vote margin. So when the central bankers met, the American pledge to reconstitute their gold if necessary was credible—but a credible illusion was not a policy.

"I was in a helpless position," Martin recalls. "My staff didn't have a program. I called Guido Carli of the Bank of Italy, a very able man, and he said, 'I'll help you.' The next day he came in with the idea of the two-tier gold market."

Under this scheme (first proposed and analyzed the previous fall by Eugene Birnbaus, an IMF, Commerce Department and White House economist, who had moved to the Chase Manhattan Bank) gold would be traded among central banks and governments acting officially at $35 an ounce—and would sell independently on a private market where private parties would pay whatever price would clear the bids and offers. The link between private dollar holders and American monetary reserves, forged in panic by Secretary Anderson in November 1960 and locked in place by Dillon the next year, was finally severed. The central bankers pledged themselves not to sell in the private market (forgoing possible profits), and for the time being they pledged also not to buy in the private market, confronting the speculators (and the South Africans and the Russians) with the danger that the price might fall *below* $35. Richard Cooper, a Yale economist later to be President Carter's Under Secretary of State for Economic Affairs, wrote a year later that it was "as if all the monetary gold on March 17 were painted indelibly blue with the claim that no new gold would be so painted in the future."

This was not at all what the speculators had expected. Overestimating the political power surpluses had given the Common Market countries (and perhaps encouraged in that overestimate by the extent to which those countries had called the tune at the 1967 Rio meeting of the IMF), they had looked for a devaluation of the dollar, an increase in the price of gold, that would give them a quick profit. They had borrowed the dollars to make their gold purchases, and were burdened with interest payments to hold assets that earned nothing. As the months passed after the March meeting, the dollar price of gold in the private market sank back toward $35, and might indeed have fallen below—except that the central banks, confronted with a possible need to write down the value of their gold reserves, finally insisted on buying in the market some more gold they could paint blue.

But what depressed the gold market and boosted the dollar in 1968 were political events, rather than economic developments. In May, the French revolted against the high time horizons of Gaullism, the insistence that the nation's workers could not be given their share of France's growing prosperity until long-range investment targets had been met. At the least, the May Days of 1968 demonstrated that gold did not buy happiness; and they compelled DeGaulle to seek financial help from America and to sell half the gold he had accumulated through the 1960s. Then, in August, Russian troops invaded Czechoslovakia, and capital fled from an apparently threatened West Germany to the United States. Whether in the absence of such events the gold buyers would have regrouped and returned to their attack is the kind of question that could be asked only much later, after some years of détente had reduced the degree of political tilt in the flow of funds.

Several loose ends remained to be tidied after the central bankers had liquidated the gold pool. Some $3 billion had disappeared from the world's metallic monetary reserves through the London gold market, and another $1 billion had vanished with the stroke of a pen when the devaluation of sterling cut the dollar price of the pounds the British ex-colonies and clients held in their reserves. Both Britain and America needed a psychological gesture from the rest of the world expressing confidence that their deficits would now cease. So the group meeting in Washington called for activation through the IMF of the new SDRs as "paper gold" to replace the real gold the system had lost. Two weeks later the Finance Ministers of the Group of 10 countries met in Stockholm and approved the necessary amendments to the IMF Charter, and sent them off for the formality of a membership vote, which took only about a year.

There remained, too, the concerns of the sterling bloc countries that had taken the losses when their reserves were devalued. They were places like Malaysia, Singapore, New Zealand, Iran, Kuwait, Kenya, Nigeria—all of which directed their trade flows through London and relied on the London market for credit. To cut their currencies loose from sterling would be an inconvenience for them, but they were not prepared to risk another November 1967. If they were to continue to hold sterling and deny themselves their rights to convert to dollars and thence to gold, they demanded a guarantee of the exchange value of their reserves. The Bank of England did not have the assets or the desire to issue that sort of guarantee.

Pushing fresh reserves into Britain to make credible a dollar guarantee Britain did not wish to give seemed to the central bankers an exceedingly risky thing to do. Disheartened by the collapse of six years' work in the gold pool and the swap markets, the Fed's Charles Coombs gave the Open Market Committee his sad opinion that it would be throwing good money after bad. But the alternatives were even less attractive. On the assurance that the money would be preserved as a fund to back written guarantees for the sterling bloc countries, the central banks that summer made long-term deposits with the Bank of England. In the months ahead, the pound did turn around; devaluation worked; Britain repaid its borrowings and closed out its swap lines. But the humiliating experience of being forced to give a guarantee of the exchange value of its currency would greatly influence Britain's reactions when the gold-convertible dollar faced its final crisis in 1971.

7

Arguing that Congress would never approve a tax increase in 1966—and fearing that it would cut down his Great Society programs—Lyndon Johnson had rejected his economic advisers' recommendations for the 1967 budget, but he did raise some extra money by "closing loopholes." The most important of these closings was the 7 percent investment tax credit, suspended for fifteen months, which removed one of the incentives Kennedy had put in place to persuade American industry that domestic investment was better than foreign. (It also contributed to ending what would be for at least fifteen years the last investment-led prosperity in America. Psychologically, the suspension of the investment tax credit confirmed what had become popular and academic majority belief; that the problems of production in America should be considered secondary to the problems of distribution. Reduced savings and investment meant slower expansion of productive capacity after 1966—which was, of course, the root cause of the devastating inflations and payments deficits that followed every expansion of demand throughout the 1970s.)

In 1967, reliance on tight money rather than budgetary restraint—though it had devastated the housing industry and nearly bankrupted the California savings and loan associations—seemed to Johnson to have been a success. The growth of the Gross National Product slowed, but unemployment remained steady below 4 percent, and the wholesale price index scarcely rose at all. Aided by low interest rates in Europe, which was suffering a mild recession, the balance of payments picture in early 1967 seemed cheerful. There was a light at the end of the tunnel in Vietnam; projections of the Defense Department budget for 1968 were jiggered to reduce the financial demands of the war. But by midsummer all this was out the window; the budget deficit for the fiscal year that began July 1 was obviously going to push $20 billion, and might be higher. In August, the President called for a temporary 10 percent surcharge on personal and corporate income taxes.

By now, the American economy was slowing down in the aftermath of the monetary restrictions a year earlier. The cities had been terrified by race riots; influential urban opinion could imagine no government policy worse than a restraint that might increase unemployment. Led by *The New York Times* in a series of urgent editorials, the opponents of the tax increase marshalled their forces in Congress. As foreign interest rates rose following the quick turnaround of the European economies, and the $2.80 pound entered its terminal agonies, capital flows accelerated toward Europe—more than $6 billion for 1967 as a whole, larger by itself (before government aid and military programs were added in) than the entire trade surplus for the year. But Congress would not move.

Johnson was deeply upset. "You know," Henry Fowler recalls, "Johnson had an intense interest in these things—to my surprise, in a way. All I had to say was, 'We've got a problem. It concerns the dollar, it concerns the pound, the stability of the international system.' His ears perked up. He was not only passively interested, he was intensely supportive. He had the gut perception of a politician that the strength of the dollar was important."

On New Year's Day 1968, for the fourth time in less than seven years, an American President submitted a new program to improve the balance of payments. At the head of Johnson's list was the domestic tax surcharge and a continuing voluntary program to restrain wages and prices ("which affect so directly our competitive position at home and in world markets"). Beyond that there were a group of severe "temporary measures" directly affecting the international flow of funds. Under the Banking Laws, the President issued orders to establish mandatory Foreign Direct Investment Controls, and authorize the Federal Reserve to turn the Voluntary Foreign Credit Restraint program into a Mandatory Foreign Credit Restraint Program. He asked "the American people to defer for the next two years all nonessential travel outside the Western Hemisphere," and instructed the Director of the Budget "to find ways of reducing the number of American civilians working [for the government] overseas."

The Commerce Department export drive was to receive a $200

million appropriation for promotion purposes, and a $500 million increase in Export-Import Bank authorizations would help establish better insurance programs for American exporters, export financing on easier terms and "direct financial support to American corporations joining together to sell abroad." The Europeans, meanwhile, would be asked to reduce or eliminate nontariff barriers to imports from America. Foreigners were to be encouraged by newly appointed task forces to visit and invest in America. The total payments swing from all these measures was estimated at $2.5 billion. Together with "factors affecting our deficit [which] will be more favorable in 1968," the program was projected to bring American payments into actual surplus by the end of the year.

At that point, clearly, the world would need the additional supply of monetary reserves to be generated through the IMF with the "activation" of Fowler's Special Drawing Rights—and Johnson called for that, too. The strength of the American commitment to SDRs is one of the stranger aspects of the decline of the dollar. As Kindleberger told a Senate committee early in 1968, "If there is difficulty in keeping the dollar convertible into gold, the addition of a third asset, which shall be as good as gold but not better than the dollar, smacks of trying to square the circle. No amount of gimmickry is likely to accomplish it." The rationale for the SDR was the need to keep the dollar scarce, but the authorization of SDRs has always come when dollars were overly plentiful.

The SDR was a step up in money creation from the established "drawing rights" member nations had in the International Monetary Fund, and even from the bancor Keynes had proposed in the negotiations preliminary to Bretton Woods. Those were both credit instruments, which enabled nations with temporary balance-of-payments problems to buy time for their resolution—either through change in the external circumstance that had made the problem (drought, strikes, etc.) or through "adjustments" to their own economies that would earn more foreign exchange or diminish the demand for it. Eventually, drawings from the IMF would have to be repaid. Though there was good reason to regard the first quarter of a country's quota at the IMF as part of national monetary reserves—this was the "gold tranche," the dollar value of the gold the nation had deposited in the Fund, available for withdrawal in other nations' currencies on demand. But the remainder of a country's IMF "quota," the "credit tranche" created by the deposit of one's own currency at the Fund, could be drawn only if the Fund's directors as bankers agreed that the prospects for its repayment were good.

From early on, the Fund had established a doctrine of "conditionality," which set up requirements for change in national domestic economic policy, steps toward an "adjustment" the Fund's economists thought necessary, before a country could draw other people's currencies out of the Fund against the credit of its deposit in its own currency. That made sense, according to the rule that no nation can be allowed to print its own reserves (which is why the Fed's "gold certificate" scheme was laughed out of Basle by the central bankers). But the purpose of holding reserves, for nations as well as for individuals, is to ensure that when trouble comes, one will retain the power to make one's own decisions— and on those grounds nations could scarcely count their "credit tranche" at the IMF as part of their reserves.

As time passed and international trade expanded on the sturdy base of fixed exchange rates, the reserve that countries were willing to count—gold holdings and "key currency" balances—diminished as a proportion of trade flows. The failure of reserves to expand as fast as trade apparently narrowed the margins of safety of the world as a whole against sudden destabilizing events. Increases in the "quotas" at the IMF, which more than doubled from 1958 to 1968, soothed some of the resulting anxiety. Still, the fact remained that drawing rights under quotas were *not* reserves, and at some point (three years was considered the norm, five years was the outside limit) the money would have to be paid back. As Gresham's Law began to operate against the dollar, questions of "reserve adequacy" assumed a new dimension.

Fowler's solution was the deliberate creation by international agreement of a new reserve asset which all the nations of the world would in fact "own." Up to a certain limit, which would have to be negotiated, each country would commit itself to pay out its own currency in return for an addition to its holdings of this new reserve on the books of the International Monetary Fund. The new Special Drawing Right would directly substitute for gold, in that a country could sell SDRs to a country designated by the Fund and receive that country's currency in return, just as it could sell gold.

The questions raised by this proposal were endless and as broad as they were deep. The era of American hegemony in the money markets had not yet ended, and the value of each unit of SDR was easy to establish: it would be a dollar (a "gold dollar," of the weight and fineness of gold at the established $35 an ounce). As all governments have always known, printing money is a profitable occupation; if an international organization was to print international money, who should receive the "seignorage," or profits, from the event? The Less Developed Countries, as they were beginning to call themselves, felt of course that these profits should go to them, on the grounds that they needed the money and had few other ways to get it. The nations that were going to supply the usable currencies for which SDRs could be traded were, in varying degrees, sympathetic to the need for aid, but also felt that the amounts and directions of their charity should be controlled by their own parliaments and not thrown into a currency pot. The problem of a "link" between SDR creation and aid to the Third World was one that would not down. It remained on the table through the disastrous "reform" negotiations of 1972-74—and, indeed, continues to disrupt IMF deliberations.

In the end, because the ideas were familiar, the negotiators decided to allocate SDRs in proportion to existing IMF quotas, with an informal pledge to the LDCs that the rich countries would use their profits from seignorage to beef up the World Bank, which made long-term loans for "reconstruction and development."

But now the Common Market countries were annoyed because their quotas at the IMF, initially set at a time when Europe was on the canvas being counted out, were far from reflecting their current status in world trade. SDRs looked to them like funny money that could be used to buy their output—or, worse, to excuse the United States and Britain from repaying their debts.

"Inevitably," Edward Bernstein, who had been present at the creation in Bretton Woods, explained patiently to the Joint Economic Committee, "power moves to those who have the resources that others are trying to borrow. No system is going to work in which real resources have to be transferred from one country to another for a fiduciary asset unless the countries that are giving the real resources feel reasonably assured that the system is working well, and not against their long-run interests." As it was mostly real European resources that would be transferred by the expenditure of SDRs, the Europeans could in the end call the tune.

What the Common Market got for consenting in principle to the first creation of SDRs was (1) an increase in their quotas sufficient to give them under the weighted voting procedures of the IMF a veto of any further manufacture of SDRs; (2) a low limit on the number of SDRs that would be created in the first three years, and a slow release of the new asset over the three years (the total American allocation in those years worked out to less than the gold that was lost in the market in the four months after the devaluation of the pound); and (3) an agreement that the system would not in fact be activated until the United States and Britain stopped pumping their currencies out to the rest of the world through payments deficits. It was this agreement that the central bankers, meeting in Washington in the gold crisis, urged their finance ministers to forget about. Nevertheless, it was not until 1970 that the first issue of SDRs actually got doled out at the International Monetary Fund.

In fact, no part of the Johnson program worked well in 1968—except the rhetoric, which turned out to be good enough. When "a coalition of illusion, blackmail and cowardice" (as DeGaulle called it) all but toppled the French government that May, the turmoil in the foreign exchange markets never turned against the dollar. Indeed, Johnson was able to be gracious to DeGaulle and supply dollars to help the franc in addition to buying back some of the gold the French had taken from America in the preceding years. That fall, speculators selling francs and buying marks were able to generate enough volume to force the first closing of the exchange markets in twenty years.

Nothing leaks out of the BIS meetings, so the speculators could not have known it, but in fact the central bankers the week before had come to the conclusion that the franc should be devalued and the mark revalued upward. This decision was not theirs to make, and the governments involved did not like the recommendation. All three German political parties had proclaimed themselves against revaluations, which could cost German jobs and profits; in France, though he felt some pull toward a devaluation large enough to give the French significant trade advantages, DeGaulle disliked the loss of grandeur involved in what would be considered a return to the bad habits of the Fourth Republic. The United States was heartily on his side; it did not wish to make French agricultural, clothing or machine-tool competition any rougher than it already was.

In this atmosphere, Karl Schiller, German finance minister, who was by the accident of rotation chairman of the Group of 10, called a meeting of finance ministers in Bonn. Fowler was in Europe visiting as a lame duck, and attended. Coombs flew from New York, Federal Reserve Board Chairman Martin and Governor Dewey Daane, who then held the Fed's foreign affairs brief, flew from Washington. Even before the foreign ministers met, the German government had voted to tax exports and subsidize imports, giving the rest of the world most of the benefits of a small mark revaluation, and the French had introduced a restrictive budget with strong foreign exchange controls in case the budget wasn't believed.

The finance ministers met and wrangled for three days, giving an object lesson in why politicians need central bankers to hide behind. The Germans were at odds with each other, but the sense of the meeting was that the French would devalue. Out in the corridors to which the finance ministers had banished them (Coombs describes a scene of Martin and Daane playing Ping-Pong before a gallery that included the managing director of the IMF), the central bankers put together a $2 billion package of support for the franc. Then DeGaulle said no, and the parities remained as they were.

Given the virulence of the French inflation following the wage increases of the summer, this solution was no solution. Less than a year later, both currencies had to change their parities; up for the Germans and down for the French. But the Americans decided to treat it as a triumph. "The United States," Fowler wrote in his last report to Lyndon Johnson, "set forth the basic principle that exchange rate changes of major financial powers should not take place without consultation between the governments of these major countries." Like other American policy pronouncements, of course, this did not bind future administrations. . . .

In the world of real trade and capital flows, the Johnson program was even less effective. Despite a further appeal as part of the March 31 speech in which he announced that he would not seek another term, Johnson was unable to get his tax increase through Congress until June. "The stalemate in the Congress on the proposed tax increase," Milton Gilbert wrote sourly from the ivory tower of the BIS, "has been watched by the rest of the world with some amazement." Then Senator George Smathers ran around the Constitutional requirement that tax bills originate in the House, tacking the 10 percent surcharge onto an appropriations bill—and selling it with the argument that it was needed for the defense of the dollar. The increase was made retroactive to April for individuals (January for corporations), holding the reported deficit of the fiscal 1968 budget to $25 billion—the largest since World War II.

Partly because the budget deficit had generated so much excess demand, the American trade surplus shrank to 40 percent of what it had been in 1967 (another reason was a long strike in the copper mines, and a strike threat against steel, which led steel consumers to import heavily to build inventory). Perversely, this masked the extent of the trouble that had been created: "If there had not been such an enormous increase of imports relative to exports," Edward Bernstein wrote, "all of the excessive demand would have had to be absorbed in an even greater rise of domestic prices and costs."

Other components of Johnson's program were a disappointment. Americans went abroad in 1968 in record numbers, raising the tourism deficit to an estimated $4 billion, by far the highest yet. Foreign direct investment by American companies also set new records, though Fowler was able to report that so far as the Treasury could discover nearly all the increase had been financed by borrowing abroad rather than in the United States.

Nevertheless, despite all the bad news, Fowler could and did claim that America during his last year at the Treasury had enjoyed an official settlements surplus and had reduced the liquidity deficit to a manageable level. As Tallulah Bankhead once said of a Maeterlinck play, there was less in this than met the eye. The settlements surplus was the direct result of the French disaster, from which France would recover. The liquidity deficit had been reduced again, as in 1968, mostly by a large short-term capital inflow, responding to American interest rates that rose to the highest levels since 1921—in a year when the Germans were holding rates down in a frantic effort to export their surplus. The biggest single shot in the arm, though nobody at the Treasury would be vulgar enough to mention it in an official report, was the final flowering of Bernard Cornfeld, whose Investors Overseas Services channeled something approaching $1 billion of European savings into the American stock market in 1968 alone.

And there was another element. The United States had always counted "above the line," as a voluntary investment in America by foreigners and thus no part of any deficit, all purchases by official foreign agencies of Treasury bonds with a maturity date more than a year away. Sales of paper with less than a year to run, however, had been "below the line," as evidence of a deficit in both the liquidity and official settlement accounts. Three years before, the Bernstein Committee had urged that no distinction be made between official purchases of long- and short-term paper—both should be considered as part of what foreigners did to "accommodate" an American deficit. This recommendation had not been accepted, and now the accounting gimmick was put to use. Friendly foreigners who expected to be holding U.S. paper all year anyway were persuaded to buy 366-day notes rather than 90-day bills. Reported sales of short-term paper to official foreigners dropped more than $1 billion; reported sales of long-term paper rose by $1.5 billion. The effects on the balance-of-payment statistics were little short of magical.

Confronted with an unpleasant situation that could not be remedied without pain in the real world, the Johnson administration exorcised the troublesome ghost by manipulating definitions. It was a characterological fault in a strange if rather wonderful President of the United States; he did things like that all the time. The world's question as to whether this fault was an individual or a national trait was about to receive some uncomfortable answers.

6 / Nixon's Nationalists

I don't give a shit about the lira.

—President Richard M. Nixon,
June 23, 1972 (expletive restored)

* * *

The Nixon administration took America back to the passive mode in the international monetary markets.

But passivity in the era of a two-tier gold market and an American trade deficit was very different from what it had been in the days when the United States had a trade surplus and could cushion the shocks of the international economy on the pillow of its gold stock.

Now the purpose of passivity was to compel foreign recognition that the United States had national interests that would have to be served by the international monetary and trade systems— and that it stood prepared to see those systems break if the fracture was necessary to eliminate American deficits.

The desire to force a crisis grew in part from foreign reluctance to share the burdens of a changing world economy and in part from the peculiar emotional makeup of this President.

Having broken apart the previous international monetary system and slammed shut the gold window, however, the administration found itself unable to force floating exchange rates on its trading partners, or to meet their demands that new American privileges must imply new American obligations.

In the end, then, the effort was made to reconstitute the fixed exchange-rate system and the Bretton Woods institutional frame, but without the restraints of gold—and without controls on the outflow of American capital.

The result was worldwide inflation, flexible exchange rates at last, and the "nonsystem" that turned over management of international finance to the private banks and the uncontrolled Euro-currency markets.

By the end of the Nixon Presidency, the United States had lost control of its dollar, in terms both of the exchange values and of the quantities available.

1

"The fact was," Richard Nixon wrote in his memoirs about the situation he found when he assumed the Presidency, "that the expansion of the Great Society was financed by deficit spending." But the federal budget that was in play when Nixon was inaugurated was a budget with a surplus—the combination of the 10 percent tax surcharge and the 4.5 percent inflation rate was pouring money into Washington. Nixon was committed to maintaining a surplus, but the spending commitments left behind by the Great Society—programs that could do nothing but grow—would thus require more taxes. The taxes requested fell on business—a permanent quietus to the investment tax credit, and a severe squeeze on the "loophole" for capital gains. So it was a Republican President, overwhelmingly the choice of the business community, who in his first months in office set the government's face against expanding investment, against the only known way of improving the productivity of American industry.

Assuming that Johnson's 1968 tax increase would immediately bite into economic activity, the Fed that summer had eased the reins on money-creation, only to find the economy much stronger than the experts had predicted; and by the time the new President was celebrating his accession to power, the screws were once again turning on the banking system.

The result was the first lesson in a great truth of the late twentieth century: that government actions repeated in similar situations do not produce similar consequences in the private sector. Having lived through the problem once, people and businesses are ready to cope when it comes back.

As in 1959 and 1966, the Fed in 1969 held down Reg Q ceilings on the interest rates the banks could pay, and sure enough the time deposits ran out of the banks to markets where they could earn more interest. But the big banks had all noticed in 1966 how convenient it was to have branches in Europe that could pull Eurodollars back for use at home; and as the domestic time deposits went out the front door, new Eurodollar deposits—bought at interest rates three and four points higher than American rates—poured through the back door. In total, about $12 billion of time deposits were removed from the banking system by market reactions to Reg Q ceilings—and about $13 billion were drawn in from Europe via the American branches abroad. As much as $4 billion of that high-interest Eurodollar money made a round trip, leaving the United States for deposit abroad and then returning, very profitably, for use at home.

Meanwhile, the European central banks had also adjusted their policies in response to what had happened in 1966. Then the drain of dollars had been like a drain of metal on the old gold standard, and had produced a contraction across the waters. Now the central banks simply added to the reserves of their own national banking systems to make up for the drain of dollars. Ever since the 1930s, economists had worried about a deflationary bias in the international monetary system (because countries with deficits had to cut back, while countries with surpluses did not necessarily have to expand). In 1969, via the Eurodollar market, the system acquired an inflationary bias. Purchased by the central banks, an inflow of dollars (like the old inflows of gold) would expand national monetary supplies, but an outflow of dollars would not be permitted to contract them. That was fair enough for the time being—the fact that the United States was fighting inflation did not mean everybody else had to deflate—but the long-term implications were frightening.

That this sea-change had occurred was concealed from view by the unsteady recovery of the pound and by the continuing crisis in the exchange rate between German marks and French francs. The November 1968 tariff and subsidy gimmicks had not worked, and money was still flooding into Germany—which was also struggling to hold down labor costs against the political infection of the very large wage increases by which the French government had won the support of the working class against the student revolutionaries. As France lost gold and Germany imported inflation (and elections were held in both countries, changing governments), the failure of the 1968 arrangements was recognized. France devalued by 11.1 percent in August, without warning; Germany revalued by 9.3 percent in October. From the European point of view, this "monetary crisis" seemed far more important than the steps being taken to counter the reflux of Eurodollars to the United States.

The franc-mark crisis of 1969 was the first monetary disturbance since World War II in which the United States took no role. Though the United States in theory still stood prepared to sell gold to national monetary authorities at $35 an ounce, nobody believed that this formal commitment would stand up against any sizable demand for metal: there were simply too many dollars outstanding. Because a fiction was being maintained, the significance of the change in the underlying reality was not entirely understood. The American monetary posture looking out at the rest of the world had returned to passivity. But whereas that passivity had once meant that the United States would do whatever the foreign situation required (buy gold or sell it), now it meant that foreigners were presumed to be big boys who would solve their own problems. The Treasury pushed—successfully, in the end—for the completion of the last formalities, Parliamentary votes and official signatures, necessary to start the issuance of SDRs from the International Monetary Fund; and Paul Volcker, who had taken over as Under Secretary for Monetary Affairs, reports that it wasn't easy. Otherwise, America lay doggo.

During the 1968 campaign, Arthur Burns had made a trip to Europe on Nixon's behalf, and had returned for a meeting in October ("in some remote place in downstate Illinois," he remembers), with advice that Nixon plan and advocate a devaluation of the dollar. The candidate brushed this aside as a possible campaign tactic, but Nixon was the first President since the payments deficit became a matter of concern not to make a statement that the United States would defend the gold (or any other) value of the dollar. His Treasury Secretary, David Kennedy, a Chicago banker who had been head of a committee studying the budget for Johnson, put out a perfunctory press release his first week in office to announce that he contemplated no change in American policies of valuing the dollar at $35 an ounce of gold.

Under Fowler, the Treasury had run a continuing seminar on American international monetary policy, chaired by Douglas Dillon and with significant inputs from Alfred Hayes of the New York Fed. The Nixon administration killed off the Dillon committee, leaving relations between the Treasury and the New York Fed to Volcker and Charles Coombs, who had been kids together in the early 1950s at 33 Liberty Street, but had grown apart. Meanwhile, Robert Solomon, the Washington-based economic consultant to the Fed on foreign matters, was developing large plans for a worldwide central bank and/or floating exchange rates, which were anathema to Coombs but the sort of large-scale initiative the Nixon administration liked to think it encouraged; and Coombs and Solomon had never got on, anyway.

This break between New York and Washington did not matter much in 1969, when money rained into America from Europe. The Treasury retired Roosa bonds, the New York Fed paid off outstanding swaps, and ended the year with only $214 million in the swap accounts. Though the trade balance and the current account showed no improvement from 1968, the hot money flows brought the liquidity balance into surplus. The official settlements balance turned positive, too, as the foreign central banks sold dollars to private parties who had private uses for them, and even put their reserve dollars into the Eurodollar market to earn higher interest.

By summer 1969, Federal Reserve Board Chairman Martin thought enough monetary restraint had been applied to stop the inflation, and the Fed eased off just a little. ("Too soon," Martin says now. "Worst mistake of my life.") In September, having relaxed the pressure on the banks enough to assure their action would not provoke a crisis, the Fed Board moved to gain some control over the inflow of Eurodollars. A 10 percent reserve requirement (the fraction that couldn't be lent) was imposed on borrowings from foreign branches, in a rather gimmicky way. Eurodollar deposits up to a total of those on the books as of March 1969 could be lent in their entirety, but everything over the March total would later be subject to reserve requirements. This stopped the import of Eurodollars, but not the growth of credit; by 1969, what I have elsewhere called the revolution in banking had been consolidated. The banks shifted their evasive action to commercial paper, new kinds of bankers' acceptances, sales of securities under repurchase agreements, and other devices.

Chairman Martin's term expired in January 1970, and Nixon replaced him with Arthur Burns, an avuncular Columbia economist who had been chairman of Eisenhower's first Council of Economic Advisers and head of the National Bureau of Economic Research, among other distinctions. Though in fact at least as close to the mainstream of economic thought as Martin, Burns had the temperament and reputation of a conservative, and a superb public persona—slow-speaking, pipe-smoking, thoughtful, gifted with a splendid talent for answering questions without telling anyone what he was thinking. Like most academics, he was a centralizer.

At the swearing-in ceremonies, Nixon said pleadingly, "Dr. Burns, please give us some money." Burns was willing to do so. Though inflationary pressures persisted, he had (correctly) diagnosed the condition of the American economy in early 1970 as one of incipient recession. The Fed quickly pumped money into the economy. Interest rates dropped like a stone (the rate on Treasury bills was halved in less than four months). Though the American trade surplus increased as recession reduced American demand for foreign as well as domestic products (and gave American producers more reason to look for foreign markets, which continued strong), money fled to the higher interest rates in Europe and the payments deficit ballooned.

Except for Volcker, who was regarded as the man paid to worry about such things, Washington initially couldn't have cared less. Like Kennedy, Nixon had commissioned a task force to give him guidance on international economic matters. Chaired by Gottfried Haberler of Harvard, the committee was greatly influenced by the monetarist theories of Milton Friedman, a long-term advocate of free-floating exchange rates rather than Bretton Woods parities. Among the participants was Harvard's Hendrik Houthakker, who would become a member of Nixon's Council of Economic Advisers, and as long ago as 1962 had called for the devaluation of the dollar. (He then had a neat, simple proof that he was right: "When unemployment and an international deficit appear at the same time, the source of the trouble can be pinned down with confidence: it is overvaluation of the dollar in terms of other currencies." The fact that the United States had a trade surplus in 1962, and that the deficit was at least in part a self-inflicted wound from defense and foreign-aid activities, did not enter into such calculations; nor was Houthakker prepared then to consider the Kindleberger question of the "balance of payments" of a bank. In fairness, Houthakker learned while in government service: testifying in 1971 as an Economic Adviser, when the dollar really *was* overvalued, he told Henry Reuss: "What really counts is our international net worth. Our international net worth is still increasing, so it is not as if we are on the way to bankruptcy.")

By the doctrines of the 1968 task force, the payments deficit of 1970 was good rather than bad because it would force the realignment of exchange rates the President's economic advisers thought had become necessary. As Houthakker later told *The Wall Street Journal,* "There was no possibility of devaluing the dollar unilaterally, since several other countries had made it clear they would devalue by an equal amount, thus nullifying our move. These countries therefore had to be persuaded by a continuing accumulation of inconvertible dollar balances." A man involved in making policy in those days points out that Houthakker in fact was not involved ("he was the cannonball on the deck"); but what Houthakker says was wanted does describe what happened.

In the first half of 1970, no harm was done by the American deficit. Britain and France had large debts to pay off at the IMF and were happy to use their surpluses for that purpose. In the aftermath of the 1969 revaluation, the mark was overvalued, and Germany, too, had a large deficit. (In fact, the Germans in 1970 sold gold to the United States for dollars, and drew dollars from the IMF to hold the mark at its new parity.) Then the Penn Central collapse and rapidly mounting unemployment forced the Fed into the most expansionary monetary policy the United States had seen since the 1950s. High-interest Eurodollar deposits became unprofitable.

Martin's Eurodollar reserve requirement on deposits acquired after March 1969 had been effective in persuading the American banks not to send back to their branches the Eurodollars they had acquired earlier. Freedom from reserve requirements (the opportunity to lend all the money) compensated reasonably well for the higher interest rates that had to be paid, and small losses could be considered an insurance premium for the margin of safety in managing the next crunch. But as the gap between interest rates in the American and European markets approached 2 percentage points, Eurodollars returned abroad in great quantity. The Fed responded by raising the reserve requirement on Eurodollars to 20 percent. ("Perhaps it should be explained," Joan Sneddon Little of the Federal Reserve Bank of Boston writes scornfully, "—lest the logic of raising reserve requirements to encourage holding Eurodollar liabilities appear somewhat backward—that the Board hoped that the threat of paying larger reserves on future borrowings would persuade the banks to maintain their costly debt. But, alas, it didn't.") From $15 billion in late 1969, the American banks' Eurodollar debts had dropped to $8 billion in late 1970—and would fall to less than $2 billion by mid-1971.

In its annual report for 1971, the Council of Economic Advisers had proclaimed the doctrine that American deficits were the foreigners' fault—as long as they insisted on running up surpluses, the United States would be unable to avoid deficits; and if they didn't like holding all those dollars, they should mend their ways. But now the 1970 trade surplus was gone, and the sums were too large: the Eurodollar outflow could not be entirely neglected.

At the beginning of 1971, the Export-Import Bank issued a security at interest rates higher than those on other American obligations, to be sold exclusively to the European branches of American banks, for the purpose of sopping up returning Eurodollars. (Such purchases would also retain the banks' exemption from reserve requirements: "Oh, what a tangled snare we bait," Mrs. Little writes, "when first we start to regulate.") In April, despite a reasoned distaste for establishing separate classes of creditors of the U.S. Government, the Treasury itself put out $1 billion of such notes, with interest rates above the notes being sold at the same time in the American market. Unfortunately, but not surprisingly, the money markets interpreted these actions as signs of weakness rather than evidence of determination.

And the weaknesses were real enough. For 1970 and the first quarter of 1971, the "official settlements" deficit ran an incredible $16.5 billion. The central banks wound up with all this money because (despite the Council of Economic Advisers) their citizenry did *not* wish to hold dollars, and under the rules of the IMF each government was responsible for maintaining the exchange value of the dollar in its own territories. Being barred from the gold window by the knowledge that it wasn't really open, the central banks grumpily went looking to invest their surplus at the best possible yields, and they put it in the Eurodollar banks, which by the end of 1970 were paying at a rate 1.5 percentage points above what American domestic banks would pay.

All the European countries were fighting inflation by restraining credit: their interest rates were even higher than the Eurodollar rates. Most of them could slow the inflow of dollars through exchange controls, but the Germans couldn't. In the first quarter of 1971, German companies borrowed $2.5 billion from the Eurobanks; when they converted the dollars to marks, the Bundesbank was the only buyer in the market.

The left hand in Frankfurt was not paying attention to what the right hand was doing. Finding itself with more dollars, the Bundesbank deposited more dollars with the Eurobanks. The "carousel," as it came to be called, generated an accelerating addition to apparent German dollar holdings, and to the quantities of Eurodollars outstanding. As of April 1, 1971, Milton Gilbert of the Bank for International Settlements reported, central bank placements in Eurodollar deposits amounted to $10 billion—up from only $3 billion at the start of the year.

Now it was the turn of the American visitors to BIS to be cross with their colleagues for irresponsible behavior, and they were. In April, Arthur Burns won from his fellow central bankers in Basle an agreement in principle that they would not deposit any more excess dollars outside the United States. Instead, they would put their money either in Treasury securities or in domestic American banks, which had sworn an oath of mickle might under the Voluntary Credit Restraint Program not to send such money abroad again.

As a further act of contrition, the Europeans eased off on their anti-inflation programs and organized a reduction of the interest rates in their own currencies, to make borrowing in Eurodollars less attractive. The Fed helped, allowing American interest rates to rise at a time when American unemployment was at 6 percent and the Nixon administration, running a budget deficit over $20 billion, wanted full cooperation from the monetary authorities to stimulate an economy still very much in the recovery room.

But it was too late. The psychology of the market had outrun the value of pledges and even actions—and the realities of the American position were too depressing. As winter turned to spring 1971, the United States trade balance fell into deficit for the first time in a century. "U.S. manufacturers," Edward Bernstein wrote grimly, "have not been able to compete with foreign producers in our home markets." Where once the American government had worried about building a trade surplus large enough to finance military and aid programs and permit capital outflows, now the American government had to worry about financing a trade deficit, too.

The dimensions of the disaster were not publicly admitted. As late as June, Treasury Under Secretary Paul Volcker and Congressman Henry Reuss were debating their differing solutions to a problem they both described as a deficit on the "basic balance" (trade, services and long-term capital flows) that ran from $2.5 billion to $3 billion a year. But the U.S. basic deficit had passed $3 billion for the second quarter of 1971 alone—and for the year 1971 would top $10 billion. The "official settlements" deficit—the quantity of dollars added to the stocks of the central banks abroad—was much greater, as the central banks wound up converting immense stocks of private dollar holdings their citizens no longer wished to keep; for the year as a whole, the official settlements deficit would, incredibly, top $30 billion. The dollar—the currency of what was unquestionably the world's most powerful economy—had collapsed; only the constant propping efforts of foreigners could hold it up.

2

The largest single source of deficit in the trade accounts was Japan. Empty of energy resources, deficient in iron, lumber, and necessary foodstuffs, the Japanese had lived by exporting since their emergence from isolation. To improve their standard of living, they needed export markets that could pay, which pretty much ruled out most of their near neighbors (especially since cooperation with the United States in the 1960s ruled out any significant trade with "Red China"). The tariff barriers of the Common Market—and of the nonmembers loosely linked in a so-called European Free Trade Association—made Europe a difficult market to penetrate for any manufactured goods also made in quantity there. Welcoming Japanese adherence to the General Agreement on Trade and Tariffs in the 1960s, the Europeans had reserved their right to maintain quotas against Japanese exports, and they did. Italy, for example, permitted the import of about 500 Japanese automobiles a year. Japan supplied only about 5 percent of European imports.

But the American market was relatively open. By 1971, the United States was importing 400,000 Japanese automobiles a year, and Japan supplied 15 percent of American imports. Organized as they were through export-oriented trading companies, Japanese industries were able to plan coordinated attacks on the American market, analyzing American tastes, costs, pricing policies, distribution systems. They did an A-1 job of producing for and selling to Americans: "The Japanese," economist Martin Bronfenbrenner of Carnegie-Mellon told the Reuss Subcommittee, ". . . have done more for the American consumer than Ralph Nader ever thought of doing." They built the world's biggest shipyards to make supertankers, and the world's most efficient steel mills.

The Japanese also did an A-1 job of protecting the domestic sales of their own industries from American competition, less by tariffs that could be protested than by the manipulation of the "traditional Japanese distribution channels" which rejected imported merchandise like an organism rejecting foreign bodies. The exchange rate between the yen and the dollar had been set at 360 to 1 by MacArthur, and had stuck there while the Japanese piled up trade surpluses. They spent a large fraction of the dollars they received from America on purchases from Australia and the oil sheikhs and the Europeans, so the bilateral deficit with Japan showed up heavily on the American balance with the rest-of-the-world.

Pushing on the Japanese had been a continuing activity of American trade representatives for fifteen years. Between 1956 and 1971 no fewer than seventy-three separate "voluntary export quotas" were negotiated with Japanese governments, but some of them failed to go into effect because the Diet wouldn't consent. (Americans were always expected to be sympathetic when Japanese domestic politics "prevented" a government from living up to its agreements, but the Japanese were always hurt or offended when protectionist sentiment was expressed in Congress. "Japan," Bronfenbrenner wrote, "reminds me of the college student who considers himself a man for purposes of burning down the ROTC building, but a little child when punishment is being considered.") To the mounting disgust of the Treasury, the State Department fought against pressuring Japan, insisting that despite their visible economic muscle, the Japanese were still "weak."

Japanese exchange controls were the tightest in the developed world; foreigners were not permitted to borrow yen. Japanese business investments abroad were tolerated only when they meshed with national plans. What could be said for them as trading partners was that they were the largest customers for American agricultural products (no small recommendation), and that they never complained about all the dollars they piled up, or threatened to take them to the gold window. But the cash value of such friendly gestures was pretty small compared to the losses the United States was suffering in the third markets from Japanese competition. And because the "traditional" Japanese internal distribution system was so inefficient and expensive, it was visibly true that Japanese goods sold at retail outside Japan for prices lower than those inside Japan. Coupled with Japanese insistence that their mounting surplus was not a "fundamental disequilibrium" which required them to revalue their currency under the rules of the IMF, the price differences looked a lot like dumping.

3

In May 1971, the international monetary system broke down under the strain of American deficits. In one week, more than $5 billion poured into the Bundesbank to buy marks at the going rate of exchange. On May 5, when $1 billion arrived at the window in the first hour of business, the Germans ceased supporting the dollar; on May 6, the German, Dutch, Belgian, Swiss, and Austrian exchange markets were closed. Over the weekend, the Swiss franc and Austrian schilling were revalued upward to new fixed rates, and the Germans announced that they would let the mark float on the exchanges, rising or falling according to demand and supply from private sources, until a sustainable level seemed to be reached. At that time, fixed exchange rates would be restored. The Belgians tried something new—yet another "two-tier" system, separating trade-related currency flows (for which the central bank would maintain a fixed rate) and capital flows (for which the market would set currency prices, without government intervention). Belgium was still operating such a system, with limited success, in 1979.

Before floating, the Germans had tried to involve all the Common Market countries in common currency action with respect to the dollar, and failed—the French were not prepared to lose the benefits they were gaining from an undervalued franc. From the American point of view, German capitulation to the speculators had further weakened the dollar and invited further raids against it, even though the move was one that would reduce German surpluses and presumably (on the Council of Economic Advisers argument that the American deficit was merely the mirror image of foreign surpluses) would contribute to assuaging the dollar's plight. Neither the Treasury nor the Fed could find out where that $5 billion inflow to the Bundesbank had come from. About $750 million seemed to have been sent abroad by the banks (which had leeway under the Voluntary Foreign Credit Restraint Program as eased by the Nixon administration), and another $500 million were to be seen in the reports nonbank corporations filed with the Treasury. But $4 billion was unaccounted for, part of the "Errors and Omissions" line in the balance of payments statements.

Toward the end of May, John Connally, Nixon's new Treasury Secretary, made a speech to an international bankers' conference in Munich, and included a pledge: "We are not going to devalue. We are not going to change the price of gold." Appearing before the Reuss Subcommittee in June, Under Secretary Volcker expressed the view that a devaluation of the dollar might not do much to help the American balance of payments—that the worst trade-flow patterns were in areas where foreigners had price advantages too great to be made up by a devaluation of a size likely to be accepted by the rest of the world. Moreover, a U.S. dollar devaluation would affect all the world's currencies. Many countries would have to devalue with us, distorting their trade relations with other countries that did not devalue, and others (especially the Japanese and the French) might come along for the ride, leaving us little better off than we had been before. Some way would have to be found to reduce the Japanese surplus, but, Volcker said, "I am not prepared to throw out the entire international monetary system because we have troubles with Japan."

Houthakker from the Council of Economic Advisers was even more soothing: "The international monetary situation, and the U.S. balance-of-payments position, are not as bad as many believe them to be." Fred Klopstock, director of international research for the New York Fed, chimed in with an assurance: "In the long run, I am not worried about the U.S. balance of payments if we manage our affairs wisely, as I am sure we will."

But Milton Gilbert came from the BIS with a very different message: "The question is, is the balance of payments worse than the U.S. officials say it is? That is where the rub comes in—it is worse than they say it is . . . There is no other country in the world that could have had the kind of deficit the United States has had over the past ten years. The dollar has been an exception because it is the reserve currency of the system. Otherwise there would have been the crisis in the dollar long before this."

Presently, the U.S. officials discovered that Gilbert was right. William Dale, a scholarly Midwesterner in a checked suit, bow tie, and horn-rimmed glasses, a graduate of the Fletcher School of diplomacy who had wound up making his career in the international end of the Treasury Department, was then the U.S. representative on the executive board of the IMF. (He later became the Fund's deputy managing director.) As early as February, he had deposited with the arriving John Connally a long memo arguing, from an IMF perspective, that the dollar had to be devalued and the price of gold had to rise. Dale remembers that the first Saturday in July he was home working on a child's bicycle when a call came from Paul Volcker. "He asked me, 'How big a deficit for June do you think would really put pressure on the dollar?' I told him, 'About two billion dollars.' He said, 'That's what we're facing. A little more than two billion dollars. Can you come over to my house this morning, and we'll talk about it?' "

The door to devaluation had opened.

4

A protégé of Lyndon Johnson's who had made a fortune as counsel to the Richardson family oil and real estate interests, John Connally had served as Secretary of the Navy in the Kennedy administration and eight years as governor of Texas. (He was riding in the Kennedy motorcade in Dallas and was wounded by the sniper who killed the President; there was briefly some thought that he had been the intended victim.) Working for a Republican President involved no great change in his attitudes, but moving to the Treasury Department was bewildering.

"I knew nothing about finance when the President asked me," Connally says. "I was trained as a lawyer. I was a Democrat coming late to a Republican administration, stepping into a department that was fully staffed, with a staff that didn't know me." But Robert Anderson urged him to accept, and he was flattered. Accepting, he hunted around for guidance, and found it in William McChesney Martin and his nineteen years as chairman of the Fed.

"I think I saw as much of John Connally as anyone when he was Secretary," Martin said recently. "He's a down-the-line fellow and he has a good mind. He wanted me to brief him on the Treasury. He and I would talk for two hours at a time, and I think I was probably the one who convinced him that in the end we had to devalue. I told him, 'The United States doesn't have the capacity to keep its balance of payments in order, and doesn't have the capacity to keep inflation under control. So we're a double failure.' Then I said, 'But if you do it, for God's sake, don't start bragging about it.' And that's exactly what they proceeded to do."

Though Connally presented himself from early on as "a bully-boy on the manicured playing fields of international finance," the fact was that initially he charmed the central bankers as he had been charming Texas millionaires all his life. They were used to politicians who took a nationalist view of international monetary matters, and felt that an American policy *admittedly* designed to serve American interests would be more predictable and less disturbing to the markets than a policy overlaid with traditional internationalist rhetoric. Connally's Munich speech laid out an indictment of foreigners for their protectionist trade policies, exchange restrictions, inadequate capital markets, and unwillingness to carry their fair share of the defense burdens. None of this was unreasonable for an American Treasury Secretary to say, and if the manner was tough, the matter was substantive. Until 1978, when the Carter administration's ten long months of pigheaded insistence on inflationary policies led to an attitude of grieving contempt toward the American government, the dollar in trouble always drew sympathetic concern if not helpful action from foreign monetary authorities.

Foreign economic policy entered into Connally's indoctrination, however, mostly through questions about the impact of foreign trade on American employment. Taking office in February, 1971, Connally found an economy rebounding strongly from the disastrous General Motors strike in the fall of 1970. But the unemployment rate was hanging at 6 percent, and the inflation rate was only a little lower. Looking abroad, a participant in the debates recalls, the administration was split: "Bill Rogers [Secretary of State] had the view that businessmen are always bitching about competition, and the U.S. is still way out in front in productivity. Maury Stans [Secretary of Commerce] had bought some gloomy thoughts of Henry Ford's, that America had become a service economy and could no longer compete internationally, and the only way we could keep our industrial jobs was through tariffs and quotas. The Burke-Hartke bill to do just that had a lot of strength in Congress."

Peter Peterson of Bell & Howell, brought on board to advise the President about international economics, recruited the monetary economist Fred Bergsten from Kissinger's staff and prepared a report for the President on *The United States in the Changing World Economy*. They went down the middle on the issues, rebuking "our view that the international competitive superiority of the U.S. was . . . so great we could easily afford concessions here and there . . . in the interest of maintaining flexible and friendly relations"—and also warning that "export 'competitiveness' not

only includes price competitiveness but marketing and technological competitiveness as well." What *really* got the President was
the estimate that "every billion dollars of [real] U.S. exports creates 60,000 to 80,000 jobs." He underlined it and for weeks
showed it to all visitors.

Arthur Burns had disconcerted Nixon by calling for a British-
style "incomes policy"; i.e., some form of control on wages and
prices to prevent fiscal and monetary expansion from raising
prices rather than production and employment. Meanwhile,
Americans were reacting in what was then their customary way to
the persistence of inflation: they were increasing their savings in
an effort to maintain the real value of what was already in the
bank. Driven by the working out of government policies set in
1968, the housing industry was moving to the biggest years in
history, but the rest of the economy had a somewhat faded look
to it when one peered beyond the short-term stimulus of catch-up
car production and car sales.

The President's economic advisers disagreed with each other.
Paul McCracken, chairman of the Council, was still a believer in
the Brookings doctrines of 1963—that vigorous American expansion would in itself solve the balance-of-payments problem by
luring capital inflows. Burns wanted fiscal stimulus and monetary
restraint (keeping interest rates high enough to discourage capital
outflows), with wage-price controls to take some of the burden of
fighting inflation off the central bank. George Shultz, director of
the budget bureau, was a Friedman-school economist who
thought that freeing up the markets domestically and internationally (floating rates) would fairly quickly resolve all the
problems.

Connally's Munich speech reflected his quick understanding
that not much could be gained from what Milton Gilbert at BIS
had wearily called "the inevitable announcement of an export
promotion program"—but that there was some small possibility
of painless improvement via increased foreign demand for U.S.
exports through action by foreigners. He gave it a shot and received some ambiguous encouragement. But America's trading

partners were being asked to give up real advantages in terms of their ability to control their own fate looking into an uncertain future. And there was always the excuse, in 1971, that any help given the Americans enabled them to persist in a Vietnam policy that was unpopular with European electorates, if not necessarily with the governments.

Connally had taken the king's shilling and would support whatever policy Nixon wished him to follow. His own preference, for reasons of temperament and political judgment, was to do something dramatic. A "summit meeting" of the President's economic advisers in Camp David at the end of June accepted the Shultz position: the economy was going to pull through without major government actions, and the foreign exchange markets would stabilize as interest rates converged (which was happening) on the two sides of the Atlantic. Japan could and would be pushed into line; though the others did not know it, Nixon was already en route to shaking Japanese security in their relations with the United States by the unprepared announcement of the opening of a dialogue with Peking. Connally's ability to handle a press conference was unrivaled in the administration; Nixon sent him out to announce the "four nos" that had been agreed upon in Camp David—no tax cut, no increase in government expenditure, no controls, no jawboning.

But, as Volcker had anticipated, publication of the frightful payments deficit of the second quarter had stimulated a flight from dollars. The virtue of the Bernstein Committee's emphasis on "official settlements" became apparent as private dollar holders rushed to the central banks to convert at the existing exchange rates, ballooning the reported deficit on the official settlements basis. Some of those dollars undoubtedly came from, or were borrowed in, the United States. Eight years before, Douglas Dillon had said, "The real danger to the United States, as to any country when it has a free exchange system, comes from its own citizens. If its own citizens lose confidence in its currency and start to try to transfer funds abroad, which they can do in very substantial volume, it is perfectly obvious that any amount of gold could be swamped very quickly." In July 1971, that beast began slouching toward Bethlehem.

"One evening that summer, I went out on the *Sequoia*," Connally recalls, referring to the President's yacht. "The President had the Secretary of State with him—Bill Rogers—and we had quite a discussion on the necessity of intensifying our firmness in international negotiations. I made a strong pitch to the President about the dollar. Rogers pretty much discounted it. He said, 'I've been listening to this since I was Attorney General for Eisenhower, at the cabinet meetings. Anderson was always warning us, but nothing ever happened.' "

Not the least of the world's concerns that summer was the threat of a steel strike in the United States. Such a strike in 1959 had established permanent relations between U.S. steel users and foreign suppliers, which through the years had been a continuing drag on the balance of payments—and the high price of the settlement had made U.S. steel production uncompetitive with that in the rest of the world, apparently forever. Some part of the deficit in June had been caused by American automobile manufacturers and others stockpiling foreign steel in anticipation of a strike at home. Now the steel companies and the unions reached agreement—on a contract which gave the workers a 30 percent raise over three years, and prompted an immediate 8 percent increase in steel prices. News of this settlement, on August 2, triggered defeat for Shultz's policy of reliance on the free market.

Albert Sindlinger, a Philadelphia-based pollster who nightly solicits the views of several hundred Americans on economic subjects (at the expense of, and for the benefit of, the automobile companies), reported in to the White House that consumer sentiment was deteriorating at an alarming and unprecedented rate. Other polls showed more than half the American public in favor of imposing wage and price controls, which Congress—over Nixon's objection—had given the President power to do. An AFL-CIO meeting had edged toward abandonment of the unions' long-standing policy in favor of free trade. Any hope that foreigners would cooperate voluntarily by revaluing their currencies against the dollar vanished with statements by the Japanese and French governments—both being inundated with dollars—that the exchange rates seemed correct.

On August 6, the Reuss Subcommittee brought in a report, *Action Now to Strengthen the U.S. Dollar,* a charming title for a document expressing "one inescapable conclusion—the dollar is overvalued." Reuss called for a reduction of military expenditures abroad, full employment at home, a "domestic price-wage-incomes policy," and especially "an appropriate realignment of dollar exchange rates." This last should be supervised by the International Monetary Fund. "If the Fund does fail to meet its responsibility," Reuss added, "the United States may have no choice but to take unilateral action to go off gold and establish new dollar parities."

A Treasury reply claimed that few members of Congress agreed with Reuss ("which was true," its author says; "didn't mean *we* disagreed")—but the exchange markets spun out of control. In February, responding to the turbulence that opened the year, the Federal Reserve Board had authorized expansion of the swap lines between the New York Fed and the various foreign central banks. Those lines had been heavily drawn on in July, and the dollars the central banks had via the swap route were, of course, exchange-rate guaranteed by the mechanism of restitution. But they had also acquired large quantities that they held naked, and they were scared—with good reason. Now several of these banks came to the New York Fed and asked for reverse swaps that would give them liabilities in dollars (and give the Fed liabilities in their currencies) to match against their uncovered holdings. In effect, they wanted an exchange-rate guarantee on the current inflow.

On August 12, the British—who had been compelled to give similar guarantees for the pound in 1968—inquired about the availability of the complete $2 billion swap line between the New York Fed and the Bank of England. Burns in Washington was kept informed, but he could see no way to close off the swap lines at this time and still maintain the cooperative central bank relations that had sustained the international monetary system for ten years. On reconsideration, the British contented themselves with $750 million worth ("what we told them they could have," Volcker says), representing guarantees against the dollars the Bank of England had been compelled to acquire in the preceding month.

Coombs flew down from New York and spent Friday morning closeted with Volcker, who put in a call for Connally, in an airplane en route to Houston for a weekend off. There is some confusion about what Volcker said. Connally is sure he was told that the British had asked for $3 billion of gold to replace the entire stock of dollars in their reserves, and that's what he told Nixon. The President responded by calling a meeting of economic advisers for that weekend—starting that night—at Camp David. Nobody from the State Department was asked to the meeting; neither was Kissinger. Connally commandeered an Air Force jet and flew immediately back to Washington, where Volcker met him at the air base; and the two men drove together, exploring alternatives, to the Presidential retreat in the Maryland hills.

It is not impossible that Volcker spoke to Connally in terms of gold—after all, he was explaining a technical situation to a layman. In fact, no large nation was demanding gold (there were some small sales to LDCs, grudgingly), because everyone knew it wouldn't be sold in major quantities. The one sizable gold sale of July—to the French—was not acquired to add to French reserves, but to permit a French repayment of outstanding debts to the IMF, which could no longer accept payment in dollars because the dollar quota was full. Indeed, the British had run down their own gold stock to repay *their* IMF debts, and had generously refrained from reconstituting it from America.

But the swap demand was functionally the same thing, and the Fed had the wind up. Burns was looking at potential losses running into the hundreds of millions of dollars if the dollar was devalued. If 'twere done when 'tis done . . . Burns added his voice to those calling for immediate and drastic action. As the Europeans went off for the biggest long weekend of their year, the panoply of American economic advisers gathered for a secret meeting with the President, arriving two by two, like the animals of Noah's Ark, in different forms of transportation to minimize the risk of discovery.

Connally proposed the Treasury's program: a ninety-day freeze on wages and prices, to be followed by lesser but still strong restraints; an investment tax credit (or "Job Development Credit") even larger than the Kennedy measure the administration had killed, usable only for domestic construction and the purchase of American-made capital goods; an end to the excise tax on automobiles to spur car sales; a 10 percent tax on the value of *all* imports (in effect a 10 percent devaluation of the dollar when spent to purchase imports); and formal closing of the gold window, permitting the American dollar to float on the international exchanges as a fiat money—take it or leave it, inconvertible to any form of reserve asset. The fact that this procedure would violate American treaty obligations under the Bretton Woods Agreements does not seem to have been mentioned by anyone—not even by Arthur Burns, who felt at Camp David and later that "there were other ways to do it. I had my say fully," Burns adds, "but Nixon had pretty much made his decision."

Connally remembers Burns's concern that closing the gold window, especially, "would precipitate a major international depression. Well, it didn't. Sure, it was a shock, but it wasn't designed as shock treatment. There was a lot of criticism because there hadn't been any prior consultation with other countries. But you don't telegraph your punches if you're going to close the gold window and put on a surcharge. Then you'd *really* have chaos."

Burns would have to tell the Basle central bankers that his side had changed the rules of the game, and he still remembers with distaste "the euphoria after the decision was reached." The United States was acknowledging, as Bill Martin told Connally, a double failure—but the people around Richard Nixon had found a way to present it as a triumph of American will and determination.* The dollar was not being devalued; the price of gold, Connally later told the press, would not change "one iota." Everybody else would have to revalue, lowering the price of gold in *their* currencies. We would make them do it.

On the way to Camp David, Herbert Stein of the Council of Economic Advisers had told William Safire, the President's speechwriter, that they were going to participate in the most momentous decision the United States government had taken in economic matters since March 4, 1933. What was done at Camp David would cast shadows far forward, across the lives of Americans (and, indeed, foreigners) yet unborn. As it happens, we have been told what was on the President's mind. "As I worked with Bill Safire on my speech that weekend," he wrote in his memoirs, "I wondered how the headlines would read: Would it be *Nixon Acts Boldly?* Or would it be *Nixon Changes Mind*"?

Thus were we governed in the United States in 1971—and perhaps not only then.

5

"The orchestration of the announcement of the Camp David decisions was the best-planned thing of its kind I've ever seen," Arthur Burns said recently. Burns himself sent telexes or personally got on the telephone to the European central bankers at their vacation retreat ("pretty late at night," Otmar Emminger recalls), and invited them to a meeting in London, where Paul Volcker, who was packed off on a Sunday plane, would fill them in. Nobody from the State Department or from Henry Kissinger's White House staff had been at Camp David: they came to Washington for briefings Sunday afternoon. Somebody thoughtfully telephoned Alfred Hayes of the New York Fed to tell him his

---

*In fairness, the final acknowledgment of a defeat often produces so great a release from prior fears and tensions that people react joyfully. R. H. S. Crossman noted in his diaries that Harold Wilson was "in tremendous form . . . a mood of real euphoria" when he faced up to the loss of the three-year battle to save the pound, in 1967.

bank was out of the foreign exchange business, and would until further notice neither buy nor sell—nor swap—currencies. The President went on television for a fifteen-minute sales pitch to the American people Sunday evening; Pierre-Paul Schweitzer, managing director of the International Monetary Fund, was invited to watch the President on a television set in Connally's office. Connally then handled the press.

In the United States, the reception was uproarious: the Dow-Jones Industrial Average rose more than thirty points on Monday. Elsewhere enthusiasm was restrained, though fear, confusion and a measure of guilt were as common as anger. The Latin Americans, Canadians and Japanese were bitter about the 10 percent import tax; the Germans were annoyed at an investment tax credit only for domestic purchases. Otmar Emminger of the Bundesbank made the first reply to Volcker's presentation in London and flatly told Volcker that German help in finding a new equilibrium level for the dollar could be expected only if the Americans were willing formally to devalue—that is, to raise the price of gold.

The French government forbade French businesses and individuals to deal in foreign currency except through the Bank of France, and adopted the Belgian "two-tier" system, with trade-related exchanges to be made at the old franc-dollar parity and capital-related exchanges to be made on an open market. The Japanese announced a determination to maintain the existing exchange rate between the dollar and the yen, and took in $4 billion at the Bank of Japan in two weeks before admitting defeat and allowing the yen to rise, with occasional interventions to keep the rise from proceeding at too rapid a pace. The Germans had already floated the mark; with judicious intervention in the markets, they allowed the total appreciation of the mark against the dollar to approach 10 percent (over and above the 10 percent of 1969). Britain and Switzerland kept exchange markets closed for a week and reopened them with stringent government supervision to prevent capital flows.

In the short term, the Camp David decisions were a brilliant performance. The world had been more or less ready to see the United States attempt a conventional devaluation, raising the price of gold and then entering into negotiations from a posture of contrition to see how much it could get away with. (The contrition would be especially appropriate because devaluation would reduce the value of the reserves so many countries held—at American urging—in the form of dollars.) Many complacently expected that the end result of these negotiations would be the "crowning" of the dollar as the world's reserve unit, backed by American pledges to maintain stability. Academic economists from Fritz Machlup to Robert Aliber had been urging for years American action to prove "that the dollar gives gold its value." Yale's Richard Cooper had noted in passing that closing the gold window "looks very attractive from the viewpoint of the United States."

Assuming that the academics were right, the United States was dealing from strength—and should behave that way. There was no need to go begging for permission to devalue; a de facto devaluation could be achieved through the 10 percent import tax, which could be countered only by illegal discriminatory duties aimed at the United States alone. Others had imposed "border taxes"—Britain in 1964, France in 1968—without rousing the wrath of GATT; indeed, the GATT rules probably permitted such actions to countries with persistent payments imbalances. (Oddly enough, the illegality was not international, but domestic. Nixon moved under alleged authority from the Trading with the Enemy Act, which was later found inapplicable for this purpose—but by then the international deal had been made and the tax removed.) Still, the British and French had planned and announced that they would drop the new tariffs when they had got their house in order. The United States, as the world's largest house, could say that it would drop the tariffs when all the others got their houses in order.

Foreigners had two problems, both serious. The 10 percent import tax hit some countries and some products harder than others, placing different nations under different strains—but since this was an international matter, there was no way to negotiate bilateral deals. Connally occasionally dropped hints that he might reduce or remove the tax for countries that cooperated by revaluing their currencies or dropping trade barriers, but that was part of the war of nerves; it couldn't be done.

And the rest of the world did, as the academics had said, need the dollar. It was the vehicle currency. Commodities from wheat to copper to cocoa to oil were invoiced in dollars. Trade between, say, Sweden and Austria was paid for not by the direct conversion of kroner into schillings (or vice versa) but via an intermediary stop in dollars. Without stable ratios between various currencies and the dollar—without fixed rates—the "cross rates" could vary ludicrously. With this in mind, the Germans proposed to their Common Market partners a "joint float" of European currencies against the dollar; but that risked pulling everyone up to the German revaluation level, and it was rejected.

Worse: every nation needs reserves that can be spent in those seasons (or years) when exports and easy borrowings don't cover necessary imports. Such reserves must be universally acceptable, and universally available. Gold was out of the question in 1971: there wasn't enough of it, and what there was lay in too few hands. Eventually, in theory, the SDRs Henry Fowler had steered through the IMF might take over, but in 1971 only $6 billion worth of those had been created—and by the rules the United States had just announced, the SDR (valued as a "gold dollar") was only a dollar under another name, anyway. "When the pound went," Jelle Zijlstra of the Netherlands Bank and the BIS said recently, "we could go to the dollar. If the dollar went, where could we go? To the moon?" Even if they had wanted to, other countries could not refuse to accept dollars—because *all* their trading partners, not just the United States, paid in dollars.

So the "prudent" creditors, to their great surprise, found themselves asking the debtor what they would have to pay. The Canadian finance minister, then serving in rotation as chairman of the Group of 10, summoned a meeting of the "deputies," at which Paul Volcker laid out the American price. It was shockingly high. Exchange rates should move sufficiently to give the United States a $13 billion "swing" in its trade balance, leaving enough surplus to pay for American military and aid commitments and to work off a little of the overhanging dollar debt. (It should be noted in passing that despite its universal acceptance, this computerized numerology of how much the United States would gain from x devaluation was doubtful stuff. As Fritz Machlup once put it, "The effects of devaluation upon income and upon trade cannot be stated unless it is known how the monetary authorities will act and react.") In addition, before the 10 percent import tax could be lifted, America's trading partners would have to abandon some of their trade restrictions to ease the export of American merchandise. Raising the price of gold was out of the question; Connally had already said no.

Then the finance ministers themselves met in London and Connally said lots of nos: he was willing to listen to other people's offers of what they might do to help the United States, but his only constructive suggestion was that the finance ministers should appoint committees to invent ground rules for a system of floating exchange rates. The great majority of the world's economists (including George Shultz at the White House, whose counsel Connally sought) believed that exchange rates determined by market forces would bring true payments balances without all the paraphernalia of reserves and interventions and decision making at international conferences. "But it was obvious," Connally says, "that we had a solid front against us. Notwithstanding the fact that the Canadians were *already* floating, they never raised a voice on our side."

Meanwhile, the fact was—and Connally understood it entirely—that all the costs of what the President was calling his New Economic Policy (after Lenin) were being borne by foreigners (including the erosion of the value of their reserves).

Until there was a deal, the United States had the floating rate system it wanted.

The English were willing to appease the Americans on gold, because it was clear that the window would not be reopened (all previous pledges not to use dollars to redeem gold were obviously canceled), and negotiations certainly should not break down over a disagreement about "the price at which the Americans will not sell gold." But the other Europeans were in no mood to write down in their own currencies the value of their gold stocks—and the IMF saw (as the Americans apparently did not: Robert Solomon still couldn't see it six years later) that failure to increase the price of gold would be the death of the gold-linked SDR. If a general revaluation that reduced the relative value of the dollar also reduced the relative value of the SDR, then no creditor nation would be willing to hold SDRs at 1.5 percent interest as against dollars at, say, 6 percent interest.

Pierre-Paul Schweitzer went on "The Today Show" to tell the world that the IMF thought the United States should make some "contribution" in the form of increasing the price of gold. This got him standing on the White House enemies list, and a year later cost him his job. (U.S. opposition to Schweitzer, who had been none too popular at the Treasury before the devaluation flap, was misguided as a matter of foreign relations. War hero and resistance leader—he had been tortured by the Nazis and still walked with a limp from the experience—he was popular with European finance ministries and with the IMF staff. His dismissal caused great resentment.) Still, the IMF institutionally sympathized with the American dilemma, and agreed that a new alignment of currencies was necessary. Staff studies at the Fund suggested that a swing of $8 to $9 billion was all the United States needed, and that such a swing could be gained by a 15 percent devaluation against the yen and the mark, 7 percent or so against the pound and the franc, something less against the other currencies. These studies leaked to the press, and presently many people were mad at Schweitzer.

Under these circumstances, the annual meeting of the IMF at the end of September, in Washington, was awaited with considerable discomfort. But Connally, at a meeting of the finance ministers just before the convention, assured everyone that the United States knew a deal had to be made and did not intend to retain the 10 percent surcharge any longer than necessary. The gold price was not a matter of great importance. ("I'd talked with the President," Connally says, "and I'd told him that in my understanding it didn't make much difference whether we devalued or the others revalued. But if he had a *political* problem about the price of gold, I ought to know it. He said he didn't have any problems.")

Connally's concessions at the IMF were in tone rather than substance: he might have taken off the war paint, but he was still at war. His performance was generally admired. Peter Jay, economics editor of the *London Times* (later British ambassador to Washington) wrote an appreciative column after Connally's IMF speech, which was rescheduled to be one of the last events of the meeting: "Balancing his conciliation on the surcharge and the gold price," Jay reported, "Mr. Connally left no one in doubt that the United States is in deadly earnest about correcting its balance-of-payments deficit, partly by exchange rate means but also, and equally important, by getting a crowbar into the unfair trading practices of Japan and the Common Market, especially nontariff barriers to industrial imports into Japan and the Six's common agricultural policy."

What Connally said was, "I do not mistake progress on understanding and agreement on procedures for the hard policy decisions necessary for a satisfactory solution . . . We are committed to ending the persistent deficit in our external payments. Indeed, at this point in time, the only question can be the means to that end, not the end itself. A monetary system dependent on United States deficits is no longer tolerable economically, financially, or politically, for you or for us." That might be conciliation, but it was certainly not compromise. And it might be noted that the day after the IMF meeting ended, the United States resumed the bombing of North Vietnam, which had been in suspense.

But there were dangers in this situation for the Americans: political dangers. "We were building bridges to our enemies," Peterson says, "and burning them to our friends." America's world leadership was in large part a function of its role at the center of the international system of money and trade, and the erosion of that role would be costly in terms of American influence. Over the long run, moreover, nations that felt themselves aggrieved and injured by a resurgent American nationalism might get together and work up means of protection; eventually, there would be economic costs, too. Everyone would have proved the point that sovereignty can win a war against prosperity; but that sort of war would be even more foolish than Vietnam.

The Netherlands embassy gave a dinner during the IMF meeting in honor of Jelle Zijlstra as chairman of the Bank for International Settlements. Arthur Burns attended, and was seated beside the guest of honor. He told Zijlstra that he was as disturbed as anyone at the prospect of mounting exchange controls and trade discrimination, but that there was no point convening an international meeting until its leaders had some notion of what deal could be worked out. "My friend," he said to Zijlstra (as Zijlstra recalls it), "we are in deep trouble. We need an honest broker. That's you."

There is some dispute between Burns and Connally as to whether the Treasury Secretary knew Burns had set up the informal, secret exploration Zijlstra then conducted, visiting all the Group of 10 capitals except Tokyo. ("The simple fact," Burns comments, "is that I got Connally's agreement to the Zijlstra mission *before* I got it under way. Connally just didn't remember.") Connally does remember Burns's insistence that the problem should be left in the hands of the central bankers, who could work it out. "I said to Burns, 'At these meetings there isn't one person in the room who has any authority except me, because the President has cloaked me with *his* authority. The central banks are arms of their governments. They have to check with their finance ministries. And the finance ministers all have to check with their heads of state.' " In principle, Burns was probably right—left alone, the central bankers would do better than the politicians—but once the governments were directly involved, as Connally saw, the Basle club was powerless.

By the time it was Connally's turn to meet with Zijlstra, he was denying that he'd been informed, and he arranged to be out of the country when the Dutchman came. This caused great offense. Zijlstra had been Prime Minister of the Netherlands before he was head of the central bank, and by protocol was entitled to the courtesy of Connally's time. But being himself a courteous man, he met with Volcker instead and got his work done.

In testimony before a Senate committee the day after the IMF meeting ended, Connally had cut back Volcker's original asking price, to a swing of $11 billion (instead of $13 billion) as the requisite for lifting the 10 percent surcharge and establishing new currency parities. Beyond that he would not go. Part of the problem was that the 10 percent surcharge was the most popular part of the New Economic Policy with the American public: it roused long-latent protectionism, the desire to get even with the foreigners, the lust for regaining jobs lost to foreign competition. Connally at the least toyed with the notion that Nixon should keep the surcharge in place for another year or so, until the elections, for political gain. Some of this had leaked abroad, and government leaders around the world felt the ground beginning to heave under their feet. Most relations between countries, after all, are commercial relations.

Complaints were sent through ambassadors to the State Department, but Secretary of State William Rogers took the position that this was a matter for Nixon and Connally. Henry Kissinger, recently returned from his triumphs in China, found that his oft-expressed belief in the primacy of politics rather than economics in international relations was not a faith for all seasons. The British ambassador was Lord Cromer, formerly head of Barings Bank and Governor of the Bank of England; Kissinger went in the evenings to Cromer for a confidential crash course in international money and trade. Then he made contact with Arthur Burns, who had been keeping a notebook of trade and exchange restrictions being adopted in other countries (Denmark, another debtor state, had actually copied Nixon's 10 percent import tax). With Pete Peterson, they formed a Gang of Three.

"Connally," says Charls Walker, who was then Deputy Secretary of the Treasury, "wanted to get all those preferences and quotas out of the Common Market, and he might have done so. But Kissinger got to the President, and said Connally was tearing up NATO."

A man who worked closely with Kissinger gives a more circumstantial account: "Henry was hearing from all the chanceries [embassies], and he decided he would have to take bureaucratic control. He knew that Nixon's election strategy for 1972 rested on summit meetings with Brezhnev and Mao, but that he couldn't go ahead with those unless he met first with the leaders of the allies. An inquiry had gone to Britain, and Ted Heath [British Prime Minister] sent back word that he could not meet with Nixon until there was progress on the international monetary front. Then Henry had control. I asked Henry once if he had put Heath up to it, and he told me it was a foolish question."

Connally scoffs. "That was the European bargaining strategy, like gold for us," he says. "They were going to make a big thing that Connally was so tough he was imperiling the alliances. I'll admit I never got any support anywhere else in government, but they never persuaded the President.

"I knew there had to be a deal soon—there is a momentum in these things, and if it went too long we would lose it. The President and I discussed who should get the credit for making the deal, and we agreed it had to be the French. Giscard d'Estaing [then finance minister] had been the leader of the other side—*outstanding*, very brilliant man, really understood the subject.

"Kissinger never had 'bureaucratic control.' The only time I talked with him was just before the meeting with Pompidou in the Azores. The way the meeting was structured, he was going to have to be with the President, and the President authorized me to tell Kissinger what we hoped to accomplish, so he would understand a little of what he was hearing."

In rotation, Connally had succeeded to the chair of the Group of 10. He called a meeting of the finance ministers at the Accademia dei Lupi in Rome on November 30. The day before, Volcker had repeated the American position at a meeting of the deputies, putting a number on the "average" revaluation the United States would demand from its partners: 11 percent. Significantly, the American delegation included the U.S. trade negotiator, who was all ready to discuss the concessions the Europeans and Japanese would make to ease the entry of American exports.

The first order of business on November 30 was a report from Otmar Emminger, then vice-president of the Bundesbank, who was chairman of the monetary Working Party in OECD. Emminger had an eighty-page paper, and said he would like to read it. Connally casually waved him to proceed. "This was one of those Renaissance palaces, with huge high ceilings," says a man who was there. "But there were a lot of people in it, and the air got stuffy. It was discovered that there was no pole to use to open the windows, and the Italian servants climbed up on each other's shoulders to reach. Emminger kept talking. White-coated waiters came in with chocolate and coffee and little cakes, and Emminger droned on. Connally was apparently asleep at the end of the table. When Emminger finished, Connally opened his eyes, slammed a hand on the table, and said, 'I suggest we go into executive session.' Emminger never forgave him."

The executive session, from which central bankers were excluded, began with finance ministers restating their governments' already well-known positions. When Giscard d'Estaing reached his emphasis on the need for a true American devaluation, an increase in the dollar price of gold, Volcker nudged Connally's arm. (Volcker was the official American representative at the meeting: Connally as chairman pro tem was presumed to be above the battle.) Connally nodded and Volcker interrupted: "Hypothetically—just for purposes of discussion—how would you respond to an offer by the United States to devalue by, say, ten or fifteen percent?" Then Connally took over: "What would the gentleman's reply be," he inquired, "if I suggested ten percent?" (Volcker says he doesn't know why Connally went for ten rather than fifteen.) Nobody in the room had been authorized to discuss numbers—and 10 percent was more than the Europeans wanted to see.

"There was forty clock minutes of silence in the room," Connally recalls appreciatively. "Then Tony Barber [British Chancellor of the Exchequer] said, 'Oh. We could never agree to such a devaluation.'

"I said, 'I'm astounded. What would you have in mind?'

"Barber said, 'Five percent.'

"I said, 'Under no circumstances could we agree—it's not enough.' "

The logjam was broken.

On December 14, Nixon, Connally, and Rogers met in the Azores with French President Georges Pompidou, Giscard, and foreign minister Couve de Mourville. They agreed to a change from $35 to $38 per ounce in the price of gold. Connally again briefed the press for Nixon, delivering himself of a homily on the central importance of preserving our alliances with our trading partners and increasing the flow of world trade. And he summoned another meeting of the Group of 10, to open only three days thereafter, at the Smithsonian Institute in Washington. Nixon and entourage (including Kissinger) went to Florida.

"Most of the time at these meetings," Connally says in disgusted recollection, "was spent in recess, as the finance ministers consulted with their home governments and the Six [the Common Market countries] consulted with each other. Whatever exchange rate changes they agreed on with us would set the exchange rates they had with each other. Friday evening at the Smithsonian, Karl Schiller [German finance minister] and Giscard came to me and Schiller said, 'We have failed to reach an accord among the Six. You are going to have to work it out.'

"The Japanese were still saying they would do nothing. I'd told them they ought to revalue the yen at least twenty-five percent, and we wouldn't settle for less than nineteen. I began to meet with these individuals. First it was Schiller. I said, 'You'll revalue fourteen percent.' He said, 'What are the French going to do?' I said, 'They will stay at the price of gold.' [This meant that the franc would, like gold, rise 8.75 percent against the devaluing dollar; this had been pretty much set in concrete by Nixon and Pompidou.]

"He said, 'The Italians?'

" 'Same as the French.'

" 'The Japanese?'

"I said, 'Seventeen percent. Whatever happens, we'll insist they revalue three percent more than you do.'

"He agreed. Giscard agreed. The Japanese minister didn't come to meetings; he had an assistant. I told the assistant, 'By ten in the morning I have to have your agreement to seventeen percent.' All these people had to check with their governments—the French cabinet met all night, because of the time difference.

"The next morning the Italians came in and said they couldn't continue the parity with the French. I went to Giscard and Schiller and said, 'The Italians are in a hell of a bad shape. Let them do what they want.' Giscard agreed. Then the Canadians insisted they weren't going back to fixed rates, and we all accepted that.

"A few minutes before ten, the Japanese deputy summoned me out of the room," Connally continues, crooking a finger to illustrate. "He told me Minister Masuta had said he could not accept seventeen percent. I turned my back on him and said I was going to hold a press conference, tell the world we had a deal but the Japanese were intransigent. He said, 'You don't understand. In 1932, the then finance minister revalued the yen by seventeen percent, started a depression, many unemployed, and he committed suicide. Can't you give my minister some other number?'

"I said, 'Sixteen point nine.'

"He said, 'Okay.' "

The total yield from the revaluations agreed upon at the Smithsonian was estimated as a swing of $8-$9 billion (the IMF target) in the U.S. balance of payments. The net devaluation of the dollar was greater (though not grossly so) than what the Zijlstra mission had proposed. The American demand for reduced barriers against American trade was referred to committee; another committee was established to work on "the reform of the international monetary system" within the framework of the IMF; the special 10 percent import tax and discriminatory investment credits and all foreign retaliation were dropped. The new fixed rates were to be held in a band of 2.25 percent around the agreed "central rates." It does not seem to have been understood that this apparently increased flexibility, in the high interest rate atmosphere of 1971, was in fact *less* than the 1 percent flexibility of the original Bretton Woods arrangements.

President Nixon flew up from Florida and addressed the meeting at the close of the deliberations, telling the assembled governors and ministers what he later told the press—that they had achieved "the most significant monetary agreement in the history of the world." He seems to have changed his mind: the Smithsonian Agreement is not mentioned in his memoirs. But Zijlstra thinks he had a point: "Remember, this was the first multilateral negotiation of change of parities since Bretton Woods. I have never understood why it could not have taken place sooner," he adds sadly, "or why it could not have been done in a more civilized manner."

Others think Connally had the best point through the period of his recalcitrance. "The fact is," said a very eminent European who cannot be named, "that the United States needed more than it got in the Smithsonian Agreement. Especially on the trade preferences, and the 'reverse preferences' the Common Market had with the Africans [i.e., the special deals that reserved a chunk of African markets for European producers]. Connally was effective because we knew we were wrong on many things. He was in a very strong position because our economies were not in the best shape in 1971, and we needed the exports. If he had held on a little longer, he might have got much more."

Connally doubts it. "Of course we should have had more," he says. "We should have had a *thirty-five* percent revaluation from the Japanese, more than we got from the Germans, more from the French. And it all came back to haunt us. The Europeans know about these things; they're very able, and they've lived through currency devaluations, monetary crises, all the economic effects. Here, nobody but the Treasury was concerned—there wasn't anybody in our government prepared to understand what we were doing."

One loose end remained to be tied up. The executive branch could not change the price of gold: that was clearly one of the prerogatives reserved to the Congress (which has responsibility for "coining money"). Four years before, Henry Reuss had written a letter to then Treasury Secretary Henry Fowler, proclaiming, "It is my determination—one that I believe is widely shared in the Congress—never to authorize an increase in the present price of gold, since to do so would not only break the faith with those who have expressed confidence in the dollar, but would unjustly reward those speculators who might seek to undermine confidence in the dollar." Devaluation had been presented as a nationalist triumph. Reuss, like everyone else, accepted it, and voted to raise the price of gold.

6

Devaluations are designed to eliminate a payments deficit, and the history of the period since World War II indicates that they perform that function fairly well (though not so well as their designers hope, because domestic inflation always eats up more of the benefit than was expected). Even the most successful devaluations, however, start off by producing perverse results. Imports in process of shipment invoiced in foreign currencies cost more because the currencies cost more; exports invoiced in the domestic currency yield the country of origin less foreign exchange, because the domestic currency buys less foreign exchange. Things get worse, in short, before they get better; economists speak of the "J-curve," which is the graphic illustration of that statement. Loans from foreign governments and central banks to tide the devaluer over the awkward descent of his J-curve are normally part of the package involved in any internationally approved devaluation. The United States, of course, did not go begging for loans, but the willingness of foreign central banks to increase their dollar holdings was in everything but name a loan—an overdraft—for the United States.

Central banks almost always cut back on the supply of credit within their jurisdiction in the aftermath of a devaluation. Sometimes the cutback is required by a rapid reflow of speculative funds that had fled this currency in the belief that it was about to be devalued. Having profited by this belief, the speculators may return their money to its source and cash in their winnings. To prevent a rapid expansion of the domestic money supply, with its inflationary effects, the central bank absorbs what it can.

More common, however, is the situation where the newly devalued currency comes under fresh attack. The payments deficit worsens on the downstroke of the J-curve, increasing the supply of the currency in foreign markets, and pundits reading the daily paper proclaim that the devaluation is "insufficient." Now the central bank must raise interest rates at home in hopes of drawing short-term capital flows to bridge the time until the J-curve turns up. A dose of deflationary pressure is recommended, too, to prevent labor unions from demanding wage increases to help their members pay the rising prices of imported goods—and also to put some domestic roadblocks in the path of manufacturers whose products are sold both domestically and for export, and who might raise their prices at home because they can do so without losing sales abroad. Inflation at home can quickly kill the trade advantages of a devaluation.

Following the Smithsonian Agreement, the Federal Reserve

Board did in fact take some hesitant steps toward tightening credit in the American markets. But the reason was the belief that the devaluation would produce great capital inflows that should be sterilized within the central bank before they made trouble. Exactly *why* the Fed's analysts thought the Smithsonian rates would attract so much money to America is not clear: the Treasury had been saying that it needed at least an $11 billion improvement in the payments balance, and nobody's computer predicted a net gain of more than $8 billion from the deal actually struck at the Smithsonian. When the predicted inflow did not materialize, the Fed in January 1972 began to ease the supply of funds to the banking system. For the full year 1972, in fact, the narrowly defined American money supply—the stuff most tightly governed by the Fed—rose an unprecedented 9 percent.

"We were very surprised at the Treasury," Paul Volcker says rather carefully, "when the Fed failed to defend the Smithsonian rates." (Jack Bennett, financial vice-president of Exxon who came down to be Volcker's assistant and later took the Under Secretary job, reports being less surprised: "Each Secretary of the Treasury," he says, "found out gradually that what he was doing was not necessarily what Burns was doing—and learned to live with it.") Burns insists that the Treasury never complained about the rapid increase in the money supply in 1972—that the White House was if anything unhappy about the rise in short-term interest rates that began in the spring despite the expansion, because loan demand was growing even faster than bank credit. Still, the fact remains that the Smithsonian era began with a reduction in the Fed's discount rate, and with interest rates on Treasury bills plunging to their lowest level since the early 1960s.

Abroad, the reaction was consternation: the last thing the reformed monetary system could support was an outflow of U.S. capital to higher rates in foreign markets. As always, the choice was especially painful for the Germans, who had no direct exchange restrictions. Otmar Emminger of the Bundesbank talked with Arthur Burns on the telephone from Frankfurt to Washington. "He seemed fearful," Emminger recalls, "of attacks by

Wright Patman [then chairman of the House Banking and Currency Committee], and of the possible loss of independence for the Fed if interest rates went up. When the Fed actually lowered American interest rates, we set ours at a very low point, against our domestic needs, in a desperate effort to save the system."

The bounds of monetary restraint were loosened everywhere. "U.S. monetary policy," Henry Fowler says, shaking his head. "The Japanese. The U.K. The Germans. The French. They were all throwing oil on the fire." Especially the British. Britain was entering the Common Market with an economy poorly equipped to compete against the more modern machinery of the Continent, and with a rights-besotted work force. Edward Heath and Anthony Barber, Tory Prime Minister and Chancellor, bought the entire package of the Kennedy-Johnson economic advisers: government-stimulated growth would generate the tax revenues to pay for the government programs, and as the economy accelerated businessmen would increase their investments, modernize their facilities, in the simple pursuit of profit. International payments would not deteriorate because Britain would become a desirable place for foreigners to make investments. But the international aspect would be secondary: on March 21, 1972, introducing a highly inflationary budget, Barber openly proclaimed that Britain would no longer take the exchange value of the pound into consideration in calculating the effects of domestic fiscal policy.

As money poured out of Her Majesty's Treasury to finance local improvements and business schemes, the British inflation rate (highest in the developed world in 1970–71), resumed its upward course, and the payments deficit increased. By June the market was ready to believe Barber had meant what he said, and the Smithsonian rates for the pound were no longer sustainable—Britain lost a third of her reserves in two weeks, defending the pound at $2.55. Sterling was set afloat, to find its own level (it was in the context of a report on this development that Nixon expressed his disinterest in the lira). The attack moved again to the dollar. Exchange markets were closed yet again, and reopened only after the Germans, the Dutch, and the Swiss had instituted the harshest capital controls those countries had seen since the 1950s.

In fact, the American inflation rate was then the lowest in the West, held down by continuing compliance with Nixon's Phase II wage and price controls. But the payments deficit continued horrific—the trade balance did not reach the turning of the J-curve until midsummer—and with interest rates low, the capital outflow was heavy. (On the official settlements basis, the American deficit in 1972 would touch $20 billion.) And beneath the surface of the 3.3 percent inflation rate, observers could see the pressures building from the rapid growth of the money supply.

Moreover, the closing of the gold window had created a peculiar asymmetry in the international settlements situation. Other nations could use their stocks of dollars to settle accounts with each other, because the dollar was still a "reserve currency." But the United States, holding virtually no foreign exchange in its own reserves and refusing to settle accounts in gold, had no usable reserve assets at all. Dollars could not be used for intervention in the markets to prop up the dollar. And the view that the American deficit was the foreigners' problem had persisted through the Smithsonian Agreement and the departure of John Connally from the Treasury. (He went to launch the cause of Democrats for Nixon.) If anything, his successor George Shultz was even more committed to the doctrine that the United States should not take responsibility for maintaining the international value of the dollar. During the worst moments of panic in July 1972, at the strong urging of Arthur Burns, Coombs of the New York Fed was allowed to activate limited swap lines and to purchase some dollars in the New York market with the foreign currencies the other central banks made available. But the authorization was quickly withdrawn.

While the currency drama was playing itself out in the markets, an even greater drama was in progress in the wheat fields of the Ukraine and China. Drought and inefficiency would produce a huge shortfall of grain supplies in the Communist countries; between them, they would buy 25 million metric tons of American wheat, helping the U.S. balance of payments by more than $1.5 billion. As 1972 proceeded, the J-curve turned up, and American manufactured goods, made cheaper by devaluation, began moving out to markets where previously they had been uncompetitive. Interest rates rose, too.

But the markets were uncomfortable with the quantities of dollars held by foreigners—especially with indications that the Germans were no longer willing to expand their dollar holdings significantly. To buy those dollars, they were printing vast quantities of marks, and they felt violent inflationary pressures on their own economy. The Bank for International Settlements noted "the awkward fact that the readjustment itself did not restore confidence in the dollar," largely because "the devaluation . . . had not been accompanied by any shift to domestic monetary and fiscal restraint."

What triggered the next collapse of the dollar, however, was a run on the lira, which the Italian government sought to defend by buying lira in the market for dollars. Both lira and dollars began finding their way to Switzerland. In January 1973, the Italians attempted to set up a two-tier exchange market, maintaining Smithsonian central rates for trade-related exchanges but permitting the lira to drop when the purpose of using it was a capital transaction. The Swiss, who had not been consulted, thereupon floated their franc, which rose rapidly. For a wonder, George Shultz's Treasury now okayed the use of whatever marks were available to take the burden off the Bundesbank.

But in fact Nixon, Shultz, and Volcker were looking for a second devaluation of the dollar in 1973. Volcker was sent on a trip around the world to inform foreign central banks and finance ministries that the United States was about to devalue by 10 percent, raising the price at which it would not sell gold to $42.22. He managed to get in and out of Tokyo unobserved by flying into an Air Force base at night and meeting the Japanese finance minister at the U.S. Embassy. (The New York Fed was not told about Volcker's mission, and learned about it via a call from the Bank of Japan, a hugely and needlessly embarrassing moment for both ends of the conversation.) German finance ministers receive in their bureaus, however, and Volcker, who is 6'7"+, was spotted easily enough in Bonn. The markets guessed what was up, and speculators began borrowing dollars like crazy. On one day in February the interest on overnight Eurodollar loans touched an annual rate of 40 percent.

Initially, these borrowed dollars went to gold, and Volcker suggested that some strategic selling of yellow metal in London might keep the system viable. The French were having none of that, presumably because they were willing to see gold rise. Having won on gold, the speculators expanded their activities to the mark, flooding the Bundesbank with $6 billion in less than two weeks, and the Germans, unwilling to print endless marks to buy endless dollars, again abandoned fixed exchange rates. The most significant monetary agreement in the history of the world had held up for less than fifteen months.

In hindsight, it seems clear enough that the world's attitudes toward money were given a disastrous twist by the American decision of 1971 to stage a one-man jailbreak from the Bretton Woods obligations. For years, economists had been arguing about the efficacy of the gold base for the world's money as a restraint on the tendency of governments to spend their way out of trouble. As numismatists can demonstrate, the emperors, kings, and princes of history have always clipped the coinage to pay their bills. In 1972, in one great burst of freedom, all the nations of the West clipped their paper "coinage" for the goal of maximum growth.

The result was pressure from all directions on the world's productive capacities. The Reuters index of commodity prices (foodstuffs, fibers and minerals) rose by 65 percent from the end of 1971 to spring 1973. Everything soared but oil. Inflation rates ran 6 percent in Germany, 7 percent in the United States and France, 10 percent in Britain, 12 percent in Italy—and in all these countries except Germany were still on the rise. Though the United States had finally moved into the good part of the J-curve in its international trade (merchandise exports rose from $50 billion in

1972 to more than $71 billion in 1973, thanks in large part to the sensational increase in agricultural prices), the dollar continued to drop against the floating Swiss franc and mark until the middle of the year, then stabilized and started up. The improvement began, slowly, in midsummer. But what gave it authority was, once again, less a matter of changing economic conditions than a matter of political urgency.

7

The Organization of Petroleum Exporting Countries (OPEC) was formed when the oil companies enforced a price reduction on the producers after the reopening of the Suez Canal ended the shortages of the late 1950s. It was an ineffective organization unable to stop the worldwide glut of oil (among the American barriers to free trade was a combination of tariffs and quotas on imported oil, protecting the high-cost producers of the United States from "unfair" competition). But American output had peaked in 1970, and world energy demand was rising rapidly. A few of the producing countries—most notably Libya—had been able to play the oil companies off against each other and to secure a larger share of the receipts for themselves. Still, some consuming nations were boycotting Libyan oil in response, and the fact was that through the commodities boom of 1972–73, oil prices had remained relatively leaden.

Then the Egyptians and Syrians sought revenge on the Israelis, and the Arab oil producers, eager to help, embargoed all sales to those nations (essentially the United States and the Netherlands) that were supporting Israel. They also reduced production by 5 percent and raised their "posted prices" from $3.05 to $5.11 per barrel (42 gallons) of oil. The Arabs noted that the oil companies were able to collect the new posted price from their customers, and did indeed obey the allocation orders. (The Europeans, however, arranged to keep the Dutch supplied after the Dutch threatened to cut off the supplies of that natural gas they shipped to Germany and France.) To their surprise, the Arabs found that prices on the spot market actually rose beyond the posted price in response to reduced production. . . . By the time the dust had settled in the desert, in early 1974, the posted price of oil had risen to $11.65 a barrel.

The United States and Canada were the only industrial powers that met most of their oil needs from domestic production—and little of what the United States imported came from the Arabs. In time of turmoil, for whatever reason, people with money tended to send it to the United States, where political stability provided a Gresham's Law preference for the dollar as a store of value. Though some oil producers accepted part of their payment in sterling (a legacy from the days when the British had policed the Gulf), oil was mostly denominated in dollars: to buy oil from the Arabs and Venezuelans or Indonesia, customers needed dollars. So the immediate impact of the OPEC action was to strengthen the dollar on the currency exchanges. In early 1974, when the bills at the new prices began to come in, the dollar briefly returned to the Smithsonian parities, up more than 15 percent against European currencies from the levels touched in June.

Some of the dollars the world now needed to pay for oil were drawn from existing reserves around the world; some were taken by purchasing dollars with other currencies (which was what strengthened the dollar). Because commodity prices were so high, some of the underdeveloped countries (now to be called Less Developed Countries, or LDCs) were reasonably well placed to put out more cash for energy. But others, including some of the industrial countries, would have to borrow. With the move to floating rates in March 1973, the United States had committed itself to abolish by the end of 1974 the Interest Equalization Tax and foreign direct investment controls that had been in effect since the Kennedy and Johnson days. It was clear from the beginning that international organizations and governments could not move fast enough to supply funds to needy consumers of oil, and that some of the money that had to be paid to the OPEC producers would have to be borrowed privately. To help ease the strain on the world's banking system, and to keep the dollar from appreciating through the Smithsonian roof, the Nixon administration in January, eleven months ahead of schedule, removed all capital controls affecting the export of dollars.

In normal times, a currency that is being borrowed for international use comes under pressure in the markets because the borrower promptly goes out to change it into the other currency he needs for his own purposes. But the international borrowers were not exchanging their dollars for other currencies when they bought oil; they simply transferred the ownership of the dollars to the oil producers. Unless the oil producers themselves decided to buy what they wanted in other countries, or to "diversify" their currency holdings, the dollar borrowings would not work to reduce the dollar's exchange value. In fact, the capital inflow from OPEC to the United States in 1974 would be almost $14 billion more than what was needed to balance the deficit in the American trade with the oil producers: the money foreigners borrowed in dollars *did* remain in dollars. And this condition might even— maybe—be stable, because as the OPEC countries increased their dollar-denominated assets they would be reluctant to take actions that reduced the value of those assets.

The payments surpluses of the OPEC nations were something new in the world. It was impossible for other nations to "adjust" their economies to eliminate their corresponding deficits, or for the OPEC nations to spend on current account even a major fraction of the money that was pouring in through 1974. (Forty percent of the capital inflow to the United States, though, did represent one-time expenditure: compensation to the oil companies for properties the OPEC countries could now painlessly nationalize.)

It was possible, though not easy, to justify what the Saudis and Kuwaitis and Libyans were doing. Their natural assets were being permanently depleted; they were entitled to build up financial assets, ownership positions in the future, after the oil was gone. On this theory, their excess funds should be invested in long-term properties; and these long-term capital flows, as the international books are kept, would balance the ledgers in a way that was comprehensible, if not cheerful, to economists. But the importing countries were less than eager to sell off their land and factories to the Arabs, who in turn were by no means ready to decide how they wished to commit their astonishing new wealth.

Driven by the inflation—which inevitably worsened when what was really a kind of excise tax on energy was imposed on the world economy—short-term interest rates had reached heights never before known in the United States or the Eurodollar market. Long-term rates were lower, on the grounds that this level of inflation would prove politically unbearable and would ultimately be reduced. The Arabs had every reason to put their money into relatively short-term deposits in the Eurodollar market, and that is what they did. Then, of course, the international banks had money they could lend to those who otherwise could not buy the oil they needed. . . . The "carousel" of the Eurodollar market was back, bigger, faster, worse in its inflationary implications, its capacity for producing ultimate disaster.

For years there had been an argument about whether the Eurodollar banks could generate new dollars with their lending, the way domestic banks generated dollars. The Fed believed not, because the only place dollars could be spent was the United States. Dollars leaking back from the Euromarket to the United States were not available to be lent again by a Eurobank; what credit creation then occurred was domestic, and the Fed had a handle on it. A borrower from a Eurobank who wished to spend outside the United States would take the proceeds of his dollar loan to, say, the Bundesbank—which bought the dollars and invested them for its own account in U.S. Treasuries. Only if the central banks returned their oversupply of dollars to the Eurobanks (as they had in 1971) could that supranational banking system develop a "multiplier."

Increasingly, however, with the passage of time, dollars *could* be spent outside the United States, because much of the commodity trade worldwide was denominated in dollars. And now, with a whoosh, there was a giant use of dollars outside the United States, to buy oil. When the oil producers placed their dollars back into the Eurobanks, they made possible a multiplication of dollar liabilities in Europe which were not claims on American banks. In principle, Eurodollar transactions passed through the Clearing House in New York, where funds were transferred on the computerized books from one Eurobank to another. In fact, a kind of dollar "clearing" grew up through overnight lending in the London market, by which the receipts of the oil exporters could be credited to the accounts of the Eurobanks and their dollar balances in New York could be protected from depletion.

An initial American million dollars paid for Arab oil might turn into several millions inside this offshore banking system. Deposited in a London Eurobank by the Arab recipient, it might be lent to the Brazilians, who would use it to buy oil from the Arabs, who would redeposit it in the London bank, etc. The asset the bank acquired in making its dollar loan was apparently a claim on Brazil, in dollars. But Brazil didn't have dollars, and the claim was really in exchange-rate-guaranteed cruzeiros. From the point of view of the Arabs who got the money, however, it all looked like the same dollars, and would be spent or invested as such.

And in practice, rather than destroy the Euromarkets, which were central to the operations of the largest American banks, the United States in crisis almost certainly would validate the dollar-denominated claims. If Gresham's Law again turned against the dollar, they would weigh on the exchange markets as heavily as the payments deficit—and in the meantime, they sustained everyone's inflation.*

---

*The question of whether lending by the Eurobanks creates dollars requires for some readers a more detailed answer than these paragraphs. (Those who are satisfied with the paragraphs may be happier if they ignore this footnote.)

Commercial banks create money by lending. When a customer brings in cash and deposits it in a checking account, his possession of "money" is in no way diminished—the checks he can write on his account are the same to him as cash. When the bank creates a demand deposit for a borrower by making him a loan, based on the customer's deposit, the borrower also has "money," and there is that

The oil price increases of late 1973 have been taken by most analysts as the ultimate example of cost-push inflation—prices went up for consumers simply because suppliers who could collect "monopoly rents" set those rents at fearful levels. But there are also analysts, most notably Jelle Zijlstra, who consider the disaster of fall 1973 to be an offshoot of demand-pull inflation, of too much money chasing too few goods. If the nations of the world had not embarked on their overstimulative economic policies of 1972–73, Zijlstra feels, the OPEC price increases simply could not have stuck. The Arabs would not have been willing to deposit in the Eurobanks a high enough proportion of their receipts to fund a credit expansion of the necessary size, and countries would not have been willing to forgo other necessities to

---

much more money in the system. The key words are "in the system"—because the checks customer and borrower write circulate through the internal clearing arrangements of the banking system, one bank's loss is another's gain and all the claims can be validated—provided nobody takes the cash out again.

When a nonfinancial corporation lends money to another such—by purchasing, say, ninety-day commercial paper issued by the borrower—no money is created. The lender has lost the use of his money for the duration of the loan, and it is merely the title to an existing sum that has changed hands. Similarly, a savings bank does not create money by lending its depositors' cash, because the borrower takes the funds right out of the savings bank system to a checking account—which is the same thing for the savings bank system as a leak of cash would be for the commercial bank system.

Those who maintain that the Eurobanks cannot create dollars rest their case on two claims: 1) that the banks "match maturities" between their deposits (which are time deposits—say for ninety days, during which time the depositor does not have the use of his money) and their loans, making their lending activities similar to transactions in commercial paper; and 2) that all checks drawn in dollars against accounts in the offshore banks leak out of the Eurobank system because the banks must "settle" their accounts every day in the New York Clearing House.

But the difference between an overnight "time" deposit and a checking account deposit is a subject for theologians rather than economists, and some minor but sizable fraction of Eurodollar deposits are overnight deposits. To the extent that the recipients of checks drawn on Eurobank accounts redeposit their money in the Eurobanks, the existence of overnight deposits makes possible a "multiplier" for the creation of dollars.

All transfers of dollar-denominated funds between the Eurobanks do indeed go through the New York Clearing House for settlement. But it may not be correct to apply to this settlement the domestic model of a post hoc transfer of reserves kept by the private banks at the Federal Reserve. Among the Eurodollar banks, the set-

divert so large a share of their reserves and resources to oil. Faced with purchasers simply unable to pay, the Arabs and their allies would have backed down. In reality, in late 1973, money was lying around ready to be taken—the land booms in all the European countries and the unprecedented run-up in commodity prices were proof of it. So the oil producers, finding they had the biggest club in the gang, came and took it—with a little help from the Eurobanks.

The availability of loans from the Arab dollar hoard persuaded weak governments in the individual countries—especially Britain, Italy, and later the United States—to draw on the proceeds of the worldwide oil tax to make up for the failure of their own citi-

---

tlement may be propter hoc, through prearranged borrowings that yield the individual bank a guaranteed balance on its transactions in the pass through the Clearing House computer. Once again, provided a substantial proportion of the receipts from Eurodollar loans are redeposited in the Eurobanks rather than in domestic American banks, there are funds in the system that do not "leak" into cash.

Whether one wishes to call the resulting multiplication of Eurodollar deposits an increase in the quantity of money is to a large extent a matter of taste. Robert Aliber of the University of Chicago proposes an "integrated" worldwide banking system in which the effect of Eurodollar depositing and lending is to reduce the effective reserve requirement on American banks, permitting the "monetary base" controlled by the Federal Reserve System to generate worldwide a larger total of bank deposits. The effect is to increase (but not greatly) the world total of dollars in circulation.

Thomas O. Waage of Baer-American Bank, a New York affiliate of a Swiss bank, contends that because he must find dollars to pay into the Clearing House for every loan he makes, the effect of Eurodollar lending is to increase the velocity rather than the quantity of dollars. But this is operationally a distinction without a difference. The indispensable truism about money is Irving Fisher's identity $MV \equiv PT$ (Money times Velocity equals Prices times Transactions). No doubt the monetarist economists are right in their insistence that quantities are important and "money matter." But monetarist analysis and prediction rest on the assumption that velocity is relatively stable—or decreasing slightly as people grow richer and hold more cash in their pockets. This has been visibly untrue in recent years. To make MV equal PT with the quantities of money reported by the Fed, it has been necessary to postulate a rapidly increasing velocity of money. If one assumes that some fraction of the Eurodollar totals should be included in the money supply, the postulate is not necessary. Even if Waage's definitions are correct, and lending by Eurobanks changes the velocity but not the quantity of dollars, the impact on the American and the world economy is the same—and so is the need for eventual validation of these dollars by American banks and monetary authorities if crisis comes.

zens to save enough to pay for the investment programs these governments considered desirable in their own economies. In Britain and Italy, this entirely inflationary government policy (carried through without appropriations, off the budget, and hence invisible to political commentators) took the form of massive official borrowings from the private market; in the United States, starting in 1976 and accelerating under the Carter administration, it would take the form of huge payments deficits. The continued and accelerating inflation enabled everyone to pretend for a while in these countries that the OPEC tax could be paid without dislocations. But someday the pretense would fail; first in Britain and Italy, finally in the United States, the costs would be enormous.

7 / Ford's Ideologues

In my period there were great problems—the exchange value of the dollar not being one of them.

> —Alan Greenspan, chairman of the Council of Economic Advisers, 1974–77

*   *   *

Political and economic circumstance combined to diminish the effectiveness of American government policy through the entire period of the Ford administration, with the oddly fruitful result that day-to-day decision making was concentrated in the hands of practical people accustomed to measuring the results rather than the intentions of their actions.

Because the United States was first in the descent to the greatest recession of the postwar period, which severely reduced American demand for imports as well as for domestic production, the pressures on the dollar evaporated.

But the urgencies of the time were such that strategic planning in American foreign economic policy virtually disappeared from the agenda.

Deprived of the solid foundation provided by American dominance—even wrongheaded dominance—the international monetary system grew increasingly fragile.

Ad hoc agreements, symbolized by "summit meetings" of the heads of state, carried the industrial economies through the trough of the recession, but created hazardous conditions for all the trading nations and their currencies in the years to come.

1

The transition between the Nixon and Ford administrations occurred legally with a sharp break—The King is Dead! Vivat Rex!—on August 8, 1974. But there was really an interregnum from the first of the year, because Nixon was unable really to pay attention to anything but his personal defense. Not just the palace guard but its officers were changing—George Shultz to William Simon at Treasury, Herbert Stein to Alan Greenspan at the Council of Economic Advisers, Paul Volcker to Jack Bennett as Under Secretary for Monetary Affairs. Roy Ash continued at the budget office. In this lineup, Arthur Burns was left end: though Nixon after the debacle of 1970 had proclaimed himself a Keynesian, the economic advisers he would bequeath to Gerald Ford were either followers of Milton Friedman or acolytes of the libertarian right.

Moreover, though no one knew it, the sea-change in the economy had arrived with the turning of the year. The great recession of 1974–75 began in December 1973, as the nation waited in lines at the gas pumps and like Burgoyne's soldiers at Saratoga, felt the world turned upside-down. In its early stages, the recession was masked by the greatest inflation since 1946, and by the hoarding of everything from toilet paper to sugar that disfigured the economic life of the nation; it would not become apparent until after the nation's economists had made fools of themselves at a White

House conference in the early fall, when President Ford vowed to Whip Inflation Now.

On the international economic agenda, the "Tokyo Round" of trade negotiations had begun; and there was reason to be satisfied with the strength of the institutions formed to promote cooperation among the industrial countries. In May 1974, as the Council of Economic Advisers reported, the OECD nations "pledged not to take unilateral action which could tend to shift deficits to other nations. Specifically . . . to avoid introducing restrictive measures affecting trade and other account flows." And they were living up to their pledge. For the time being, at least, the inflationary impact of devaluations kept everyone from seeking to escape trade deficits by that route, and the possible relief via quotas or tariffs was trivial beside the oil burden.

On the other hand, the effort to "reform" the international monetary system, pledged in the Smithsonian Agreement, was winding down in a failure nobody wanted to admit. The first six months of discussions about reform had been devoted to the question of *who* should be the reformers. The LDCs had been left out of the discussions in 1971 because they were not members of the Group of 10. This was a problem for them, because the question of where they were to buy their needs and sell their products would be greatly influenced by the relative values of the currencies of the developed world that were set by the Group of 10. (Indeed, one of the reasons for the August 15 exercise had been American displeasure at the extent to which an overvalued dollar had reduced the competitiveness of American goods and services not merely in Japan and the Common Market, but also in the markets of Latin America and Asia.) As a united group, the LDCs had enough votes at the International Monetary Fund to block any amendments to the Articles of Agreement.

From the American point of view, the processes that had brought about the Smithsonian Agreement were highly unsatisfactory. Connally had found himself alone in the Group of 10, a debtor surrounded by creditors. Wrapping themselves in the mantle of pious internationalism that comes so naturally to

Americans who are misbehaving, John Connally and his successor George Shultz demanded a forum at which the voices of the poor would be heard and their votes would be counted—a debtors' club, in short, to balance the creditors' club. ("U.S. officials hoped," George Shultz later wrote, "—mistakenly as it turned out—that an alliance between the United States and the less developed countries might be possible.") But no such forum existed, and its invention took a while. What emerged was the Committee of 20, delegates appointed by the constituencies that elected executive directors to the executive board (a lower-level body than the Board of Governors) of the IMF.

The C-20, their ministers, their deputies, their bureau, their friends and associates met every couple of months or so from late 1972 to late 1974, wasting time, energy, intelligence and money. (Meetings associated with monetary matters are lavish, with first-class air travel, big black limousines, hotel suites, *grands crus classés*, and gray caviar: these are the fellows who print the money they spend.) At the large meetings of the deputies—with about 200 people in attendance authorized to speak—the work was carried forth through discussions of an "annotated agenda" prepared by the bureau. These discussions, wrote John Williamson, a British economist then with the IMF, "varied from direct answers to the questions posed to discursive philosophical contributions, from serious analysis to repetitive statements of aspirations, and from brisk challenges to other Deputies to attempts to synthesize compromise solutions. What struck someone accustomed to the interplay of seminars or academic conferences was the rarity of contributions in the latter categories; indeed, the proceedings were aptly characterized by Jeremy Morse [of the Bank of England; director of the C-20 bureau] ... as a 'multilateral monologue.' " And the communiqués that were the output of the meetings were described by Paul Volcker as "vacuous sentences."

What the Europeans wanted from monetary reform was some sort of "asset settlement" by nations that were running payments deficits. They resented the ease with which the United States could buy other people's products, invest abroad, maintain military forces around the world, and exert political leverage through lending—simply by running its own printing press. Old-fashioned economists used to write about "seignorage"—the profits a king (later, a government) derived from the power to coin or print money. In the view of the Europeans, the United States had for some years enjoyed worldwide seignorage, and this had to stop. All new reserve creation should be through the IMF, and a country with a surplus should have the right to compel deficit countries to transfer SDRs in payment—the way countries before 1971 officially (before 1968 in principle, before 1961 in reality) had the right to force the United States to disgorge gold.

American commentators were and are unimpressed with the argument for asset settlement, pointing out that most of the dollars the United States has pushed into the world are invested here by their holders, who collect interest on the investments. The interest presumably sops up nearly all the seignorage. But, of course, the interest itself is paid out of the printing press.

What the Americans wanted was continued opportunity to export dollars, plus "symmetry." As the world turned, some countries would have a payments surplus and some would have a payments deficit. (Presumably it wouldn't be the same countries all the time, but the movement from one status to the other might occur rather slowly.) As the Bretton Woods system was organized, the pressures to "adjust" lay mostly on the countries with a deficit, which could be pushed to deflate their economies, depreciate their currencies, raise interest rates, reduce government deficits, and do something to reduce imports and increase exports. The Americans felt that whatever new monetary system was negotiated should with at least equal force compel countries with a surplus to inflate their economies, appreciate their currencies, lower interest rates, and do something to increase imports and decrease exports.

The procedure Shultz suggested was the establishment of a "reserve indicator" for each nation; whenever that nation's official reserves rose above the indicator ceiling, all sorts of awful sanctions could legally be applied to its exports and its capital imports. "The United States," says Joseph Gold, an English lawyer who retired in 1979 after a generation as general counsel to the IMF, "was very keen on sanctions, and wanted them to be *automatic,* on the theory that public opinion would more easily accept automatic sanctions. I thought that misconceived the operations of the Fund." The points made by Shultz were identical with those Keynes had hammered at Harry White in 1943–44. As Professor Posthuma of the Netherlands Bank said some years ago, "I have heard all the arguments before; only the countries using them change from time to time."

What the Less Developed Countries wanted was money. The success of the OPEC countries had emboldened them to attempt all sorts of commodity corners, none of which worked. Very slowly the LDCs came to realize that the quadrupling of oil prices would not only raise the price of the energy they needed but also cut their earnings from their own sales. (The balloon in commodity prices burst toward the end of 1974.) They thereupon began to demand the politicization of markets and to proclaim in all the international organizations where votes were one to a country the imminent arrival of a New International Economic Order. The real result was to turn the United Nations and most of its specialized affiliates into great bazaars for exotic beggars who shook their bowls at passersby and cursed the givers. The C–20 meetings, haunted by a Third World "steering committee" of 24 members, were inevitably no exception. Specifically, the LDCs wanted all new issues of SDRs allocated to them (this was called "the link") as an aid program. But they also supported the American insistence that nations must be permitted to hold their reserves in whatever form they wished, because they wanted to earn the maximum interest on what money they had.

One of the few items on which general agreement was reached in the first year's work was that the reformed system, like the unreformed one, would be based on "stable but adjustable" exchange rates. Meeting only a month or so after the markets had been swamped by the 1973 speculative flows—$8 billion, $6 billion to Germany alone, in the first ten days of February—the ministers of the C-20 simply ignored the fact that all the major currencies were floating on the exchange markets with reference to the dollar. But once the oil pirates of the Gulf had raided the coffers, it became obvious that exchange rates would have to be flexible to absorb the varying punishments meted out to other people's balance sheets by $50-billion-a-year OPEC surpluses. Clearly, the Arabs could not have rights of "asset settlement" with the United States even for the dollars America created to pay for oil for itself—let alone for the dollars created in loans to other countries that needed dollars to buy their oil. And to apply "symmetry" provisions to Saudi Arabia and Kuwait, penalizing them for building up their surpluses, was an attractive idea but an obvious nonstarter. Failing anything better, the C-20 in early 1974 grudgingly approved for an "interim period" a floating exchange rate "regime" for all currencies.

One question did get resolved at the Rome meeting in January 1974. The SDR had been pegged to the "gold dollar"—the dollar as valued prior to August 15, 1971—and had appreciated as the dollar devalued with relation to gold. With rates floating, and the dollar entirely separated from gold, this was no longer a suitable standard. The solution, credited by Williamson to Jacques J. Polak, chief of research at IMF and the senior inhabitant, was an SDR pegged to a "basket of currencies."

As originally established, the new SDR was worth 40¢ U.S. plus 33 Deutsche pfennig, plus 4.5 British pence, plus 44 French centimes, plus 26 yen, etc., through the complete list of the currencies from the sixteen countries that had done 1 percent or more of world trade in 1968–72.

This left out the oil states, none of which before 1974 had accounted for 1 percent of world trade. In spring 1978, the IMF got around to recognizing the change in status of the oil countries, and rearranged the basket to add the Iranian rial and the Saudi riyal. This was an interesting problem, because in fact these countries did not do their international trade in their own currencies—they worked in dollars. It made an even more interesting problem at the end of that year, when Iran erupted and the value of the rial became a question like the nature of Unidentified Flying Objects (another matter international organizations troubled themselves with in 1978). But all the problems associated with the actual use of SDR were interesting, confusing, and ultimately—this is what *really* doomed the reform movements—not worth solving. As Janos Fekete of the Hungarian State Bank put it, "People don't like these cocktails of currencies that have to be mixed every day. They want something simple—like gold, or dollars."

The basic use of the SDR was as a reserve—a "paper gold"—that could be transferred between central banks as an asset settlement to clear the books of surpluses or deficits. But a central bank's indebtedness normally would be expressed in terms of a currency used in private transactions, so the central bank in actually using SDRs would call upon the IMF to supply that needed currency, and the IMF in turn would call upon the proprietors of that currency to supply it for SDRs. Surplus countries would thus wind up with credits in SDRs like gold in the vault.

Now, central banks were willing to hold gold (indeed, they were reluctant to part with it) because in the inflationary atmosphere of the 1970s, it seemed so likely to increase in value. They could decide to hold foreign exchange because that money was useful day-to-day; because they earned interest on their use of it; or because it was politically or economically inconvenient to refuse to buy the currency of a significant trading partner. But why, other than the mechanism of compulsion built into the IMF rules (and it was pretty widely understood that any attempt actually to force surplus countries to do things they didn't want to do would probably bust the system), should any nation wish to hold SDRs? As Milton Gilbert wrote in the 1969 Report of the Bank for International Settlements, welcoming (if that is the word for it) the first Special Drawing Rights, "One waits to see by experience if Gresham's Law will operate and which bad money will drive out what good—gold, dollars, or SDRs."

If central banks were to be willing to hold SDRs as part of their assets, obviously they would have to earn interest on them. What should that interest rate be? The United States (which had a blocking veto in the IMF, and could scarcely be ignored in any case) was of course unwilling to see interest rates on SDRs as high as the interest rates on dollars, because the exchange-rate risk on SDRs was clearly less than that on dollars (if the dollar as one-third of the SDR cocktail lost exchange value, the other two-thirds would be gaining), and nations that could earn as much on SDRs would dump the dollars they were holding. Moreover, the LDCs which were the likely borrowers of SDRs wanted to see interest rates as low as possible. The first issues of SDRs in 1970 had carried an interest rate of 1.5 percent; by 1974, short-term interest rates were averaging about 10 percent in the five currencies actually borrowed across national boundaries. (As of 1978, incidentally, the weightings used to calculate this average were 49 percent for the U.S., 18 percent for Germany, and 11 percent each for Britain, France, and Japan.) Clearly, to make SDRs attractive, that derisory 1.5 percent would have to rise.

The compromise solution arrived at in June 1974 was 5 percent, about half the market rate. If this was all they could earn on SDR accumulations, the surplus countries were entirely unwilling to approve any further issues of SDRs. In 1976, the interest rate was raised to 60 percent of the world average, which was insufficient sweetener for the pot. In 1978, as part of an agreement to raise the total quantity of issued SDRs by another $12 billion or so over five years, the interest rate was raised to 80 percent of the average.

There remained the question of the "link," the use of seignorage from SDRs to help the Less Developed Countries. "The question at issue here," as John Williamson wrote, "was not whether the monetary characteristics of the SDR could be improved, but whether the SDR scheme could also be used to advance the objective of transferring real resources for development without prejudicing its primary function of providing a monetary asset for central banks."

The answer was no, though Williamson thought it could be

done. If the SDR was to be acceptable as a store of value, the world had to have great confidence that its issuance would not be a subject of political pressure—and the LDCs have an all but religious belief in the desirability and efficacy of political pressure. The United States especially insisted that if the IMF were to acquire new charitable purposes, the thing should be done in an open-and-aboveboard manner and not through the technicalities of reserve creation. A compromise was achieved by which the IMF became the home for special loan funds to tide the poor countries over the worst dislocations arising from the oil crisis. It was hoped that the Arabs would be generous contributors to these funds, but the hopes were disappointed. Later, more money was found for the LDCs through the sale of one-sixth of the IMF's gold hoard, with the proceeds allocated for assistance to the poor.

The root unreality of the discussions in the C-20 was the failure of the assumptions that had led to the initial approval of the SDR device in the late 1960s. "A dozen years ago," the 1978 IMF Annual Report explained, "when the establishment of the SDR facility was being considered, the volume of global reserves was held to be determined by the availability of newly produced gold for monetary purposes, by Fund policies on credit tranche drawings, and by the deficits of reserve currency countries, particularly the United States. It was widely thought at the time that only small additions to reserves could be expected from increases in monetary gold and also generally concluded that the system should not continue to rely on U.S. deficits for its liquidity needs. This was the background that led to the view that allocations of SDRs were required to augment an inelastic supply of reserves in order to prevent a global shortage of liquidity. The situation today is very different. The freedom and efficiency of private international capital markets is such that for creditworthy countries operating within their borrowing limits the supply of reserves is highly elastic. For these countries, which account for the bulk of international transactions, the quantity of reserves can adapt flexibility to changes in demand, and earlier tests of adequacy are thus less applicable."

From 1970 to 1977, to give the thing numbers, global official holdings of reserve assets—measuring in SDR, valuing gold at market—had risen from SDR 95.8 billion to SDR 343.3 billion. IMF credits and SDR allocations amounted to a little more than 11 percent of the total in 1970; in 1977, after a doubling of quotas and the fulfillment of the initial SDR allocation, the International Monetary Fund component in world reserves was down to 6.6 percent. Foreign exchange holdings, which had been just over four times the total of IMF-related reserves in 1970, were almost eight times the IMF total by 1977. The IMF and the C-20, in other words, were working not at the center of the international monetary system but on the periphery.

From the IMF point of view, the growth of world reserves mediated through the Eurocurrency banks has both positive and negative aspects. Positively, a more liquid world is a world where trade flows more freely, and charity to the LDCs tends to rise. Negatively, inflation is worsened, and greater hardships are imposed on those countries which cannot borrow in the private market or have exhausted their credit. And from the realms of fiction—but truth, as is well known, can be stranger than—comes a neuroticism about a day when the deposits run out of the banks, and the "country loans" can no longer be refinanced as they come due. In a *banking* sense, oddly enough, the new "nonsystem" makes the IMF civil service cadre more important than ever: a great deal of the private and even government lending that dwarfs the IMF's resources is now conditioned upon IMF findings that a borrowing government will follow policies that will enable it to repay its drawings from the Fund—and thus, by implication, its other debts.

From the American point of view, the system is immensely dangerous: it multiplies claims denominated in dollars which are not really claims against American banks but cannot be distinguished from the real thing by those who receive them as payments. If the Saudis decide they would rather hold marks than dollars, they can shift the dollars multiplied through the London interbank market just as easily as they can shift legitimate dollars created by the Federal Reserve. When they do so, the balance of payments of the United States shows an outflow of funds on the "official settlements" basis, though on the American side the transaction is actually a wash—the dollars bought by the Bundesbank are returned to the United States and replaced on the Eurodollar market with new loans from American banks. (If the Bundesbank itself lends the dollars back into the Euromarket, the official settlements deficit can grow even though no part of the transaction has anything to do with the United States.) Nobody—literally nobody—can ever get the figures straight. Thus, even in 1975, a year when an American *surplus* on current account reached the whopping total of $22.4 billion in IMF definitions, official foreign claims on the United States, the settlements deficit, rose by $5.3 billion. That's elasticity a rubber band could envy.

Parts of this unprecedented system had locked in place in 1971, when the world banking system had to handle the first appallingly large outpouring of dollars from the United States. OPEC pressure concentrated everyone's mind in the private sector; the Council of Economic Advisers estimated that more than one-third of the OPEC surplus of 1974 was deposited in the Eurobanks to earn interest. Once the market (with the help from the Federal Reserve Bank of New York) had shaken off the horror of the failure of Germany's Herstatt Bank in summer 1974, the giant banks set about perfecting the Euromarket.

The C-20 haggled about irrelevancies in SDR creation while the Eurocurrency market became the true international monetary system and the real issues to be resolved were those of control of the Eurobanks. The Ford administration watched these institutions grow not merely with benign neglect but with encouragement. ("Large-scale official borrowings in foreign financial markets," the 1976 Economic Report noted complacently, "has demonstrated the ability of countries to create liquidity through debt operations.") This was a free market; the people around President Ford believed with all their heart and soul (especially after Paul Volcker was replaced at Treasury by Jack Bennett) that the free market always solves problems, never creates them.

2

Having roared into simultaneous boom in 1973, the industrial nations in 1974 all reined in their money supplies and, when possible, their budget deficits; and by the end of the year all of them had marched in lockstep into the Great Recession. By June 1975, industrial production had dropped 13 percent in the United States, almost 10 percent in Germany, more than 10 percent in every other European country, almost 17 percent in Japan.

In terms of the value of the dollar, the results were spectacular: the dollar rose 7 percent against the French franc, 10 percent against the mark, 14 percent against the yen, 18 percent against the pound and 22 percent against the lira from the third quarter of 1973 to the third quarter of 1975. The rise reflected not capital flows but a drastic swing in the trade balance, to an unprecedented $16 billion surplus. Imports fell and the value of exports rose as most commodity prices collapsed but farm prices stayed high because the world was still winding down from the food shortages and hunger scares of 1974. It was a stroke of great good fortune for the future of world trade that the time of maximum American unemployment coincided with a trade surplus, dampening what might otherwise have been irresistible protectionist pressures in Congress. (When your country is consuming more foreign products than foreigners take from your producers, it is easy to make a superficially plausible argument that restrictions on trade will increase employment; but the argument looks like the folly it is when foreigners are buying more from your work force than you are buying from theirs.)

Meanwhile, the great stabilizer of the welfare state—the fact that government spending continues as the economy turns down, while tax take diminishes—pumped money into the American economy through the federal deficit. In his 1975 budget message, President Ford called for a 12 percent tax rebate to increase purchasing power fast. But even before that rebate had passed the Congress, the stabilizers had gripped and the recession had bottomed out. Nobody could be sure of that at the time, of course, and the bottom was very low, with seven million unemployed. Moreover, it was all but impossible for observers at the time to take the leap of faith that the very speed and depth of the recession—the dumping of inventories at distressed prices and the shutoff of orders—would make the budget stabilizers, which maintain demand, more effective.

An activist Democratic Congress elected in the aftermath of Nixon's disgrace began inventing expensive countercyclical programs to stimulate a bigger and better recovery, and by the end of the first session, the United States was committed to budget deficits of about $60 billion each for the 1976 and 1977 fiscal years. By January 1976, the Council of Economic Advisers was warning (unheeded) of "a significant danger . . . that, instead of smoothing economic fluctuations, discretionary changes in policy aimed at demand management may themselves become a source of economic instability."

Looked at from a longer perspective, the sudden and enormous trade surplus of 1975 should have been discouraging. Nearly half the $14 billion swing in the trade balance had been accounted for by reduced imports of manufactured goods. Net national income had dropped by roughly $26 billion; more than a quarter of the associated reduction in national consumption was in the area of imported merchandise. To return to a concept left to germinate in the first chapter, the American "income elasticity of demand" for imports had grown very high—people were spending an unprecedentedly large fraction of their marginal disposable income for imports. If recession by reducing income at the margin cut back imports so dramatically, recovery was all but certain to increase them at a fast pace.

And so it proved. Edward Bernstein provides the figures: between 1975 and 1977, 28.6 percent of the increase in domestic expenditure for goods went to buy imports—while only 9 percent of the increase in domestic production of goods left the country as exports. The shattering trade deficits of 1977–78, and the collapse of the dollar on the world exchanges, were forecast by the trade surplus of 1975. But the dollar was strong in 1975 and most of 1976 ("I can't honestly say we planned it that way," Treasury Secretary William Simon comments breezily), and the Ford administration—not to mention Congress—had other things on its mind.

3

Along the headlands of economic analysis lie several gardens where sirens dwell, who lure the unwary policy-maker to luxuriant ease and then struggling servitude. They are nonpolitical places, where economists of left and right persuasion can join in celebrating the truth of certain assumptions of their discipline, wellsprings of definition yielding sweet liquors that take the reason prisoner. One of these dangerous oases—the author struggles to escape the sirens of metaphor—is the concept of free-floating exchange rates among the currencies used in international trade. It was vigorously promoted in the 1950s by a range of academics from the British socialist James Meade to the American protocapitalist Milton Friedman, both pretty much for the same reason: national independence. To Meade, fixed exchange rates and the need to defend them restrained the socialist state from measures to increase jobs, redistribute income and force people to accept services instead of goods; to Friedman, fixed exchange rates were loci of infection from which foreign notions of the regulated economy spread to reduce the efficiency of capitalist enterprise.

"Exchange rates adjust themselves continuously," Friedman told the Reuss Subcommittee in 1963, describing the beauties of floating rates, "and market forces determine the magnitude of each change. There is no need for any official to decide by how much the market rate should rise or fall. This is the method of the free market, the method that we adopt unquestioningly in a private enterprise economy for the bulk of goods and services. It is no less available for the price of one money in terms of another ... All countries, and not just the United States, can proceed to liberalize [trade] boldly and confidently only if they have reasonable assurance that the resulting trade expansion will be balanced and will not interfere with major domestic objectives. Floating exchange rates, and so far as I can see only floating exchange rates, provide this assurance. They do so because they are an automatic mechanism for protecting the domestic economy from the possibility that liberalization will produce a serious imbalance in international payments ... It is not the least of the virtues of floating exchange rates that we would again become master in our own house."

The theory of floating exchange rates rests on the unexceptionable—indeed, true—principle that both demand and supply are functions of price. The purpose of exporting, as is sometimes forgotten, is to pay for necessary or desired imports. If imports go down in price, there will be more demand for them, requiring more exports—which may be impossible, unless the price of the exports goes down, too. But imports are denominated in foreign currencies, and exports in the domestic currency. To equilibrate the demand for and the supply of international trade goods, the obvious mechanism is the relative price of the currencies in which they are traded. If a country cannot export enough at current prices to pay for the imports it wants at current prices, a drop in the exchange value of its currency will take care of the problem, raising the price of imports (in the domestic currency) to reduce demand at home and lowering the price of exports (in foreign currencies) to increase demand abroad, until the market is cleared.

The real world is, of course, much more complicated than that. Just for starters, there are the capital flows—demands for a foreign currency for the purpose of lending at high interest rates in a foreign market, or investing in attractive foreign business opportunities. There are remittances: in 1979, the U.S. Embassy in

London was sending out 15,600 checks a month, for $3.5 million, to Social Security and other U.S. government pension recipients living in Britain. For years, Turkey's balance of payments retained an appearance of plausibility because Turkish workers in Germany were sending marks home to their families. There are tourists, returns on previous investments, fees on patents and copyrights, insurance premiums and payouts, the costs of maintaining one's nationals abroad (in embassies, offices, banks, military installations), etcetera, truly ad infinitum.

To which the Friedmanite answer is that the market feels all these pressures more accurately than the Commerce Department can count the numbers. The world changes—economies grow and decline; new products enter into international trade; new markets open up to be serviced; inflation rates vary. Governments seek stability and make insufficient allowance for change. Speculators buying and selling in forward markets—trading in currencies for delivery in one or three or six months—will sense the significance of developments in the different economies. And, "because they are risking their own money," they are more likely to be careful than governments would be, and more likely to get it right. "The more flexible the exchange rate," wrote Sidney Rolfe and James L. Burtle, "the faster will be the return to, and the more persistent will be, the equilibrium."

"People who believe in the market system thoroughly," Charles Kindleberger objected, "would auction off the places in every trolley car to get full utilization of capacity.... But the lady shopping would like to know what the price of trolley cars is going to be that day, and what it is going to be the next day and the next day after that." The Friedmanite reply is that the forward market takes care of that problem, too—it is available for use by importers, exporters, borrowers, and lenders as well as speculators. For what is only a small premium (closely related to the difference in interest rates in the two countries involved), the commercial user of foreign exchange can assure himself of the price he will have to pay or will receive in his own currency on the day his supplier presents the bill or his customer has to pay.

Under a floating rate regime, in theory, governments would not need reserves at all. A deficit would no longer be financed by transfer of reserve assets: it would melt away with changes in the exchange rate. Best of all, nobody would have to worry about deficits and surpluses. "A system of floating exchange rates," wrote Yale's Richard Cooper (later to be Carter's Under Secretary of State for Economic Affairs), "has the apparent virtue of solving the balance of payments problem, since exchange rates always adjust themselves to maintain balance at all times."

If a national economy became uncompetitive internationally, the problem under floating rates, economist Fritz Machlup told the Reuss Subcommittee, would "change its mode of appearance in that it replaces troublesome payments balances with troublesome price movements." Robert Solomon, long-time adviser to the Federal Reserve Board, noted happily after his retirement a difference between the situations of the United States recovering from recession in 1976 and 1961: under floating rates, "concern over the U.S. balance of payments deficit had become a thing of the past." As sometimes happens when theory is imposed upon reality, his timing proved faulty.

Once the gold window had been closed (though this was not recognized for a while), the United States was inevitably committed to a theory of floating rates: it had no reserves with which to intervene in the currency markets to defend fixed rates. This was fine with George Shultz, by training and conviction a free-floater (he prefers the phrase "market-determined rates"), but as long as Paul Volcker was Under Secretary for Monetary Affairs, there was a locus of resistance at the Treasury. And there was resistance elsewhere. The State Department felt an institutional preference for stability in all international relations. Burns at the Fed shared the central bankers' distaste for abandoning a game in which they knew the mini-max solutions they could live with and replacing it with what might be a more dangerous game. But once Volcker had been replaced by Jack Bennett (and Shultz by William Simon from the Wall Street bond house of Salomon Brothers), the dynamics of American reality were not merely accepted but gleefully welcomed by the Americans who were in charge of international monetary negotiations.

Since 1974, the International Monetary Fund standard had been the Special Drawing Right, itself a floating unit measured by the exchange rates of the currencies in its basket. The only surviving fixed reference point was gold, and the academic economists had been urging the demonetization of gold for years. Once the C-20 had been reconstituted as the "Interim Committee" of the IMF ("Interim" because its purpose now was to provide a fig leaf for the violation of the fixed-rate clauses in the treaties, until such time as amendments could be hammered out), the new American negotiating team set its cap for full approval of floating rates, the demonetization of gold, and the elimination of the word "convertibility," which seemed to imply some obligation to provide reserve assets to the holder of a currency. (What was substituted in determining the authority of the IMF to lend money the borrowers could use, which was where the issue arose in a floating system, was the phrase "freely usable currency," itself defined as a currency "widely used to make payments for international transactions" and "widely traded in the principal exchange markets." And you thought you had troubles.) Burns, who had not liked the closing of the gold window in 1971, also did not like the elimination of the gold link in 1975, but he was overruled. The French wanted a return to fixed rates and official uses for gold, and could not be overruled.

At the first post-Nixon summit meeting, on the Caribbean island of Martinique, the Americans thought they had a deal: an agreement to let central banks use gold in their dealings with each other, at market-related prices rather than the $42.22 at which nobody (not just Americans) would sell metal. But comparisons between what Giscard d'Estaing was saying and what Under Secretary Jack Bennett was saying shortly demonstrated that there was no deal, and also that Bennett had depleted his usefulness in negotiations with the French. (Part of the problem was an error in negotiating strategy; as one of the participants puts it, "The American Treasury thought the way to persuade the French was to work with the Germans.") Edwin H. Yeo, monetary economist and vice-chairman of the Pittsburgh National Bank, was brought in to take Bennett's place, and a meeting of the Big Five finance ministers and central bank governors was called for Washington at the end of August to precede the last Interim Committee meeting before the 1975 IMF annual convention.

The negotiations were stuck not just on definitions but on national beliefs when Simon commandeered the Presidential yacht *Sequoia* for a reception which, not by accident, turned into a working session, and Simon instructed the captain to keep the ship circling in the river until further notice. Confronted with the immediate danger of spending the rest of their lives in the stifling weather of Washington in August, the conferees reached an agreement to abolish the fixed price at which gold was not traded; to eliminate the use of gold in transactions with the IMF; to redistribute one-sixth of the IMF gold stock to member nations (at $42.22 an ounce) according to their original contributions and sell by auction at market prices (then about $140 an ounce) another one-sixth of the hoard, for the benefit of the LDCs; to permit free exchange of gold between central banks at market prices; but to prohibit central banks from buying new gold in the private market for two years. After the two years, everybody would be free to buy; Simon said to Henry Reuss and others that this wouldn't happen, but he was wrong.

It is interesting to note that the Less Developed Countries benefiting from the Trust Fund include all the OPEC nations but not Israel—and include also Argentina and Brazil (the second largest recipients of proceeds from the gold sales), Romania, Yugoslavia and Portugal but not (though it is a member of the Fund) the Republic of China. The IMF is not *exactly* like other international agencies, but it's in the system.*

On the question of the new exchange rate regime, no agreement was possible even on the circling *Sequoia*. Finally the German finance minister suggested that since the problem was

---

*Three of the richer Arab states and Yugoslavia, however, have turned their receipts back to IMF to be distributed to poorer countries.

between the Americans and the French—and the others could live with whatever they could agree upon—the question should be negotiated bilaterally, with everyone else promising to accept anything acceptable to those two parties. The negotiators were to be the deputies of the two Treasuries—Edwin Yeo and Jacques de Larosière. "We had carte blanche," Yeo recalls in wonderment; "it was an incredible thing." They began meeting secretly (which meant in Paris), every other week or so.

Meanwhile, Henry Fowler went through the roof about the gold agreement, and broke his rule against criticizing his successors at the Treasury. "For decades," he told the Reuss Subcommittee, "the United States has been a party to the accumulation of dollar balances in the reserve holdings of central banks for countries rich and poor around the world. An integral part of this process was the implied assurance that the dollars so accumulated ... could be converted at will into gold ... When this practice and position was unilaterally terminated by the announcement of President Nixon on August 15, 1971, the United States, in my opinion, assumed something of a moral and political obligation. It is obliged to insist that the future role of gold in the monetary system should be resolved in a manner that would not visit a discrimination or inequity on those countries whose reserve assets were largely in dollars."

Instead, Fowler insisted, the Interim Committee agreement should be seen as "conferring large windfall increases in official reserves on a few large gold-holding developed countries while the less developed ones grope for crumbs to keep their economies alive." The figures he presented were convincing, too: the Group of 10 countries plus Switzerland held a total of $107 billion in reserves in 1975, of which $37 billion was in the gold to be more than tripled (it would later be sextupled) in value; the rest of the world held $75 billion in reserves, of which only $7 billion was in gold. But there was no way to demonetize gold so long as it was the only commodity with a fixed price—and ultimately no way to float the dollar *legally* without also floating gold. The French were still fighting for a new regime of fixed exchange rates; allowing them to value their gold hoard at market prices was the necessary bribe if they (and the Common Market allies who would not move without them) were to accept amendments to the IMF agreements.

Describing the deal Yeo and de Larosière reached between themselves, the English economist John Williamson scornfully called it "a complete victory for the United States. . . . The dollar is once again unrivalled and the pretensions of the IMF to conduct a world monetary system have been brought to naught . . . French diplomatic sensibilities were modified by France's being given the responsibility of conceding to US wishes . . ." But Yeo stresses that Article IV of the IMF under the Second Amendment, which is what he and de Larosière (who became managing director of the IMF) wrote in their meetings, does not enshrine "the Treasury doxology. The central point in Article IV," Yeo says, "is that stable exchange rates are a desirable end, but that a particular system of exchange rates would not and could not offer stability. This was not the Treasury position, and it was not the French position. We said that these systems made up by economists become political men, lacking practical support but revealing a beautiful symmetry, are not the way you can run the world. The thrust is that if you want stability, you have to stop holding meetings of eminent people to discuss exchange rates, and start managing your economies properly. And if you want to make a move toward substantive reform, you have to expand IMF surveillance. Which is what we did."

Under the terms of the agreement Yeo and de Larosière gave their principals at the Rambouillet meeting of the heads of state of the Big Five in late 1975, each nation can choose its own exchange-rate procedures—free floating, managed floating, pegged to SDRs, pegged to another country's currency, pegged to whatever basket the country likes, pegged to anything but gold, within whatever margins the country wishes to choose. The United States chose to float. Unless a country has announced a fixed-rate arrangement, its central bank is supposed to buy or sell in the market only "to counter disorderly conditions or erratic fluctuations."

The IMF is left free to reinstitute a pegged-rate system by an 85 percent vote (which guarantees that the United States, retaining 19.96 percent of the votes under the new quota arrangements, would have a veto); but even if a pegged system is established, no country that doesn't want to join it may be forced to join. All countries are forbidden to manipulate exchange rates to gain advantages at the expense of others, and the IMF is to exercise "surveillance" not only over actions in the exchange markets but also over all nations' domestic policies with the goal of promoting stability in the exchanges. The IMF executive directors urged the amendment-drafters to require a "decision" following the periodic surveillance, to give the IMF at least a semblance of teeth; but both the United States and France gravely doubted whether when great powers are involved, the IMF should be privileged to bark, let alone bite.

Having been approved by the Big Five, the Second Amendment to Article IV sailed through the meeting of the Interim Committee in Jamaica in January 1976. Simon said it would be the last monetary reform for a long time, and that it was an accomplishment in every way comparable with Bretton Woods. Exactly what it means is still, to say the least, unclear. One thing it does mean, which has been highly significant but largely unnoticed, is that the world's central banks, front-and-center in all currency crises through the 1960s, have been relegated to the periphery. For better or worse, the action is now in Washington, not Basle. The politicians are in control.

All these negotiations, incidentally, were carried through during the year of the big American trade surplus. Despite its continuous advocacy of floating rates, the United States still had by law an Exchange Stabilization Fund set up by Franklin Roosevelt in the 1930s to sell dollars into the market, holding down their exchange value and assuring that American trade would not be hampered by an overvalued currency. Throughout the year, that Fund was active in pursuit of its original purpose, and by the end of December it held no less than $8 billion of foreign currencies. The Treasury doxology was no better than the other doxology in controlling human behavior.

4

"The floating exchange rate regime has served the United States well," Henry Reuss said in late fall 1975. There have been few dissenters, if only because nobody can imagine how a fixed-rate regime could have held together at all under the batterings of the middle six years of the 1970s. Just as the private Eurobanks proved more capable than anyone had expected in meeting the world's need for "reserves" after the oil price rises, business firms have proved much more resilient than anyone could have imagined in the face of rapid changes of the effective "prices" at which international trade is accomplished.

Yet the fact is that none of the theoretical postulates of floating proved out. The theories were false in a world where governments manipulate interest rates and the banking system's reserves as their central tool for managing domestic economies. Given free convertibility between two currencies, a higher interest rate in one of them will draw funds from the other. Under a fixed-rate "regime," the result is a payments deficit which has to be financed or adjusted for; under a floating-rate regime it shows up as a change in the exchange rate. If the two countries are relatively "open" to each other's trade, which is what the theory expects will be promoted by floating rates, the result will be to worsen inflation in the country with the low interest rates (and thus a depreciating currency) and reduce production in the country with the high interest rates (and thus an appreciating currency) until such time as the two governments reconcile their policies.

Far from becoming "masters in their own house" by the institution of floating rates, the governments lose their power to use monetary policy in pursuit of domestic objectives. In 1976, while Americans were celebrating the liberating effects of floating exchange rates, Rinaldo Ossola was explaining to an international meeting why Italy, despite high unemployment, was raising interest rates: "Balance-of-payments difficulties . . . forced us to tighten monetary policy . . . , and to subordinate its conduct to external objectives . . . In theory it is well known that floating exchange rates allow national monetary policy to be independent of external constraints. However, in the present world, where inflationary biases exist . . . , the choice of depreciating the exchange rate until external equilibrium is reached does not exist in practice. Continued depreciation of the lira would only have aggravated our inflation, worsened our terms of trade, and postponed the stabilization of our economy. . . . Capital outflows had to be stemmed through a tight monetary policy. This is generally the case for countries in weak balance-of-payments positions."

Fritz Machlup in 1938 had demonstrated that what would *really* link economies tightly to each other was not the gold standard, which permitted central banks to keep their banking systems insulated for a while if desired, but floating rates with international transactions accomplished through private banks. Since floating became a reality, the members of the Common Market have kept struggling to establish a fixed exchange rate system among themselves, to float as a unit against the dollar. This has been interpreted in the press as expressing a desire for greater unification of their economies, but in fact what makes a "snake" or "European Monetary System" necessary is the need for the individual nations of the EEC to maintain a degree of independence in their policies. With full convertibility and floating rates, each would be completely at the mercy of the others' domestic decisions. With fixed rates within a band of permissible variation, and the possibility of central bank intervention in the markets to keep all the currencies within the band, governments can at least cushion the shock of changes in their trading partners' policies.

"It is one of the strangest things about the 1970s," says Jelle

Zijlstra. "God's grace dawned upon us: floating was the great discovered truth. Mr. Market knows best. We must never go back to the follies of Bretton Woods. But governments today are supposed to have a view of the most silly and ridiculous things. Why should they not care about the value of the national currency?"

Worse: the institutions lose their sense of the roles they are supposed to play. "I remember I was at a meeting once," Edward Bernstein says, "and the Governor of the Bank of Canada said the situation had become very disruptive. The market was looking to the authorities to tell them what to do, and the authorities were all looking to the market for guidance."

Convertibility is the key, not "exchange-rate regimes" or the nature of reserves. Given full convertibility, the degree to which one nation's policies depend on another's is a function of how deeply their economies are intertwined. In a world of interdependence, everyone's independence is circumscribed—and the more a country relies on foreign trade for either goods or jobs, the less independence it can hope to have. Fixed rates are, in Robert Roosa's fine phrase, "an armed truce"; they buy time for reflection, adjustment, or negotiation. Floating rates set all against all in a Hobbesian economic universe. The more flexible prices become internationally through changes in exchange rates, the less control nations can hope to have over the domestic prices of those goods most easily transferred across borders. Since money is transferred with a touch on a keyboard, and the interest rate is the price for money, full convertibility and floating rates *necessarily* defeat those central bank controls that lie at the heart of the government's influence on the private economy. Masters in our own house, indeed!

Floating rates also, visibly, failed to eliminate payments surpluses and deficits from the world scene. Diehard advocates argue that this was because the float was "managed" (or, as the Germans said, "dirty"), with governments intervening in the market to buy or sell currencies at rates other than those the market left alone would have determined. ("There is no doubt," Jack Bennett said in early 1979, "that holdings of U.S. Treasury bills by foreign governments are higher than they would have been if they had not chosen to promote their exports and deter their imports.") But since "intervention" is inevitable in a regime of full convertibility (every action by the central bank to change the level of bank reserves and interest rates constitutes "managing" the float, or requires action in the markets to neutralize its exchange rate effects), it is hard to see how a "clean" float is conceptually—let alone practically—possible.

Moreover, as we have seen, devaluations in their early stages produce perverse effects (the "J-curve"), so that short-term fluctuations in the exchange markets are likely to show short-term results opposite to those that would "automatically" stabilize the market, and to feed upon themselves. Shrewd speculators risking their own money might indeed help to balance such changes, but if it takes one to three *years* before the "volume effects" of a devaluation show up, which is what most observers of the international trade scene believe, the speculators need longer time horizons and even more guts than people of speculative temperament are likely to have. Anyway, there are few forward markets as much as a year out, and virtually none beyond a year, because buyers and sellers in international trade don't know a year in advance what money they will need or receive.

Because both trade and payments deficits persist and must be financed (a balance is a balance), the need for reserves is by no means diminished in a floating-rate regime, and may even be enhanced. Certainly that was the view of the 1978 annual meeting of the International Monetary Fund, which recognized the passage of the Second Amendment validating floating rates and at the same time put through increases in the IMF credit system against which nations in trouble can draw foreign currencies. Central banks must buy and sell currencies in the forward market to give their nations' exporters and importers some assurance that normal corporate planning is still possible. In 1978, when the dollar was depressed by mounting deficits and the absence of comprehensible American policy, some $50 billion in official intervention was needed to keep the dollar from falling to sea level;

in the first four months of 1979, when the United States had much higher interest rates than most of the industrial democracies and mounting oil prices created a growing need for dollars abroad, no less than $60 billion in official intervention was required to keep the dollar from rising to the sky.

"I have come to believe that the lack of resiliency in exchange markets is an inherent characteristic of those markets," Scott Pardee, senior vice-president of the New York Fed, told a meeting of the FOREX Association of Canada in early 1979. ". . . The fact that a particular currency is declining is flashed around the world in seconds. Market commentary and the news services quickly provide an explanation for the decline . . . Sometimes these explanations are farfetched, but the conjunction of a decline in a currency plus a plausible explanation for the decline can trigger a widespread reaction in the same direction . . . This reaction itself adds credence to the explanation . . . Once a rate begins to move, both the risk seeker and the risk avoider may suddenly be on the same side of the market."

The extent to which movements in exchange rates were sudden and rapid (rather than smooth and slow, as theory had predicted) was masked from American commentators by the use of "weighted averages"—especially the weighted average published by the Morgan Guaranty Trust, which gave a single number for the motion of the dollar as against the currencies of major American trading partners "weighted" according to the value of the trade. That meant the fluctuation of the American dollar with reference to the Canadian dollar had by far the greatest weight, and the value of the dollar in terms of South American currencies was highly significant. But the United States had always perceived a difference of kind, not just degree, between the dollar and the cruzeiro; and so, of course, had the rest of the world. "Anyway," says a U.S. Treasury attaché in Europe, "people in a market don't look at trade weights. They look at individual currencies."

Edward Bernstein, whose consulting service is influential all over the world, had been pointing out the extreme volatility of the dollar by comparison with the European currencies, the fact that during the thirty-six months from the beginning of 1973 to the end of 1975, there were six periods during which the dollar had risen or fallen by 10 percent or more against the European joint float over a period of as little as three or four months. (Between other currencies, rates sometimes moved 10 percent in two weeks.) "Simon," Bernstein recalls, "invited me to a meeting at the Treasury. We had quite a collection—Costanzo from Citibank, people from Morgan and Chase, all the ex-Under Secretaries, Roosa, academics, Arthur Burns. Simon said, 'Have you ever stopped to think what it would have been if we'd had a fixed-rate system? When you look at it on a trade-weighted basis, the fluctuations have been very small.'

"I said, 'What does that mean? You include Latin America, with its tradition of devaluing, as an offset against Europe. Nobody does business in trade-weighted exchanges. If you insist on weighting, do it by the exports of the Group of 10, not by the American bilateral trade figures.' As we were leaving, Burns said to me, 'That was very well done'—and the Fed began to use an index weighted by the Group of 10 trade figures."

That floating rates were imposing unexpected burdens on industry was illustrated by the need for (and then the flap over) new accounting rules for reporting the results of international enterprise. Prior to 1976, American companies with operations abroad could choose their tactics in calculating the effects of currency changes on the P&L and balance sheets of their foreign affiliates. They could translate all foreign currency numbers into dollars, or take gains and losses only for exchange-rate changes affecting current assets and liabilities (inventory, accounts payable and receivable, short-term loans), or write up and down their monetary (as opposed to real) assets and liabilities abroad. There was here a fertile field for jiggery-pokery, and the use of annual adjustments (some "deferrals") could conceal significant impact from exchange-rate changes during the year. The Financial Accounting Standards Board pondered the issues, which are more various than anyone who is not an accountant could ever imagine, and in

THE FATE OF THE DOLLAR

October 1975 came down from Mount Sinai with Rule 8, which took effect at the start of 1976.

FAS/8, which accountants demand be followed before they will certify a statement, requires companies to keep a running record of the value in dollars, at that day's exchange rate, of all inventory acquired, and to report the value of that inventory in those terms in every quarterly statement. All financial items—capital, working capital, short-term and long-term debt, accounts receivable and payable—must be revised quarterly to show dollar value as of the last day of the reporting period, with gains or losses on the "translation" to dollars brought right down to the bottom line. Sales by the subsidiary company in the currency of the country where it operates can be taken as a total for the quarter and converted to dollars for reporting purposes over the average of the three months. Plant and equipment, however, must be carried on the books at "historical cost," the exchange rate of the time of their construction or acquisition.

Companies which invest in strong-currency countries are penalized by FAS/8 because their debts in an appreciated currency must be increased on the dollar books at home, while their fixed assets and inventory continue to be valued at the "historical" exchange rate. Ruth Pleak of Des Moines tells the sad story of ICN Pharmaceuticals, a California drug company which bought a German manufacturer, paying mostly through a D-mark borrowing in Germany. The company was a success, carried the interest charges on the loan easily, and returned a profit. Nevertheless, ICN had to take a $5 million foreign-currency-translation loss, which put it in the red worldwide for 1976, when an appreciation of the mark was interpreted to increase the reported debt on the loan to buy the factory—but could not be used to show an increase in the value of the factory itself.

With sales translated at the average exchange rate for the period and inventories carried at historical rates, Alan Teck of New York's Chemical Bank points out, "the relationship between sales and costs of goods can be greatly distorted." But all sorts of things get bollixed—deferred taxes, mergers, stockholdings, etc. And everything has to be reported every quarter, up or down. John Y. Gray of Ernst & Ernst noted when FAS/8 was only six months old that "Large swings in foreign currency exchange rates since the issuance of the Statement . . . have affected the earnings of some companies to the extent that bankers, securities analysts and others have been surprised. Quarterly earnings have reacted sharply to changes in exchange rates . . . Many companies have increased their activity in the hedging area (e.g., forward exchange contracts) and other companies are now engaging in hedging activities which had not considered doing so previously."

To avoid big swings in reported profits, which could affect stock prices, credit ratings, customer relations, and even executive salaries, companies went to the banks for help in protecting themselves from what they considered distorting mirrors. One line of defense was to borrow for all foreign needs in dollars, which would guarantee against ugly surprises in the form of debt revaluation at the end of the quarter. (Eight years earlier, Lyndon Johnson had instituted an Office of Direct Foreign Investment to force American multinationals to stop exporting dollars and meet their financial needs abroad by borrowing in the local markets; now the U.S. accounting board was in effect forcing them to use, and weaken, the U.S. currency.) But the most popular remedy was to operate in the forward markets. In many currencies, of course, there *was* no forward market of any substance, and then the multinational might be advised by its bank to find a currency *like* the one desired for hedging purposes. Everybody hedged everything: Citicorp executive vice-president G. A. Costanzo, head of the foreign department, reports that his bank, our second largest, has hedged the capital in each of its locally incorporated branches and owned affiliates around the world.

The foreign exchange markets began to hum with activity. "If we wanted to devise a better marketing tool," Gerald Kramer of Chase told *Business Week,* "we could not have come up with anything better than FASB-8. Once companies see the volatility in their earnings, they come to us and say, 'My God, what are we going to do?' " One New York bank in London reported to *Busi-*

ness Week in December 1976 that its trading room was making $150,000 a day "just by trading sterling for its corporate clients."

And when you think of what was happening to sterling that fall, the boast takes on interesting dimensions.

5

Coming to power in 1974 in the aftermath of a coal strike that had reduced British industry to three-day-a-week operations, Harold Wilson's Labour party found an economy torn apart with inflation, suffering the world's worst trade deficit ($11.7 billion for the year), and entering into a recession. Catch-up from a disastrous first quarter made the second half of 1974 deceptively robust (Britain was the only one of the seven largest industrial countries to show a growth in Gross National Product in the second half of 1974), but inflation got steadily worse. At the end of 1974, Saudi Arabia, which had traditionally sold a quarter of its oil output in pounds, announced that in the future only dollars would be acceptable. In 1975, the economy plunged, and traditional Keynesian stimuli failed to brake it. The budget deficit reached 8 percent of GNP; the "deflator" (the measurement of overall inflation) reached past 28 percent. That fall, Labour announced a shift in policy, from measures aimed at stimulating consumer demand to measures aimed at increasing investment in ailing industries. Nothing helped: while the rest of the world straggled up the slope of recovery, Britain continued to decline.

It will come as no surprise that the government blamed the failure of Britain's recovery on an overvalued pound, hovering just over $2 as 1976 began. What had kept the pound high, however, was a combination of government and industrial decisions difficult to reverse. In the private market, the oil companies were bringing money by the shipload to Britain to pay for drilling and setting up of the infrastructure of the North Sea oil fields. Governmentally, Britain had been meeting its domestic budget deficits by borrowing abroad, for the terrifying reason that the British would no longer buy their own government's paper at any interest rate the government could consider paying. Between energy investment from abroad and official borrowings, foreign money was being converted to pounds at an exchange rate that did not reflect the impact on export prices of the continuing inflation.

In March 1976, overcoming some qualms at the Bank of England, Her Majesty's Treasury began to plot a devaluation, which turned out not to be a contradiction in terms in the era of floating rates. But the plot, Stephen Fay and Hugo Young reported two years later in the *Sunday Times,* "had to be kept quite secret. If it was ever known, or suspected, that a fall in sterling was official government policy, the process could get rapidly out of hand as sterling holders [whose 1968 exchange-rate guarantee, once renewed, had run out in 1974] rushed to sell their pounds."

The centerpiece of the plan was to be a reduction in the Bank of England's Minimum Lending Rate (the equivalent of the Federal Reserve discount rate) in the teeth of the continuing inflation. Then, Fay and Young report, "the Bank had a stratagem known as 'backing into' a devaluation—appearing to fight a fall while covertly seeking it. 'We intended to shout "Rape!" but not loud enough for anyone to hear,' said an insider." But the scheme was accidentally blown on the Friday before it was to begin, when the trading desk sold pounds into a market that had started the day strong but was declining before the Bank's order reached the dealers. Britain was pledged not to engage in competitive devaluations, by the OECD agreement of 1974, and central banks do not sell their currencies into a declining market. The dealers panicked. The pound dropped in one week to $1.90, which was where the government wanted it—and continued down. The Bank of England had nowhere near enough foreign exchange to brake the fall by purchasing in the markets.

In early June, with the pound just over $1.70, Jelle Zijlstra of the Netherlands Bank called Gordon Richardson, Governor of the Bank of England, and told him that this nonsense had gone far enough—Britain had an obligation to defend sterling. Richardson called Arthur Burns, and the two of them (plus Zijlstra, wearing his other hat as chairman of the Bank for International Settlements) arranged with their colleagues in the other central banks for a defense fund of $5.3 billion, of which $2 billion would be provided by the United States. Treasury approval would be required, however, for American participation: Under Secretary Edwin Yeo was waiting for an invitation to come to London.

James Callaghan had succeeded Harold Wilson as Prime Minister. Having been Chancellor of the Exchequer at the time of the 1967 devaluation, he knew a great deal about monetary pressures and hated the whole business. He especially resented the International Monetary Fund, the soulless economists who had come to Britain in 1965 under the direction of Jacques Polak (by 1976 the senior economic adviser of the Fund) and had imposed "conditions" on the sovereign government of the United Kingdom before authorizing the loan that kept the pound at $2.80 for two years after it should have been devalued. Zijlstra offered him a way to stabilize the pound (which was of course necessary—the price of Britain's imports had skyrocketed, and was wrecking the government's "incomes policy") without subjecting his government to IMF scrutiny. He invited Yeo and received a shock.

The *Sunday Times* reporters quote Yeo as saying, "The trouble in Britain was that people had a higher standard of living than the country was earning. The Tories had lost control of monetary policy and, after 1974, Labour lost control of budgetary policy." Yeo was prepared to put up the $2 billion for the American piece of Zijlstra's package, but only for six months. After that, any outstanding debt on the support package would have to be financed through the IMF. Callaghan was trapped.

On June 28, the leaders of the Western world met in one of those economic summits, this one in Puerto Rico. Treasury Secretary William Simon remembers sitting around a swimming pool with Callaghan, who asked him how much time he thought Britain had before the complete collapse of sterling. "I said," Simon recalls, " 'Through the summer. You Europeans are smarter than we are, you take the summer off. When people come back from vacations, I wouldn't be surprised to see the pound go to a buck and a half.' He was horrified."

On July 22, Chancellor of the Exchequer Denis Healey brought in a revised budget that was as far as Labour's left would let the government go: it cut several billion dollars off the Public Sector Borrowing Requirements, which were the root of the financial disaster, but failed to instill any sense of emergency in the country or the government. And when people came back from vacation, sure enough, as Simon had predicted, the pound went into shock. Healey and Richardson got as far as the airport on their way to the late-September annual meeting of the IMF (held in Manila in 1976) when they were recalled by their subordinates to face a new run on the pound of unmanageable dimensions. Alone among the nations of the world, Britain was represented at Manila by civil servants rather than ministers and central bank governors.

On September 29, the Bank of England raised the Minimum Lending Rate to a previously unimaginable 15 percent, and the government announced that it would apply to the IMF for a loan. "Political officials on both sides of the Atlantic," the *Sunday Times* team reported, "were numbly aware of the possibility of a bankrupt Britain with inflation fed by unmanageable increases in import costs, spiralling up to 60 to 70 per cent, unemployment rampant as factories closed, and devastating effects on world trade." The IMF team of six, headed by an Australian economist, arrived on November 1 and hid from the press in Mayfair's Brown's Hotel. After a quick look at the books in Her Majesty's Treasury, they told Callaghan and Healey that a condition of IMF assistance would be an additional reduction of about $7 billion in public-sector borrowing, over and above what had been announced in July.

Callaghan now opted for a "political" solution. Arguing that the real problem was not the current borrowings but the reserve currency burden represented by the sterling balances, he went secretly to Germany's Helmut Schmidt as a fellow Socialist to ask help in funding those balances, after which (money being fungible) he would have no need for IMF drawings. He thought he got encouragement from Schmidt. While continuing to negotiate with the Germans, he sent Harold Lever to see Gerald Ford in the White House. Lever, an intellectual businessman who had married a great fortune, had gone into politics as a maverick but was on Labour's front bench (he had the cabinet post of Chancellor of the Duchy of Lancaster, which carries no operating responsibilities). He had from the beginning opposed what he called "the mongrel system of floating rates. You can't imagine how alone I was. My speech from the front bench opposing the floating rate was greeted in stony silence on both sides of the aisle." He was personally friendly with Treasury Secretary Simon; an energetic, friendly, confident man of the kind politicians like because he gives them sure answers to questions.

Lever met with Ford, who had just been defeated for reelection, and with Kissinger. His message, in effect, was that the retiring administration should not take responsibility for the collapse of the Atlantic alliance and the world economy. What was working against him, though it was hard for the British in crisis to understand the force of the argument, was that Britain was not the only country appealing for money from the IMF: Portugal and Spain, not to mention Peru and Zaire, were being compelled to accept distasteful conditions to win approval of their drawings. At a meeting of the National Security Council called specifically to consider Britain's plight (and to give Kissinger backing in his request to Ford to make a personal appeal to the IMF on Britain's behalf), Simon and Arthur Burns told the President they could not conceivably accept what the politicians wanted. "I didn't exactly say I'd quit," Simon recalls. "But I let them know I'd blast them out of the water if they politicized the IMF." He had talked with Schmidt, who was not, it turned out, as sympathetic as Callaghan had led Lever to believe.

Ford wanted to give Lever something nice to take home from his visit to America, and told him that the United States would help Callaghan get out from under the sterling balances and the reserve currency role. Then he authorized Yeo to tell Lever that of course this support would be given only *after* Callaghan had made his deal with the IMF. Several confusing newspaper stories resulted.

In the British cabinet, a left-wing caucus had formed under the leadership of Anthony Wedgwood-Benn, the Peronist of the Labour party. Benn's proposal was for an economic Fortress Britannia, with import surcharges and rigid exchange controls, to free the nation from the grip of the bankers. Lever pointed out sourly that it would be necessary for the troops to sally forth from Fortress Britannia at regular intervals to borrow money, even under the most favorable of Benn's hypotheses. Others suggested that the Commonwealth countries might not react really favorably to an import surcharge against their goods, and that failure to apply the surcharge equitably against all might trigger a trade war Britain could only lose. By the time debate was over, Callaghan was ready to bargain for whatever he could get from the IMF; Healey had reached that conclusion some months before.

The deal as struck cut British social services by about $5 billion, and provided sufficient backing for the pound to make its defense credible—especially at $1.55, to which it had fallen. At that price, British goods would be highly competitive in the world; coupled with the arrival of North Sea oil, the pound might even be the beneficiary of the export-led boom the Treasury had hoped to stimulate from the beginning. In 1977, Britain would show a surplus on current account and a whopping capital inflow of almost $12 billion—and would become the largest buyer of the Treasury bills the United States had to sell that year to balance its own books in the face of the worst trade, current account and liquidity deficits in history.

By then, the money-changers in the international banks were no longer profiting hugely from customers protecting themselves in the forward market against the instability of the pound. The bankers were striking it rich in the dollar.

8 / Carter's Incompetents

The problem of the sterling balances . . . is an ever-verdant reminder
. . . that urgent national requirements and international circumstances
can lead to a prejudicial buildup of holdings which, though still enjoying status as valid claims against national production, can lose all semblance of being validated on demand. . . . What is to prevent such a
situation from developing if priority political objectives draw the
United States into financing internationally on the cuff, in abuse of the
international status accorded its banking facilities and ancillary short-
term instruments?

> —Judd Palk, manager, interna-
> tional project, National Industrial
> Conference Board, 1965

* * *

The foreign sector has acted as a drag on the speed of expansion in the
U.S. economy.

> —Economic Report of the Presi-
> dent, 1978

* * *

The President had been told by the young men around the White
House that it didn't matter what happened to the dollar—it was only
ten percent of GNP.

> —George Ball, former Under Sec-
> retary of State, 1979

* * *

Jimmy Carter brought to an increasingly centralized American government a cadre of decision makers whose compre-
hension of the institutional machinery they were to control was
limited by their inexperience and their essentially amateur orien-
tation—by their belief that the "issues" they had read about all
their lives in the newspapers were, in fact, the important questions of policy.

Virtually all the market-oriented officials in the Treasury Department returned to the private sector with the end of the Ford
administration, and the influence of Arthur Burns as Chairman
of the Federal Reserve Board was greatly reduced by White

House attitudes prior to his replacement at the end of his term in January 1978.

The experienced people who returned to government with the return of the Democrats were blindly slotted into jobs where neither their temperament nor their beliefs permitted them to express the institutional views inescapably implied by their positions.

Moreover, the severely politicized nature of the Nixon and Ford administrations had denied the experience of the period 1969–77 to virtually all plausible candidates for major posts in the Carter administration.

As a result, the advisory cadre, much of it most impressive both on paper and in person, was suffering from a cultural lag, perceiving the problems of the late 1970s in terms appropriate to the 1960s, but entirely unsuitable to the difficulties that faced the incoming government.

The policies actually adopted in the international arena were not unlike those of the first Nixon administration—but without the understanding that they invited a crisis in the monetary system and without any plans to manage the crisis when it came.

After twenty months of inflationary actions deeply damaging to both the domestic economy and the exchange value of the dollar, the Carter White House in the fall of 1978 reversed the thrust of its policies, but was unable to explain to politically significant supporters—indeed, to itself—the necessity for the change.

1

By the end of 1976, when Simon and Yeo were beating on the British for their irresponsibility, the American current account had swung into deficit at an annual rate of $12 billion, and the dollar had depreciated in six months by almost 10 percent against the D-mark and its associates in northern Europe. Several of the economists consulted by the incoming Carter administration were still arguing the Brookings Institution case of 1963, that further expansion of the United States economy would take care of the problem.

"Over the past fifteen years," Robert Solomon, now retired to Brookings from the Fed, wrote in a paper for the Atlantic Council in 1977, "it has become evident that when a large industrial country goes into recession its currency tends to weaken, and when its aggregate demand is booming, its currency tends to strengthen. Even though the current account surplus increases in recession and decreases [!] in a boom, changes in capital flows tend to overwhelm these movements in the current account, as interest rates fall in recession and rise during a boom period relative to interest rates in other countries." Laurence S. Klein of the Wharton School, reputedly the new President's favorite economist, told the Joint Economic Committee early in 1977 that this happy state was already blessing America: "The attractiveness of the U.S. economy for world investors has meant that capital has been flowing in, giving strength to the position of the dollar, and there is every reason to believe that such strength will continue."

This was not, however, the view of most of the economists who flocked to advise Carter during the interregnum and to work for his administration. "We never thought American expansion would help the balance of payments," says Anthony Solomon, an amiable, handsomely bearded New York economist and businessman who had served as Under Secretary of State and retired to be a sculptor at a Maryland estate before Carter lured him back to Washington to be Under Secretary of Treasury for Monetary Affairs. In fact, the predominant opinion in the new administration was that the American deficit was the result of the failure by the other large industrial countries to recover fast enough from the 1974–75 recession. It was *because* the United States was moving faster up the cycle that America had so large a payments deficit.

The remedy was for the surplus countries, especially Germany and Japan, to give a good macroeconomic heave to their economies—big budget deficits and easy money—to stimulate domestic demand, a significant part of which would be satisfied by imports.

THE FATE OF THE DOLLAR

In the first weeks of the new administration, Vice-President Walter Mondale was sent around the world to introduce himself to the various heads of state and tell them the United States expected them to pull their weight as importers. (Included in his entourage were Under Secretary of State for Foreign Affairs Richard Cooper and Treasury Assistant Secretary for International Monetary Affairs C. Fred Bergsten, to speak strongly to their opposite numbers.) Treasury Secretary Michael Blumenthal confided to the Joint Economic Committee that he did not think Mondale and his experts had got quite enough in the way of pledges, and the administration would keep pushing.

The problem was not an easy one. As long as the OPEC countries were piling up surpluses, there was a deficit to be divided among the rest of the world. If all that deficit lay upon the LDCs, which was roughly the case in 1975 when the United States had a surplus, the poor nations of the world would soon use up their credit from even the most optimistic Eurobanks. It could be argued (and certainly was felt) that developed countries which maintained a payments surplus were behaving *immorally*—especially when they had unemployed workers and underemployed productive facilities. (Japanese industry was working at under 80 percent of capacity; but it should be remembered, and often isn't, that Japan had suffered dangerous payments deficits in 1973–75.)

What would make the world a better place to live in would be a deliberate political decision by the industrial countries in surplus to be the "locomotive" of economic growth for the international community. The United States was already a little engine that could, straining up the hill; but the Europeans and the Japanese had failed to stoke their fires. Neither the British, braked by IMF restrictions, nor the Italians could offer any strength (the lira had dropped from 630 to the dollar in mid–1975 to 875 to the dollar at the end of 1976); but the computers all said that the Germans could raise their growth targets by 1 percent, and the Japanese by 2 percent, without risking inflation. What the United States was asking from these countries was not a *sacrifice*, after all: we were telling them to let their people live better. . . .

In any event, the Carter administration was going to drive the American economy full speed ahead. There was a (false) perception among the economic advisers that the recovery had slackened, and a strong desire to use the federal budget to make social problems go away. The Ford administration had left a deficit of about $57 billion for 1977; the newcomers would whomp that up by $10 billion or so, mostly through a $50-per-head credit to be handed out in April and May, and would plan to return to $57 billion deficit (as against Ford's proposed $47 billion) in fiscal 1978. The record fails to show any consideration whatever of the impact these policies might have on the exchange value of the dollar. To the extent that an international risk was considered, it seems likely that the Carter administration—like the Nixon administration eight years before—had some hopes of resolving the nation's payments difficulties by pushing the dollar down. "Exchange rates," Treasury Secretary Blumenthal told the Joint Economic Committee somewhat ominously in early February, "must play their proper role in bringing about an international adjustment."

The economy remained strong—so strong that the President dropped his $50-per-head rebate plan (never very popular among economists, who are more likely than politicians to credit consumers with reasonably high time horizons). What with improved receipts and a failure to spend all the appropriations, the 1977 deficit was "only" $45 billion.

At a London Economic Summit in the spring of 1977—where a president trained as an engineer finessed his way to his own satisfaction through the awkward fact that the heads of the British, German and French governments were all trained economists who had served as ministers of finance—commitments were gathered from the Germans and Japanese to raise *their* domestic budget deficits and increase the apparent wealth and spending power of their citizenry. Meanwhile, the trade deficit kept growing, but the dollar stayed up with reference to the European currencies, though it did fall 9 percent against the yen in the first half of the year (restoring the cross-rate between the yen and the mark to its levels of a year before, absolutely essential if the Common Market were not to slam embargoes on what little Japanese merchandise they bought).

On the silly Morgan Guaranty "trade-weighted index," the dollar actually rose in the first half of 1977, because the Canadian dollar (its largest component) had entered a crisis phase—three years of wage and price controls administered by a government that had proclaimed the obsolescence of market economics had left Canada with much higher inflation, unemployment, and trade deficits than the United States. Part of the support for the dollar in those six months came from the rise in oil prices, which compelled foreigners to find dollars to pay the oil producers, who accepted only dollars (and who had continued their 1976 patterns of investing those dollars, which favored the United States). But much of it derived from dollar buying in the market by the German, Swiss, and Japanese central banks, which were preventing what would otherwise be substantial appreciation of their own currencies in dollar terms.

There was a kind of triangular trade going: the United States imported much more than it exported and made up only part of the difference with repatriated earnings on investments, services, fees, etc.; the dollars that went abroad were converted to local currencies at the existing market rate by their recipients; then the foreign central banks, loaded with dollars after these conversions, bought U.S. Treasury paper, thereby financing the American domestic budget deficit. This was a crazy way to run the world, and everyone outside the United States saw that it could not be sustained for any long period of time.

The Europeans complained that the need to print their currencies to buy dollars was inflating their money supply and hindering any fiscal stimulus they might wish to administer in response to American political pressure. The Americans, off the record, were telling the Europeans (and especially the Japanese, whose bilateral trade surplus with the United States had risen to a rate of $7 billion a year and was climbing) that part of the problem was their insistence on "intervening" in the currency markets to maintain the exchange value of the dollar. If the dollar depreciated, increasing American import prices and reducing American export prices, the United States trade deficit would begin to drop.

The Carter administration was focused primarily on unemployment in America, being fed by the arrival on the job market of the enormous birth cohorts of the late 1950s (birth cohorts that were 50 percent larger than those that had sought work in the 1950s, 25 percent larger than those seeking employment in the 1960s). An "overvalued" dollar cost jobs in the export industries and destroyed jobs in import-competing industries. After a contentious meeting of the OECD in Paris in June, Secretary Blumenthal gave a press briefing at which he called for the Germans and Japanese (especially but not exclusively) to free the exchange markets and let their currencies rise against the dollar.

In early 1979, Blumenthal gave an interview to *Fortune* magazine, in which he claimed that "I never said that I wanted the dollar to decline." This was noted in conversation with a man at the Fed who has high responsibilities in the foreign exchange market, and he winced. "June 24, 1977," he said. "None of us will ever forget it." There is no question that the United States *did* want the dollar to decline and *did* say so, both privately and publicly. "I remember I was testifying before a Congressional committee," Arthur Burns says, "and I emphasized the importance of a stable dollar on international markets. I was asked if that was not inconsistent with Treasury policy. I kept a straight face and said it wasn't. Blumenthal was furious."

As the dollar crisis neared climax in fall 1978, Dr. Erik Hoffmeyer, governor of the Danish National Bank, complained bitterly, "You have created a system where you do not follow the rules." Janos Fekete, deputy president of the Hungarian National Bank, who had bet a good piece of his country's reserves on the strength of the dollar with no special support for such actions from the Hungarians' great protector to the East, was still livid about the 1977 statements: "We are dealing with the markets," he said, "we are all bandits together. And here come these newcomers and they don't *understand.* Absolutely unheard of," he added, "for a finance minister to talk down his own currency."

Henry Reuss commented mildly that he thought the dollar *was* overvalued in 1977: "The Japanese had been rigging the market to prop the dollar, sell all the color television sets and cars and cameras. Blumenthal was right to say he was damned if he would cooperate. But we were all slow to recognize the tremendous overhang of foreign dollars at a time when there was so much bad news, and of course it got out of hand."

Unfortunately, it was always going to get out of hand. "The British experience was a textbook on this sort of thing," Edwin Yeo says sorrowfully. "But nobody read the textbook. Blumenthal thought the Treasury staff was no good, infiltrated by me, so conservative they wore shiny neckties."

From the arrival of floating rates through 1976, American international monetary policy had been made by money-market men serving in Washington—Volcker, Bennett, Yeo (reinforced by Simon). Floating rates had always carried a great risk of inflation. ("One possible consequence of flexible exchange rates," Henry Wallich of Yale, later a Governor of the Fed, had warned the Reuss Subcommittee in 1963, was "a worldwide acceleration of inflation. . . . If exchange rates go down, wages will rise, and exchange rates cannot recover.") Facing that risk now was a cadre of policy makers not one of whom had ever in his life worked a day in a money market. "Blumenthal," Arthur Burns says, "had a large experience in foreign trade, but knew *nothing* about foreign exchange—literally nothing. Solomon also knew nothing about international money markets. And they had nobody in Treasury to lean on. Anyway, at Treasury, staff people have no independent position; they never speak up."

2

One part of the nation's trade deficit could not be blamed on the macroeconomic parsimony of foreigners: the growing U.S.

appetite for imported oil. And as long as the gas was available at the pump, the public took no great interest in the problem: the turnaround in the petroleum trade had been too fast for the culture to absorb.

In the 1950s and early 1960s, the American oil industry had fought great battles in Congress to keep out by quotas or tariffs low-cost foreign oil, especially oil from the Persian Gulf. The Texas Railroad Commission restricted the output of wells in that state, allegedly for reasons of conservation but also, clearly as part of a price-fixing scheme. In 1956 and 1967, when the running war between Israel and the Arabs had cut off the Europeans from their usual sources of supply, the United States was able to increase production and supply its allies with their needs. Oil suppliers and natural gas suppliers fought each other for both industrial and home-heating markets.

But by 1971, when Peter Peterson organized his *tour d'horizon* of foreign economic relations for Richard Nixon, it was clear that the United States was losing self-sufficiency in energy: "Unless there are some major breakthroughs in cleaner domestic energy resources . . . our trade deficit will continue to increase and we will consume more and more relative to what we produce. Some would say that oil imports, for example, could climb by $12 billion by the end of this decade, unless we find domestic alternatives."

American oil production had stopped growing (in fact, 1970 would prove to have been the peak year); annual usage of natural gas far exceeded annual additions to known reserves. American export earnings in the years to come would have to cover the costs of imported oil as well as the imports which had always been on the agenda. And then, of course, just as imports began to represent a significant proportion of American energy consumption, OPEC quadrupled the price of imported oil.

This was an extremely awkward development in an economy where other cost structures rested on a low cost for energy. Americans drove large, wasteful automobiles (which had just been made about 20 percent more wasteful by environmental legislation that reduced engine efficiency to eliminate emissions—by means requiring unleaded fuel that also took more crude oil per gallon of gasoline). American commercial and residential buildings had been built with minimal insulation because it was cheaper (especially for the builder) to heat or cool the surrounding air than to produce a thermal-resistant shell. American industrial productivity had been boosted in part by finding ways to substitute low-cost energy for high-wage labor. And now the low-cost energy was vanishing.

Government reaction to the oil shock was something less than a model of foresighted policy-making. The first perceived necessity was to protect American consumers from the price increases by government controls—essentially on prices alone, though some gestures were made toward telling refineries how to allocate raw stock among various petroleum products. A body of theory was developed and publicized to defend this decision. Oil, it was said, was exempt from the normal laws of economics: demand was inelastic and would not be reduced by higher prices; supply could not be increased by higher prices because, after all, there was only so much oil in the ground.

Meanwhile, the Europeans let energy prices rise, with considerable improvement in the efficiency of energy utilization; as Jelle Zijlstra of the gas-rich Netherlands likes to point out, it is the countries with no domestic oil supplies—Japan, Germany, Switzerland—that have had the payments surpluses. And, of course, the Europeans (with small cars that drove short distances, fewer appliances, no tradition of overheating in winter and no great need to cool in summer) had always used less energy than Americans: a 1972 study indicated that residential energy use per capita in West Germany was less than half the American levels.

In the United States, price controls without rationing led to both short-term and long-term dilemmas, both deriving from the fact that petroleum is a commodity, the same stuff whether produced domestically or abroad. Short-term, the government faced the fact that different refineries had relied on domestic or imported oil. There was no way to hold down the price of imported oil. Thus the refinery dependent on imports could not compete against the refinery with a domestic supply. To equalize the costs of the commodity to its processors, the government had to establish a detailed program of "entitlements" by which refineries could gain the privilege of processing price-controlled domestic oil only by purchasing high-priced foreign oil. The system actually *promoted* imports, at a time when announced national policy was to reduce imports.

Long-term, the dilemma was that all the low-cost oil likely to be found in the United States had already been found. Price controls fixed at the *average* domestic cost would cut production quickly by driving out of business all the wells from which oil cost more, and would bring domestic exploration to a halt. Even those most insistent that high prices wouldn't produce more oil did admit that uniformly low prices would reduce current production. (Why this asymmetry should exist was never explored, despite the fascinating challenge of creating such a theory.) Price controls set high enough to make Alaskan oil pay, or to stimulate the use of tertiary recovery methods to pump more of the older basins up to the surface, would carry the controlled price near the Arab price. It became necessary to invent many new categories for separately characterizing a single commodity—new oil, old oil, new-old oil, oil from wells that produced less than ten barrels a day, oil from wells that required injections of one kind or another to keep delivering. Books of rules and regulations grew, and interest in exploring for oil in America concomitantly declined.

In 1975, President Ford and his advisers decided the knot could not be untied, and gave Congress a simple proposal (which President Carter and his advisers would resurrect four years later)—let the price rise to the world level, and put a windfall profits tax on the oil companies to keep them from making too much on their older, low-cost producing facilities. This was overwhelmingly rejected by Congress, which instead produced at the end of the year a Rube Goldberg bill that actually cut back by a few cents per gallon the cost of petroleum products to the American consumer.

In 1977 President Carter decided that the great crusade of his first term (other than the elimination of waste and corruption, of course) would have to be the reduction of energy use and the expansion of energy supply. For this purpose he issued a call to a Moral Equivalent of War (Russell Baker of *The New York Times* helpfully supplied the acronym MEOW). But the bill introduced for the administration was calculated to be defended in terms of its fairness (leveling out the burdens imposed) rather than in terms of its effectiveness. The longer the program lay before Congress, the worse it looked as a way actually to narrow the gap between domestic production and consumption—and the more reluctant legislators became to adopt something that the more articulate sectors of their constituencies never ceased to denounce as unfair. In 1977, the cost of imported oil touched $45 billion.

The composition of American oil imports was also changing. In 1973, almost 30 percent of imported oil was from Canada, and about 12 percent was from Venezuela, both countries all but certain to spend the proceeds in the United States. By 1978, these two countries accounted for only 6 percent of the greatly expanded American import, and even the addition of Mexico to the supplies (at 6 percent all by itself) did little to improve levels of confidence that dollars for oil would return to America to buy American output. By contrast, the share of Algeria, Libya, and the Gulf emirates and sheikhdoms in American imports rose from about 12 percent in 1973 to at least 33 percent in 1978—and these countries were far more closely tied to European economies.

There were policy implications here beyond the energy program itself, which were not understood by either the Carter administration or Congress. The 1976 deficits had not weighed on the dollar in part because the OPEC countries had invested their surplus in the United States. For this investment to continue—which was presumably in the OPEC interest, too, for they wished to swap the depletion of their oil reserves for long-term earning assets in some stable environment—the value of the paper the OPEC countries were acquiring had to be sustained. If American inflation exceeded that in the other industrialized countries, there was a danger that OPEC would find other places to put its money, leaving the United States with a deficit on energy imports that would become much more painful to finance.

Moreover, the composition of American exports had been changing. Fifteen years before, Charles Kindleberger had warned the Joint Economic Committee that the pattern of tariff reductions planned under the Trade Expansion Act of 1962, coupled with the growth of lending tied to the purchase of American exports, might be counterproductive for the long-run competitive position of the United States: exports would indeed expand, "but in familiar products, protected markets and away from the sharply competitive areas where the technological change is most rapid. This increase in exports may be said to slow down growth because it permits the economy to evade the necessity for facing structural changes. . . . A significant portion of our exports are or are in process of becoming high-cost exports to protected markets." Kindleberger contrasted the 1962 situation with that of the Marshall Plan days: "During the European Recovery Program, Europe wanted the goods, and the aid financing was a necessary accompaniment. At the present time, on the other hand, Latin America and Asia want the financing, and are obliged to take goods under our tied-loan arrangements."

There was a tendency at the State Department for Americans to pat themselves on the back because the United States absorbed so much larger a share of Less Developed Country exports than the Europeans or the Japanese did, and sold more to the poorer nations, much of it on concessionary terms. On the other side of this coin, there was a reduction in the quality of the currencies American exporters were earning. If the oil exporters would not accept Ghanaian cedis in payment (and, very sensibly, they wouldn't), a surplus on American trade with Ghana was of limited utility to the United States. A discouragingly large portion of our sales to LDCs was arms. And in our dealings with the LDCs, we were to some degree, through multinational companies and through loans that financed the export of capital equipment, setting up foreign competitors not only against our exporters but also against American manufacturers in the home market.

THE FATE OF THE DOLLAR

There remained the problem that had turned up so shockingly with the giant swing from surplus to deficit in 1975–76—the very great income elasticity of demand for imports, the tendency of Americans, as they got richer, to spend an increasing share of their added income for foreign products. No doubt the American deficit would be somewhat diminished if the surplus currency countries in Europe and Japan beefed up their domestic demand. But the evidence argued that in a year when everyone was prosperous, the U.S. trade balance would deteriorate because Europeans and Japanese growing richer would expand their consumption of our goods less rapidly than we gobbled theirs. A mounting share of our exports was agricultural, at best relatively unresponsive to income growth abroad, at worst endangered by the spread of agricultural subsidies in other countries and by the improvement of foreign farming techniques, most of them carried abroad by Americans and donated (or sold for a small fee).

Finally, we were still buying foreign properties and securities. "Americans," Paul Volcker said thoughtfully the other day, "were brought up to invest abroad, not to export." But now we had neither the trade surpluses nor the volume of domestic savings that might justify such uses of the dollar abroad. Through the 1970s, though their population is only half of ours and their GNP considerably less than that, the Japanese had been saving more in absolute terms than Americans had been saving; even the Germans, with one-quarter the American population, saved almost as much in total. It was only because the dollar was the world currency that American investors had easy access to funds they could use abroad.

In the 1960s, DeGaulle had objected to the use of overvalued American dollars to acquire other people's land and industry. But in those days, it was at least arguable that the most highly developed economy should be exporting capital, that the surplus of American savings over domestic investment opportunity needed an outlet, and that foreigners were benefiting by the employment of American savings to strengthen their industrial base. "The United States," said James Tobin of Yale in 1965, "did not abuse the privileged position of owning a printing press for international money. We did not flood Europe with worthless paper, forcing them into inflation while we carted home the products of their toil and thrift." By 1977, that boast could no longer be made. Total domination of the monetary system by the dollar—promoted in fact if not always overtly by Treasury Secretaries from Connally on—had created a situation where Americans were able to use the savings of foreigners to expand American ownership of foreign enterprise.

Dollars created by American banks (and to some extent by foreign banks operating in the Euromarkets) were turning up as marks and francs and yen in the domestic economies of our trading partners, impairing their prospects for managing a noninflationary growth of their own economies. That other dollars were turning up at the central banks of the LDCs was a hypocrite's justification for an economic policy that encouraged Americans to consume and purchase more than the value of their production. And, having put the dollars out, the United States was now telling the world to let the exchanges float free so the dollar-denominated reserves they had accumulated would be worth less. Against this background of outrageous conduct, the Carter administration lectured the rest of the world about its political, economic, and moral misbehavior. In the reactions of our allies there appeared the echo of G. K. Chesterton's rollicking complaint about self-righteous attitudes of the 1920s: "I do not mind the swindle, but I do not like the swank."

The ambivalence of American policy—aimlessness is perhaps the better word—turned up in the fall 1977 hearings of the Reuss Subcommittee. Treasury Under Secretary Solomon was anxious to assure the folks that everything was going fine. Although foreign central banks were in process of buying no less than $30 billion of U.S. Treasury bills in 1977 alone—a clear example of foreign "accommodation" for a trade deficit—Solomon told the committee, "We are financing this deficit through a fully autonomous net inflow of foreign capital." Then he added, "The dollar has remained relatively strong in the foreign exchange markets.

As of September 30, the rate, measured on a trade-weighted basis against the other industrial countries, was actually stronger than it was at the beginning of 1976. It was strong because investors have confidence in the future of the U.S. economy."

Reuss himself was annoyed at Japanese market interventions: the Japanese, he said, "have through various official and unofficial means done a good deal to see that the yen's external value was as low as it could be goosed." But when Laurence Krause of the Brookings Institution urged deliberate action by the United States to push down the exchange value of the dollar, Reuss pointed out that such conduct would violate our IMF obligations. In the Report of the Subcommittee, Reuss conceded that "The composition of the current U.S. trade deficit limits the utility of dollar depreciation as a tool for curbing the disequilibrium"— and insisted that "If the United States is to have a large and persistent trade deficit, it must also have a policy for financing and gradually reducing the deficit that is credible to U.S. residents and foreigners alike."

But the Report grew truly lyrical only when contemplating the beauties of a depreciated currency: "A lower exchange value for the dollar . . . creates additional jobs in export and import-competing industries. It makes travel in the United States easier for foreigners to afford, it bolsters the revenues of our international airlines, and it encourages the sale of consulting and engineering services abroad. Given a rising stock market, a cheaper dollar encourages foreigners to invest in financial assets. Dollar depreciation and modest wage increases have encouraged foreign direct investors to establish manufacturing operations within the United States. The same factors have stanched the flood of American direct investment abroad and the transfer of jobs across our boundaries. These benefits should not be overlooked, and so long as they result from the workings of economic forces in exchange markets rather than government manipulation, we should feel no embarrassment about enjoying them."

In the fourth quarter of 1977, Reuss had a lot to enjoy. The American money supply was expanding at the fastest rate since

1972; the new fiscal year had begun with a budget deficit projected to be $10 billion larger than the year before (of unprecedented size for the third year of a recovery, well into the red even by the most permissive "high-employment" standards); interest rates were relatively low, and steps by the Fed to raise them slightly had drawn deliberately publicized wrath from the Council of Economic Advisers and the White House staff; the trade deficit was greater than ever, and rising. In the face of such news, no power on earth could maintain the value of the dollar: holders of dollars, domestic as well as foreign, were prepared to offer as many as the central banks of the strong currency countries would take, in exchange for marks, Swiss francs and yen. In the last months of 1977, the dollar dropped in virtually free fall—by 14 percent against the Swiss franc, 9.6 percent against the yen, 8.8 percent against the mark, 8.4 percent against the previously ailing pound.

On December 9 the Group of Five (U.S., U.K., Germany, France, and Japan) held a meeting of finance ministers in Paris, at which Blumenthal refused even to consider American actions to support the exchange value of the dollar. *The New York Times* explained that "the American trade deficit is not considered to be as serious a problem here as it is held to be in European capitals, with Washington officials pointing out that it represents no more than a modest 3 percent of the national output of goods and services." Looked at from abroad, these words meant that the government thought Americans should not worry about taking from the rest of the world—in return for paper which their government was now saying should be allowed to decline in value—goods and services equal each year to roughly six years' worth of their foreign aid. What price human rights?

That weekend, after the BIS meeting in Basle, Fritz Leutwiler, president of the Swiss National Bank, brushed off reporters with the words, "What's the use of making a statement if we haven't got anything new to say?" In the aftermath of those meetings, Burns persuaded Blumenthal that this game could not be played so rough as that: the Arabs, who sold oil for dollars, were getting upset about American reluctance to maintain the value of their hoards.

On December 21, 1977, a White House statement was issued to the effect that "the recent exchange market disorders are not justified." ("I stuck into a Presidential statement," Burns remembers happily, "a comment that the United States had the responsibility to preserve the integrity of the dollar.") The *Times* news story then quoted "top Administration officials" as asserting that "the dollar would now reverse its course and begin to rise." An economics commentary by Leonard Silk reported that "belief is growing in foreign exchange markets that the dollar has been oversold and will be rallying in the months ahead."

But in fact little was happening in the markets: the Fed's drawings on its swap lines with the Bundesbank had just nudged beyond the $200 million mark, and market intervention in New York was slow and grudging. Words stopped the dollar's descent briefly, and then it resumed. Now, however, the President himself went abroad, on the trip that was later celebrated night after night on television screens for the New Year's Day banquet at which he expressed his delight at being in Iran in the presence of a Shah whose people loved him so much. Quite by accident, because the plane needed a refueling stop, this trip included a visit with King Khalid of Saudi Arabia. Carter was very impressed with the King, and took to heart his warning that oil prices—which the Saudis had just kept level for the coming year at an angry meeting of the OPEC ministers—would have to rise if the dollar kept falling. From Air Force One, the President issued a statement that the United States would soon be taking steps to stabilize the exchange value of the dollar.

On January 4, 1978, a joint statement by the Treasury and the Fed proclaimed an intention to intervene to protect the dollar, and announced a new Treasury swap line with the Bundesbank to supplement the existing Federal Reserve credits. The discount rate was raised by half a percent. The dollar jumped 6 percent on the exchanges as the Fed for the first time really leaned on the market—by the end of January the swaps drawn on the Bundesbank were up by about $1.3 billion from their October level, taking the Fed and the Treasury borrowings together.

In that atmosphere, Arthur Burns—whose replacement as Chairman of the Fed had just been announced—went off for a valedictory trip to Basle with stopovers at several of the major European central banks. For some time, he had been urging the Treasury and President Carter to give earnest of American good intentions by taking more of the risk of any future market depreciation of the dollar. His proposal was to sell paper denominated in currencies other than the dollar (which would have to be paid off for more dollars if the dollar went down), using the proceeds to intervene in the currency markets. By taking Swiss francs and marks out of their domestic economies for intervention purposes, the United States would relieve its partners of the inflationary pressure they suffered when they had to print their money to buy ours. Now Burns took his proposal outside the American government, to the foreigners who would be buying the paper. The Swiss were enthusiastic; the four big privately owned banks said they were prepared to market $3 billion worth of francs for an American issue "this afternoon." Burns called Emminger, mentioned a total figure of $10 billion for U.S. sales in foreign currencies, and Emminger said the Germans would be happy to take their share.

"I worked out a plan with my staff," Burns says, "and told them to work it out with the Treasury staff. The Treasury staff refused to look at it—they had instructions from Blumenthal not even to talk about it. Emminger sent people here to discuss the proposal with the Treasury; Blumenthal wouldn't agree to see them unless it was understood that the sale of U.S. paper in foreign denominations would not be brought up at the meeting. My plan was substantially what they did months later, on November first. If they had done it in January, we'd have an eight percent prime now [he was speaking in January 1979, when the prime was 11¾%], and the dollar would be worth decidedly more in the exchanges."

This statement was carried delicately to the Treasury, where it was received discontentedly. "The January fourth package," Anthony Solomon said, recalling the atmosphere of early 1978, "was at Burns's initiative. He did also in a rather casual way suggest the sale of bonds. I wouldn't go along with that. In January we would have been blown out of the water—the current account deficit in the first quarter was going to be horrendous. I wasn't going to buck the market—it would have been the height of folly. All the trends were going in the wrong direction."

Another Treasury spokesman was even more forceful. "I always got on with Arthur," he said, "but you have to remember that Arthur Burns is not a great team player. If he was so eager to intervene on a major scale in January, he had large unused swap lines he could have drawn for the purpose. But then his beloved Fed would have lost the money. He wanted to intervene with the proceeds of our bonds sales, so the Treasury would lose the money."

Whether these attitudes were post hoc or truly held at the time is a question that cannot be answered. They do not explain why Treasury spokesmen in the weeks before and after Christmas 1977 were telling the press not just that the markets would stabilize but that the dollar would now begin to rise. Or, perhaps even more interesting, why the press agreed, and printed analyses predicting a resurgence of the dollar at the start of a quarter when the U.S. trade deficit would run at an unforgettable annual rate of $48 billion, less than one-fourth of which was oil. Those first three months of 1978 were, in fact, the quarter Alaskan oil came on stream and U.S. energy imports diminished.

3

In Paris on January 4, 1978, the same day the Treasury and the Fed made their joint announcement of measures to support the dollar, the President in a major speech set forth his economic agenda for the coming year: "America's efforts will be directed toward maintaining the strength of the dollar," he said, "injecting new purchasing power into the economy through a major tax cut, reducing unemployment and bringing inflation under control." Obviously, one cannot control inflation or support the strength of the dollar by injecting new purchasing power into the economy: Carter couldn't mean it. Then the Economic Report of the President and the Council of Economic Advisers landed on Congressional desks—and by God, Carter did mean it.

Not since Herbert Hoover sought to balance the budget at the depths of the Depression has an economic policy been so harmful to the nation as that of the Carter administration at the beginning of 1978. Despite the visible acceleration of inflation in 1977 (to 6.8 percent in consumer prices, from 4.8 percent in 1976), the Council of Economic Advisers rebuked the Fed for its "unsettling" increases in short-term interest rates, and argued that money supply could be permitted to grow more rapidly because the velocity of money was slowing. (In reality, velocity was increasing.) In its projections for the economy in 1978, the Council assumed that "Personal saving will expand by approximately one-third." (In reality, personal saving was declining.) Productivity increases almost five times those that were actually achievin in the year were projected to defend a proposed 1979 budget deficit of $62 billion against any charge that it might be just a little inflationary.

For foreigners, there was no comfort at all. The President admitted that the $18 billion deficit on current account in 1977 (as he then estimated it) "while not a cause for alarm . . . is a matter of concern." On the value of the dollar, he insisted that "Under the flexible exchange system basic economic forces must continue to be the fundamental determinant of the value of currencies"; the most he would give is that "we will not permit speculative activities in currency markets to disrupt our economy or those of our trading partners." The Council added firmly: "For large countries like the United States, where the economic cost of changing domestic growth is large relative to the improvement in the current account that would result, it is not appropriate to modify domestic objectives . . . in order to reduce the current account deficit."

In the Congressional hearings on the 1978 Economic Report, Council chairman Charles Schultze added insult to injury. One of the reasons a large budget deficit was necessary, he told the Joint Economic Committee, was that "the current account deficit . . . represents a drain on the stream of national income: it means that we are sending more dollars abroad through purchases of goods and services than are returning to our country to buy goods and services here." The root theory of international trade held that deficits and surpluses were to some extent self-correcting because the deficit by draining money (initially gold) would tend to deflate the economy that was importing too much, reducing demand for imports; while the surpluses would inflate the economy that was exporting too much, reducing its capacity to export.

The United States had been hammering on the Germans and Japanese to permit reflation—and in fact had forced them to expand their money supplies rapidly to accommodate the enormous outflow of dollars. But it would not permit the deficit to have even a marginal deflationary effect at home: the government would supply, through increased deficits, the money that was lost abroad. Operationally, Schultze was saying that the savings of foreigners would be coerced into purchases of U.S. Treasury issues, through the medium of our trade deficit.

Otmar Emminger read Schultze's comments in his starkly modern office in the Bundesbank in suburban Frankfurt. He is a lean, long-headed man with a fringe of brown hair and watery brown eyes, immaculate, *echt Deutsch,* with a rather sour expression that conceals a rather expansive personality. He remembered back to 1959, "when my good friend Bill Martin wrote a consoling letter to a Congressman who had written him expressing concern about the deflationary effect of the loss of gold. Bill said, 'Of course, the Fed will make up the difference.' I thought to myself—having been brought up as a classical central banker—only the United States could afford such a letter. In those days, it *could* afford such a letter."

What the Carter administration was doing was far more pernicious: it was building into the federal budget new expenditures (many of them "uncontrollable" in later years) to be funded by foreigners out of the excess dollars they received from the U.S. payments deficit. If and when that deficit was reduced or eliminated (which was the administration's stated goal), these expenditures would have to be financed by higher taxes, which the public was unwilling to pay, or by the hidden tax of rising inflation. Martin's Fed ran an accordion that could contract as well as expand, and he could in theory cut down the money supply when the payments deficit eased. But the federal budget is a balloon that never shrinks.

In fairness to Schultze, the Congressmen and Senators before whom he was appearing were even more bloodthirsty for inflation than the Council. The President had proposed a $62 billion deficit for fiscal 1979, but Chairman Richard Bolling of the Joint Economic Committee opened the hearings on the Economic Report with the comment that "There appears to be a broad consensus that more stimulus is needed."

The staff report prepared for the Committee denounced the rise in the discount rate that had accompanied the January 4 announcement of the new swap lines with the Bundesbank: "Such use of monetary policy for international objectives has long been opposed by the JEC and it is to be hoped that the Committee will strongly insist on reversal of the unfortunate retrogression of monetary policy." A Wharton School economist was paraded forth with an econometric projection that showed a loss of 250,000 jobs and 200,000 housing starts if interest rates rose by 1 percentage point. (In the event, interest rates would rise by 3 percentage points, but jobs would increase by half a million more than the Wharton projection *without* interest rate increases, and housing starts would be slightly higher than the projection without a rise in interest costs.) Henry Reuss chewed out Henry Wallich, appearing for the Fed: "Really," Reuss said, "we cannot stand for ruining the domestic economy just because somebody thinks it will make a few foreign bankers happy."

After the upward blip in early 1978, the dollar sank like a stone, and the stock market followed. The Fed intervened against the mark (the United States and Europe were both quite prepared to see the yen rise forever) by almost three-quarters of a billion dollars in ten trading days in February (splitting the prospective losses evenly between the System and the Treasury). On March 13, the German and American governments announced a new program of joint intervention, including an increase to $4 billion of marks available to the Fed. The dollar had briefly fallen below the level of two marks but now massive support—a total intervention that probably exceeded $8 billion at its peak ($2.84 billion of it American under the swap lines)—brought the dollar's head back above that waterline. The Fed also drew on swap lines with the Swiss National Bank, though here a much greater share of the burden of intervention was left to the Swiss, who instituted the harshest exchange controls in their history, forbidding foreigners to buy Swiss securities (and restricting their access, where possible, to franc-denominated securities issued outside Switzerland), and expanding the "negative interest rate"—a fee of 2 percent per quarter—on foreign-owned deposits in Swiss banks.

At the end of March 1978, Blumenthal had to go to Mexico City for a meeting of the Interim Committee (the successor to the Committee of 20) of the International Monetary Fund. He was not looking forward to the trip, and he needed a major statement of reassurance that he could take with him. By now, Schultze was scared, too, and joined with Blumenthal in a statement that inflation, not unemployment, was the great danger confronting the American economy; the administration's policies would have to be reoriented to fight inflation. Significantly, William Miller, the new Federal Reserve Board Chairman, did not join in the statement. Through the disasters of the first quarter, the discount rate and money market interest rates in the United States had remained steady, and the growth of the narrowly defined money stock was accelerating (in the second quarter of 1978, in fact, it would rise at the fastest pace for any three months in American history).

At Mexico City, Blumenthal was presented with a suggestion by Johannes Witteveen, the retiring managing director of the IMF—a proposal for a "substitution account" which would permit central banks to trade their dollar holdings for a new issue of SDRs, placing much of the risk of a continuing dollar devaluation on the United States. But there was nothing in it for the Treasury because these dollar holdings were now being invested (in many cases automatically, by computer program) in the Treasury Bills that Blumenthal had to sell anyway to fund the massive domestic deficit. Blumenthal issued a statement to the press refusing even to discuss the possibility of a substitution account, and everyone went home.

Thus far, the public record. There is reason to believe that on their return home, the European central bankers planned a daring and original coup to get the monkey of the payments deficit off their backs. Most investment abroad by Europeans is guided by banks. And most European governments administer their banks through systems of fairly explicit guidance. In early April 1978, according to reports that were current among the financial and economic attachés of the European embassies abroad, the central banks suggested confidentially to the private banks that for European investors the American stock market was awfully low (as it was), given the mounting properity of the United States, the high profits of the corporations, and the cheap dollar. The purchase of shares on the American stock exchanges would be more profitable for everybody than the conversion of dollars to local currencies, which could not be invested so profitably right now if only because the central banks had been forced to print so much money to absorb previous dollar inflows.

Guided or spontaneous, the European private banks in April flung their customers' money at the New York Stock Exchange. Share prices rose like free balloons in the heaviest trading days in history. And despite the continuing U.S. payments deficit (still worsening on the downstroke of the J-curve, as devaluation upped the price of imports and reduced receipts from exports), the new private demand for American investments enabled the central banks to reduce their holdings of U.S. Treasuries. The "errors and omissions" (or "statistical discrepancy") line in the balance of payments rose to almost $9 billion, in America's favor.

But the boom in the dollar was short-lived. Congress kept fiddling with the energy bill and hanging ornaments on the Christmas tree of the tax cut. With the domestic economy in boom, American manufacturers still lacked interest in exports, while consumers were fascinated by imports. Foreign competitors were benefiting from a "virtuous circle" in their appreciating currency: because so many of the raw materials in international trade were denominated in dollars (especially but not exclusively oil), the rising mark and yen reduced costs in Germany and Japan. Meanwhile, stagnant productivity with rising wages (and increased costs for those raw materials and semifinished manufactures *not* denominated in dollars) was lifting the American price level more rapidly than price levels elsewhere. Official Washington still gave little sign that it understood the gravity of American international economic problems. As Paul Volcker put it at the end of the year, in the annual report of the New York Fed, "the credibility and coherence of United States economic policies became a serious issue for holders, and prospective holders, of dollars."

The inflow of investment dollars ceased; the stock market retreated; the dollar again, in the charming phrase of the market, "came on offer." Now the central banks of the smaller European powers and the LDCs weighed in, "diversifying" their reserves from dollars into other currencies. Several countries, most notably Argentina and Brazil, borrowed heavily in the Eurodollar markets and used the proceeds to buy marks and Swiss francs. The Swiss extended their "negative interest rate" penalty to deposits in Swiss banks by foreign central banks and governments.

In mid-July 1978, the heads of state of the Big Five held another economic summit meeting, this one in Bonn. The United States still had sufficient clout to compel the Germans and Japanese to pledge stimulative efforts in their own economies (which in fact had not grown much in the fifteen months since the London summit of 1977: appreciating currencies were beginning to weigh on their export industries, which were earning more but producing less). But now the rest of the world was unwilling to let the United States parade its virtues.

Even the OECD economists had given up on the "locomotive" theory, and now felt the United States through reckless stimulation of its own economy was endangering the stability of the economic world. American exports were higher because depreciation of the currency had reduced their prices abroad—but imports were up, too. President Carter was compelled by the pressure of his colleagues to promise not only a reduction in American energy consumption but also a lid on American inflation. (Summit meetings, of course, are places where man proposes. God disposes later, and if He gets it wrong, that's His fault.) The markets were not impressed; in the three weeks after the summit, the dollar dropped more steeply than ever before.

4

Prior to the Bonn meeting of 1978, the nine nations of the expanded Common Market had held their own summit in Bremen, and had resolved to establish somehow an oasis of currency stability—a European Monetary System with its own unit of account (the European Currency Unit, or "Ecu," a charming conceit returning to use the word that had represented the smallest French coin in the nineteenth century). Everybody was annoyed at America's inability to handle its problems—and angry about the enormous competitive advantage devaluation was giving the United States in international trade. ("My colleagues from the other countries keep telling me," said one of the Americans working in the Multilateral Trade Negotiations then proceeding in Geneva, "that the meetings spend all their time haggling about whether a tariff should be seven percent or five percent, while our monetary authorities back home organize the world to place a twenty percent surcharge on American imports and give a twenty percent subsidy to American exports.") But the crisis problem for the Europeans was less the fall of the dollar itself than the impact of that fall on the cross-rates among other currencies.

The dollar was the "vehicle" for convertibility of the currencies even of adjacent European countries which did a good deal of trade with each other. In the days of fixed exchange rates, these arrangements were convenient for bankers and traders, and did no harm to anyone. But once the rates began to float, there was a danger that the value of one currency with relation to the dollar might be affected by factors that did not apply to the other, changing relative prices in the trade between the two countries for no reason related to that trade. The Germans were conscious of this problem from the Smithsonian days, when they felt that the 2.25 percent permissible fluctuation between currencies (which meant a possible 4.5 percent between two currencies traded through the vehicle of the dollar) was too wide within Europe, where trade was incessant and central to domestic economies. (Countries like Denmark, Belgium, Austria and the Netherlands export more than a third of their total output, and import correspondingly.) So the Germans organized a "snake" (a 1 percent maximum deviation from fixed "cross-rates" for the North European currencies) inside the "tunnel" of the 2.25 percent deviation permitted by the Smithsonian agreement—and had to watch most of their partners drop out of the snake as inflation proceeded at different speeds in the different countries.

That was a nuisance, but there was economic logic to it. In 1978, with the exchange rates between the dollar and other large currencies dictated by Gresham's Law questions rather than by relative purchasing power or even interest rates, the logic was gone. Two European currencies especially were considered safe havens for dollar holders in flight: Germany's and Switzerland's.

Both reduced their interest rates to the lowest levels ever (in Switzerland, government paper sold for less than 1 percent a year), hoping to make their currencies unattractive to investors. But still the money poured in.

Between March 1976 and March 1978 (*after* the French elections which the center-right had won), the French franc depreciated by about 25 percent against the German mark. Something less than half of that drop can be explained by the difference in the inflation rates of the two countries. Most of the rest represents a Gresham's Law feeling *by dollar holders* that the mark was a better store of value than the franc. There was no flight of francs to marks; but capital flows from the vehicle currency, choosing this exit rather than that, produced the same effect. Trade and tourism were distorted, and there were peculiar developments like the ludicrous mushrooming of shopping centers around Strasbourg to serve German housewives from across the Rhine who had discovered that the same number of marks bought them more food or fashion or furniture on the other side of the bridge. This phenomenon was created in Washington, but Washington never thought about it at all.

As late as 1976, Donald Cameron of the Chase Bank could write that "sophisticated observers look to . . . cross rates as a possible indication of future movements . . . because . . . cross rates tend to vary only temporarily from their natural or historical range." Now all that was out the window: cross-rates were being determined not by the relative economic performance of the two countries but by the relative attractiveness of their currencies to dollar-holders fleeing the dollar.

The disaster was the Swiss franc. The ability to feel sorry for the Swiss is a scarce talent, but the collapse of the dollar did turn into a horror story for them, because theirs was the ultimate Gresham's Law preference—the Swiss franc was paper gold beyond the dreamings of the SDR. In the 1960s, the exchange rate between the mark and the franc was rough parity, with the mark slightly more highly valued—a mark bought about 115 Swiss centimes, give or take 2 percent. The countries made their money in different ways—the Swiss relied heavily on invisibles, tourism, financial services—but there were areas, like machine tools, pharmaceuticals and other chemicals, where they competed. In fact, machinery and metals accounted for 45 percent of Swiss exports and Swiss employment.

Switzerland's 1972–74 inflation had been worse than Germany's; it lifted the mark to a value of 125 centimes. Switzerland's push on the brakes had been harder than that of any other country—after all, the overwhelming majority of the workers made unemployed by government action were foreigners—"guest workers" who could and would be sent home. As a result, the franc rose just above parity with the mark at the end of 1975, then fell back slowly to the point where the mark bought about 110 centimes in early 1977. Then came the deluge. From July 1, 1977 to late September 1978, the dollar fell roughly 20 percent against the D-mark; it fell more than 38 percent against the Swiss franc. The result was to send the Swiss franc soaring in the cross-rate against the German mark, to the point where the mark bought only 77 centimes. And because the Austrian schilling was pegged to the D-mark, Swiss prices from a foreign point of view also rose more than 20 percent by comparison with Austrian prices, simply because of the currency warp.

"Swiss firms," wrote a Swiss industrialist, "are confronted . . . with a currency situation that no longer has anything to do with real economic conditions. In the twelve months between September 1977 and September 1978 . . . the Swiss franc . . . appreciated against the currencies of our 15 major trading partners by 35.4% on an export-weighted basis, which even allowing for inflation differentials, represents a real rise in value of 28%. Moreover, two-thirds of this upvaluation occurred in August and September, 1978. Thus, in the space of just two months, the prices of Swiss products on foreign markets rose by some 20% . . . The machinery and metal industry has had to sell at lower prices than in 1977." As that phrase indicates, the firms took their losses, "taking on work," the industrialist put it delicately, "primarily for the sake of maintaining the level." There is reason to believe that the

Swiss National Bank helped under the table with forward transactions that blunted the knife. But that couldn't go on for long.

The same thing on a smaller scale was happening to the Germans in comparison with much of the rest of Europe, and tomorrow it could happen to others. France, which had installed the most admired economist in the country as premier, was still the best diversified and fundamentally strongest economy in Europe (it had grown more rapidly than any other in 1962–72); with moderate luck on the political front, the French franc could be a candidate for Gresham's Law refuge in the 1980s. And all French governments, of whatever political coloration, detest uncontrolled currency fluctuations.

The European Monetary System was designed to establish parities among the currencies of the Common Market countries. These parities would be expected to move at regular intervals to reflect changes in underlying costs and inflation conditions in the different countries, and the band of flexibility within which trading could occur under the rules was for some countries very wide. (Italy, with a cost-of-living indexing system for wages that made inflation look painless to the labor unions, was given a 6 percent leeway for the lira.) What was important was that cross-rates would be set by reference to the Ecu, the value of a weighted basket of EMS currencies, rather than the dollar—and central bank intervention to hold a currency within the permissible band of fluctuation would be done directly in the currencies of the partner countries rather than through the dollar. With each currency also trading individually against the dollar in world markets, EMS was obviously subject to attack from speculators when any of its components neared the edge of a permissible range, but the resources and sophistication were there to make such attacks risky for the speculators.

About this development, as about so much else that had to do with the Common Market, American attitudes were ambivalent. If the Ecu became established, and moved into use for private as well as official transactions, it might become a serious rival to the dollar as a unit of account in pricing commodities, which would be a blow to the dollar and to the United States. On the other hand, much of the American problem in managing its currency internationally had from the beginning been the absence of other places for countries and corporations to borrow. Over the long run, the health of the dollar requires either capital controls which could do damage to the word economy (and might not work anyway) or the creation of other reserve and vehicle currencies. The fact that EMS would use its own currencies rather than the dollar for intervention purposes was in itself a help to the dollar (probably), because it would eliminate what was from the American point of view an extraneous use of the American currency. Finally, given the apparent absence of self-control by the United States, there was something to be said for having a rival reserve currency, responsibly managed, to keep American economic policy from repeating the follies of 1966–68, 1972, and 1978.

No doubt the reasons the Europeans were pressing ahead with EMS at this time constituted a rebuke to the United States and its administration of the world's reserve currency. The Treasury Department's nose was therefore out of joint. "The instinctive reaction at Treasury," says a State Department man who works on these problems, "was, 'My God, we can't have these people making these decisions without us.' " The State Department staff solicited a meeting with Richard Cooper, their boss as Under Secretary of State for Economic Affairs; and Cooper solicited a meeting with Blumenthal. The two men agreed, as did Henry Wallich at the Fed, that "we can't afford to be seen as sabotaging EMS."

This decision may or may not have been communicated to the Treasury staff. Lisle Widman, Deputy Assistant Secretary for International Affairs, sent out to the Treasury attachés in the embassies of the major financial centers a list of two dozen or so questions about EMS to which the staff would like the attaché to get answers. "We wanted to know," Widman recalls, "whether this thing was going to develop in such a way that the market would perceive the Europeans going off to run their own regional monetary system, leaving the IMF to the developing countries. Our second concern was: Would the Europeans, in effect, fix the dollar rate, and deprive the United States of control over its exchange rate? We didn't want to get back to the Bretton Woods system again. And we didn't want to see an EMS that would lead to a remonetization of gold."

The State Department man says disgustedly, "Widman's questions were of the order of 'How do you know you won't be murdered in your bed some night if you join this thing?' Everyone in Europe said, 'Aha! The Treasury's against EMS.' We were furious."

5

In this atmosphere, with EMS on the drawing board and the dollar on the floor, the hundred-odd Governors of the International Monetary Fund and their retainers met in Washington at the end of September 1978. In the giant ballroom of the Sheraton-Park Hotel finance ministers and governors of central banks addressed acres of empty chairs while meetings not on any agenda swirled through corridors and hotel rooms. The contrast between the optimism prevailing on the podium and the bewildered disappointment in the corridors was eerie. President Carter delivered a reassuring statement. A man who has been at every IMF meeting since 1946 listened to it with a sense of disorientation he did not entirely understand—until he realized that "this was the first time an American President gave a speech to IMF that clearly had *no* input from the Treasury; it had all been written by the White House staff."

Treasury representatives were shocked by the failure of their opposite numbers to give credence to their claims that "the fundamentals" were improving for the dollar: the volume effects from the previous dollar depreciations were being felt in American exports, they said, and the trade balance was certain to improve. During the summer, Anthony Solomon had delivered himself of the heartfelt opinion that "the market is irrational," with no sense whatever that this statement translated immediately in the minds of his audience to a confession that he didn't understand what was going on. But the American deficit on merchandise trade was up from $31 billion in 1977 to $34 billion in 1978; the deficit on current account was up from just over $15 billion to just under $16 billion. Foreign official holdings of U.S. Treasury paper had risen $37 billion in 1977 and would have to rise $34 billion in 1978 to accommodate the American payments deficit and its psychological consequences. There had been too many dollars out there before these two years—now the weight on the market, all the people and governments who held dollars and wished they held something else, was crushing.

All the international agencies were predicting that the United States balance of payments would benefit by perhaps $10 billion from the 1977–78 depreciation of the dollar. "In September in Washington," Otmar Emminger remarked a few months later, "a U.S. official said to me, angrily, 'Why don't the speculators honor those figures? OECD, IMF, all the research groups agree.' I had to explain to that high official that even if this is true you have another year of deficit, ten billion, fifteen billion dollars. There's an autonomous deficit in the capital flow. It may be half of what it was in 1978, but it's still going to be ten, fifteen billion dollars. Who is to absorb it?" The answer eventually would be short-term capital flows drawn by interest rates much higher in the United States than elsewhere; but that answer was still some months down the road.

To help the return of dollars to the United States, the Fed in August 1978 removed the reserve requirement on Eurodollar deposits placed in American banks by their foreign branches, a requirement originally instituted by Chairman Martin in 1969 and variously manipulated in the years since. But there was plenty of money around for the banks to lend after Chairman Miller's great binge of expansionary credit policy through the first three quarters of 1978. Only $1 billion or so of repatriated Eurodollars appeared on home office books in the first months after they were made reserve-free.

Having seen no progress at the Interim Committee meetings

that directly preceded the IMF Convention, the Swiss in October 1978 decided to take their fate in their own hands. Leutwiler announced that Switzerland found intolerable any cross-rate that gave fewer than 85 centimes to the mark, and would simply print francs and sell them on the exchanges until the franc had sufficiently depreciated—whatever risks that might involve in terms of domestic inflation. In the first three days of October, the Swiss National Bank had to create $4.5 billion worth of francs (expanding the Swiss money supply by 10 percent) to satisfy demand and convince the world of its commitment. This outpouring of paper effectively removed the link between the Swiss franc and gold, which until October 1978, had been moving in tandem against the world's currencies; a year later, the fact that the franc no longer qualified as an acceptable substitute for gold would help power the rocket that drove gold prices to preposterous peaks.

By agreement with the Bundesbank, Leutwiler bought only dollars with his francs, trying to push the franc down without pushing the mark up. The disorder in the market, however, rebounded against the dollar, which after a brief pause to digest the banquet of francs resumed its downward course.

6

After the IMF meeting, President Carter and his advisers turned their attention to inflation, which was now at an "underlying rate" of more than 8 percent. Inflation fed the depreciation of the dollar, and in turn fed upon it. The price of imports rose. Foreigners could raise their bids in dollars in American commodities markets without raising their cost in terms of their own currencies. American producers could raise their prices more freely because they would no longer feel competitive pressures from imports. (Such factors apparently were not considered by the Council of Economic Advisers when it estimated that a 10 percent decline in the exchange value of the dollar produced only a 1 percent increase in the American price level.)

THE FATE OF THE DOLLAR

Meeting after meeting in the White House pondered the question of what the Carter administration should now do about the inflation it had so aggressively invited for twenty months. The debate was won by those who argued that the administration had to avoid any restriction which might look as though it would increase unemployment. Pledges would be given about the fiscal 1980 budget, still a year away from coming into effect, and an effort would be made to put the monkey on the back of the private sector by blathering about wage-and-price guidelines.

Announcement of the program was postponed until Congress had passed a stripped-down version of the President's energy legislation, then scheduled for October 24, 1978. That afternoon, a White House briefing outlined the President's message for a gathering of senior economic officials from all the Departments. The State Department representatives noted with horror that the program did not even mention international economic policy.

The President's televised speech was well received by political figures and by the press, all of whom detested the divisive debates that would follow any real effort to reduce demand by diminishing the spendable income of either individuals or governments. Meanwhile, Congress proceeded with the tax cut, following through on the President's January pledge to boost purchasing power—though now, obviously, if one were serious about inflation, the need was to restrict the growth of purchasing power. A Congressional initiative forced administration support of the Humphrey-Hawkins bill, a vague proposal for national economic planning that gave the reduction of unemployment far higher priority than the control of inflation. The Fed took no action to give the President's program a monetary component; it began to dawn upon observers that Carter had put into the Chairman's job, which carries the institutional role of guarding the value of monetary accumulations, a man whose previous experience as a business executive gave him a borrower's perspective.

Domestically and abroad, the markets reacted with something like shock to these renewed demonstrations of fecklessness in America. In the genteel words of Alan Holmes, Manager of the

Fed's Open Market Committee, the President's program was "greeted unenthusiastically in the exchange markets." The stock market headed south, and the dollar simply collapsed. By Friday, October 27, there *was* no international exchange market: everybody was offering dollars, and nobody was bidding. In New York, the branches of the Swiss banks were borrowing their petty cash needs every morning rather than risk going to bed at night holding dollars.

Washington was flooded with terrifying reports from embassies in all the major trading countries; the Treasury and the Fed received warnings from the international banks that in the absence of significant steps by Washington they would have to widen the spreads between bid and offer on the dollar to such an extent that the currency would lose its utility as a vehicle for international trade. The President called Blumenthal to a meeting in the Oval Office. It is reliably reported to have been the first time that the two men had met privately, without the presence of at least one of "the White House kids," since the flap over Bert Lance had poisoned relations between the White House staff and the Treasury in summer 1977.

Some time in summer 1978, Blumenthal had undergone a conversion experience, and had come to understand that the losses the United States could suffer from a continuously depreciating currency were far greater than any gains it might thereby enjoy. It is widely believed (though specifically denied by the man who should know best) that the agent of this conversion was James Ammerman, the U.S. Treasury attaché in London, who in August made an unscheduled, uninvited, and unannounced return to the United States, bringing with him personal experience of the mounting panic in the London market. Coincidentally or otherwise, Blumenthal soon after Ammerman's visit began warning any who would listen that the administration was risking disaster with its monetary policies.

That disaster now crouched visibly at the White House door. The President asked Blumenthal to give him a description of what might happen, and Blumenthal did so. Domestic inflation would soar as the price of imports rose uncontrollably (this included oil) and foreigners bought heavily with their appreciated currencies in the American commodity markets. Other nations would hastily erect import barriers against American exports, to protect themselves against the flood of goods made cheap only by the cheap dollar. International trade would diminish drastically, with losses for all participants. Third World countries, which still held most of their reserves in dollars, would be bankrupted, and interest rates on the dollar abroad—and thus, soon, at home—would fly into the high teens and maybe worse. American influence abroad, whatever triumphs might be achieved with Sadat and Begin, would plummet. Blumenthal is reported to have added, as an afterthought, that the President would have to face these problems with a new Secretary of the Treasury.

Grimly, Carter authorized Blumenthal to put together a package to defend the dollar. Once again, William Dale at the IMF got a call on a Saturday, this time from Anthony Solomon: the United States would be asking for $5 billion worth of SDRs from various facilities (including, nostalgically, the old General Arrangement to Borrow, long disused); most of them would be converted to marks. Solomon assumed there would be no problem about that. Dale commented that if this was the entire measure of the administration's support, it would be blowing in the wind. Solomon assured him much more was in work, and outlined the package—Dale has by his desk a framed piece of yellow legal-pad paper on which he scribbled the numbers beside his home telephone: $10 billion of Treasuries denominated in foreign currencies (à la Arthur Burns); gold sales of 1.5 million ounces a month ($400 million at market prices) for as long as necessary; increases of the swap lines to $6 billion with the Germans, $5 billion with the Japanese, $4 billion with the Swiss. The total was $30 billion of new foreign exchange and reserve assets, to be used to purchase the dollars on offer, and the world was to be given to understand (what might or might not be true) that there was more where this came from.

The German, Japanese,* and Swiss governments instantly agreed in principle—nothing was worked out in detail for weeks—to the issuance of Treasury securities denominated in their currency, and promised satisfactory arrangements for selling them. (In the end, to the Treasury's relief, the Japanese found it hard to fit such securities into their traditional market system; but the yen fell with the Shah, anyway, so it made no difference.) The central banks were eager to cooperate.

Federal Reserve Chairman Miller had panicked, too; he offered as the Fed's contribution a 1 percentage point rise in the discount rate, an increase in reserve requirements on large certificates of deposit, and a pledge to brake increases in the money supply. This would be announced—something that had never happened before—by the President rather than by the Fed. It was the first time since the Great Depression that the discount rate had gone up by 1 percentage point in a single step. With the discount rate at 9½ percent in America (a historic high) as against 3½ percent in Germany and Japan (historic lows), surely the arbitrageurs would be willing to hold dollars.

Over the weekend, the London *Sunday Times* guessed that a major initiative was afoot. Solomon violently (and, of course, properly—and, strangely, successfully) denied the story. By Monday the package was complete. A very few people were informed on Tuesday, and on Wednesday a visibly upset and angry President Carter, flanked by Blumenthal and Miller, made his announcement. This was November 1, All Saints' Day, and most of the markets in Europe were closed. In America, the stock market shot up, and the dollar rose by up to 5 percent against various currencies.

The impression was that the United States had regained con-

* The Carter administration's decision to help the Japanese hold down the yen, thus keeping Japan's exports competitive in world markets, was an act of considerable political courage and statesmanship, which yielded dividends in U.S.-Japanese relations in 1979. The Japanese, whatever their vices, do have the amiable quality of remembering who their friends are and what their friends have done for them.

trol of its destiny, which was 180° wrong. But the United States had begun to express an interest in its destiny, and that was crucial.

7

The old guard fired one last little parting shot. "The dollar decline is only part of a larger world currency story," Robert Solomon, now retired from the Fed to the Brookings Institution, wrote in *The New Republic*. ". . . It takes two to tango. The dollar problem is not purely an American problem . . . The leaders of other countries may find it politically convenient to blame the United States for some of their domestic problems, but unless they deal with their own problems—by improving the domestic performance of their own economies—the yen problem, the mark problem, and the Swiss franc problem will be prolonged. And for as long as it lasts, it will continue to be labeled, incorrectly, a dollar problem. . . . [The support actions] may have come just as the markets were turning around anyway . . ."

The earth turns and the world changes—but the Established Advisers (especially, perhaps, those at the Brookings Institution) never change their Advice.

9 / The State of the Dollar

Lighthouse, him no good for fog. Lighthouse, him whistle, him blow, him ring bell, him raise hell, but fog come in just the same.
—anonymous West Coast Indian, quoted by William L. Prosser, law professor

*   *   *

The worst episodes in recent monetary history—the great inflations— have been marked by the subjection of central bankers to overriding political pressures.
—R. S. Sayers (1956)

*   *   *

F oreign exchange transactions are conducted through dealers who both buy and sell, and at any given time each of them will have either an inventory of a currency or an "oversold" position in that currency. These positions are in part a matter of choice, in part an inescapable aspect of serving customers who cannot be turned away. Bids and offers will be influenced by dealers' positions because the quantities involved are enormous and the "spreads"—the gap between the lower price at which they bid to purchase and the higher price at which they offer to sell—are very narrow. With the yen at 200, the quotes might be to buy at 199.92 yen to the dollar, sell at 200.08 yen to the dollar. On a $1 million transaction (which is absolute minimum in this mar-

ket), the yield to the dealer on a turnover at these prices is $160—
or $1,600 on the more likely $10 million transaction. On the other
hand, the interest cost of carrying an average $50 million "book"
during the course of the year runs about $20,000 per working day
in a high-interest-rate environment, and foreign exchange dealers
don't come cheap.

When prices are moving rapidly, the losses (or gains) on the
inventory or oversold position can overwhelm the trading profits
in a few anguished seconds. But it is also true, as Al Costanzo of
Citicorp cheerfully concedes, that trading departments make
their money not by serving customers to earn a minuscule spread
but by being right more often than they are wrong in deciding
whether to hold inventories or go short.

In principle, the dealers attempt to keep themselves "covered"
in the forward market for any excess purchases or sales they are
making today, and the real "play" is between the "spot" market
and the "forward" market at various times ahead—usually thirty,
sixty, or ninety days. Bets can be and are laid off constantly as the
dealers "adjust" their positions. And this is, as the big banks love
to point out, a twenty-four-hour-a-day market, where traders
keep computer terminals in their bedrooms and get up at four in
the morning to catch the simultaneous closing of the Tokyo market and opening of the European market. "The day begins," says
the man who runs one of the largest "forex" dealing operations,
"in Singapore, which hands over the position to Bahrain, which
passes it on to London, which gives over to New York, which
hands over to San Francisco, which turns it over to Hong Kong."

During the steepest part of the dollar's slide, there was some
indication that a few of the banks (including some American
banks) were selling in Singapore and Bahrain to start the price
down, then purchasing at a profit when the market opened low in
London. Very naughty; very hard to prove; not, of course, the
source of the dollar's troubles, though it did lead some European
bankers to marvel at how little patriotism the Americans had.
(Perhaps it should be noted in passing that Swiss banks may not
have short positions in foreign currencies—that is, they are not

permitted to seek foreign exchange trading profits by betting that the franc will rise.)

"You find the extremes in the foreign exchange market," says Walter Hoadley, chief economist of the Bank of America. "The trader mentality of twenty seconds and the theorist mentality of thirty years. And the real world is somewhere in between."

Carter's November 1 initiative found the market on balance deeply oversold—dealers had contracts to deliver dollars (mostly to governments and central banks) well in excess of their contracts to receive them. And some of the contracts for the dealers to receive dollars represented an oversold position by their customers, who didn't know exactly where they were going to get those dollars for delivery. Their scramble to assure themselves of dollars to satisfy contracts pushed up the dollar's international value in the days after the U.S. announcement, and the central banks (including the Fed) gleefully made life harder for the speculators by purchasing for their own accounts at key moments of the rise to spring the "bear trap."

Still, there were all those dollars out there, many of them in the hands of people, corporations and LDC central banks which saw the improvements in the dollar's exchange rate as a God-given opportunity to get out. Soon after the November 1 announcement, Blumenthal made a trip to the Gulf to point out to the sheikhs how much better off they were with the dollar healthy again, and returned home with statements that the next increase in oil prices would be modest. When the increase turned out to be large (14.5 percent in stages for 1979—not really surprising, considering that in 1977–78, as in 1972–73, the Western nations had flooded the world with money that was up for grabs), the dollar suffered because traders feared they had been deceived again. Significantly, the upheavals in Iran, the sort of thing that once might have triggered a flight to political stability in the United States, acted initially as a depressant on the dollar.

In December 1978, the dollar lost about half of its November gains, and a fair fraction of Carter's $30 billion support fund had to be spent—a source in Britain who is in a position to know says that counting some unpublicized guarantees, the total was over $9 billion at its peak; the official figures (Treasury and the Fed, interestingly, put out two different sets of numbers) indicated less than $7 billion. A first large issue of D-mark-denominated Treasury paper was sold (very easily: the coupon rate was set almost two percentage points higher than what large borrowers had to pay the banks for marks, allowing what looked like a fat safe return, though the profits slimmed down considerably in 1979, when bank interest rates rose as part of the Germans' renewed fight against inflation).

Then the market turned decisively. In January, the "oversold" positions from October on the typical ninety-day forward contract had to be bought in. ("People had *terrific* losses," Emminger said with great satisfaction.) German manufacturers with Iranian contracts had sold their anticipated dollar receipts in the forward market, and in the absence of the receipts had to scare up dollars. In March, when the forward contracts written during the December slump had to be paid off, it developed that surprising numbers of Japanese banks and traders had sold the dollar short and were on the hook. But the biggest single element, beyond doubt, was the oil price rise, which once again, as in December 1973, started a rush for dollars to pay for the oil.

Once it became credible that the dollar would stop dropping (at least for a while), the interest rates in the dollar markets became irresistibly attractive. For those who believed the dollar would actually rise against foreign currencies, it was an imperative of profit to keep one's assets in the higher-yielding currency, especially if one could borrow in the lower-interest currency. "Leads and lags" began benefiting instead of punishing the dollar. Foreign governments sold billions of dollars worth of U.S. Treasuries to meet the private demand for dollars; the Fed paid off most of the outstanding swaps; the Treasury accumulated foreign currencies, intervening to brake the dollar's rise.

By spring 1979, roughly half the dollar's losses of 1978 had been recouped, and for the first quarter there was a $20 billion plus for the United States on the "errors and omissions" line. In

April and May, both the Fed and the foreign central banks were selling dollars for other currencies virtually every day, to keep the dollar from rising too fast. U.S. Treasury bills held by the Fed for foreign owners dropped by $40 billion from late 1978 to mid-1979. All the swap lines were closed out, at a profit to the Treasury and the Fed; and the last of the Swiss-franc Roosa bonds were finally paid off.

But the appearance was deceptive. The dollars acquired by private holders from governments (at rising prices in the exchange markets) did not stay in the United States: they went into the Eurodollar banks. Some of these dollars were employed there to help finance third countries' oil purchases. Others—more than $15 billion worth—made a round trip and returned to America as loans to the home office from the foreign branches of American banks—the "Eurodollar deposits" so conveniently freed from reserve requirements in August 1978. The hot money had been reconstituted and would be available out there for renewed attack when the dollar next began to fall behind the pack.

There are fashions in currency valuation as in everything else. In 1978, speculators were looking at trade deficits, anticipated inflation rates, and apparent political will (and capacity) to manage domestic economic difficulties. On these criteria, the world in 1978 liked the D-mark, the yen, the Swiss franc, the Austrian schilling and (once the left-wing political threat was beaten back in March) the French franc. On these criteria, the world then distrusted the dollar, the Italian lira, the Danish kroner, and the Canadian dollar.

In 1979, fashions changed, and for a while the speculators were looking at nothing more than the height of interest rates. "You can understand what's wrong with the world," a central banker said in April 1979, "when you realize that the strong currencies this spring are the dollar, the lira, the Danish kroner and the pound." The governments of the industrial democracies were reported to be seeking stability in the exchanges (i.e., everybody was taking advice from the Bundesbank). If exchange rates were going to be more or less stable, then the places to borrow were

THE FATE OF THE DOLLAR

Switzerland (which was trying to export money as a way to fight inflation), Japan (holding down its payments surplus for political reasons), and Germany. The place to park the money was the dollar, for which borrowers would pay interest rates more than double those paid by mark or yen borrowers, more than six times those paid by borrowers of Swiss francs.

Houses built on such foundations will not stand. In the second half of June 1979, the fact that the dollar was still fragile was suddenly (and to many shockingly) demonstrated. The American economy had begun to turn down, and interest rates appeared to be softening despite double-digit inflation; and bungling by the Energy Department in the management of the fuel crisis had once again cast doubt not only on the competence of the incumbent administration but on the capacity of an American government structured into isolated mission-centered bureaucracies. Interest rates were moving up in Germany and Japan in response to rising domestic price levels. The Arabs, swimming in dollars after the rapid run-up of oil prices, had indicated that they planned to "diversify" their holdings. There were rumors of renewed war in the Middle East as the Syrians considered their options in the conflict between Israel and the Palestinian terrorists based in Lebanese camps. Off on the horizon, the stability of the European Monetary System in its first months seemed to presage the possibility of oil sales denominated in Ecu rather than in dollars. The convergence of these concerns sent the dollar skidding (down 3 percent in one week against the yen, mark, pound, Swiss and French francs) despite intervention by American and foreign authorities that ran to as much as half a billion dollars a day.

Further increases in OPEC prices in June 1979 failed to generate the customary improvement in the status of the dollar (partly because the oil companies had anticipated the jump, acquiring extra dollars through the spring); the visible inconsequence of another of those ridiculous Economic Summit meetings at the end of the month, in Tokyo, did generate the customary distrust of American government and policy. This distrust was then deepened drastically by President Carter's disappearance to the mountaintop of Camp David, his reappearance with a highly controversial production-oriented government-dominated energy program unfortunately presented as a consensus statement, and then his dismissal from his cabinet of Blumenthal and Energy Secretary James Schlesinger, known to be advocates of gas and oil price decontrol, the only energy program foreign governments could take seriously. Panic conditions not unlike those of October 1978 reappeared in the exchange markets, though now the flight was mostly to the pound, invigorated by the rapid growth of North Sea oil production and the financial stringencies the new Tory government was beginning to impose on the British economy.

The markets steadied briefly when William Miller was moved out of his immediately influential, operating position at the Federal Reserve Board to a more policy-oriented and less independent job as Treasury Secretary, to which he was better suited by temperament and in which his increasingly obvious limitations would do less harm. Then Miller in his first statement as Secretary-designate suggested that the yen was undervalued and should rise with relation to the dollar, thus indicating that neither he nor the Treasury had learned much from the experience of the previous two years—and the rumor arose that David Rockefeller, who is not greatly admired by his fellow bankers in America or elsewhere, would become the new Chairman of the Federal Reserve Board. The price of gold passed $300 an ounce.

The Federal Reserve Bank of New York, as agent for the Federal Reserve System and the Treasury, sold marks to buy dollars in all the world's markets, spending every pfennig of the foreign exchange acquired in the brief springtime of the dollar's strength, and taking on new swap debts of more than $2 billion at the Bundesbank (plus some tens of millions from the Swiss). In February 1978, the expenditure of $750 million in marks in ten days had been considered extraordinary by all participants; in mid-July 1979, American purchases of marks ran as high as *$500 million a day*. And the markets would not stabilize.

Once again, alarming reports from ambassadors abroad

303

flooded into Washington; the international banks brought pressure on the Treasury and the White House; and Arthur Burns from his vacation retreat in Vermont raised specters before the eyes of businessmen and politicians who had access to the President. In the teeth of reports that the Gross National Product had declined in the second quarter, the Fed moved to raise interest rates to hold short-term capital in the country—and Carter appointed as the new Chairman Paul Volcker, president of the New York Federal Reserve Bank, who had been the firmest and loudest voice for monetary restraint and high interest rates on the System's Open Market Committee.

Rarely can a man have been worth so much cash money to his country as Paul Volcker was in the first week after his appointment. Down more than six percent against the mark since the beginning of June, the dollar regained nearly half of its losses in the last week of July, and $7 billion of Treasury paper was sold at an interest rate at least 1/4 of 1 percent lower than would have been required in the absence of this appointment. The extent to which the Carter administration had sought the man rather than the man seeking the job was made evident in Volcker's hard-line statements on the need to reduce inflation "quickly," both at press conferences and in his confirmation hearings before the Senate Banking Committee (where, of course, he was a familiar figure from his time as Under Secretary for Monetary Affairs in the Nixon administration).

Miller, still talking, toed the new line with a statement that the United States would not permit the exchange value of the dollar to drop further under any circumstances (contradicting his assertion a few days before that the dollar should fall vis-à-vis the yen). The only sour note in the orchestration was a report from Henry Reuss's committee to the effect that high interest rates were not slowing inflation and would lift unemployment, and that it was bad policy to postpone "exchange-rate adjustments" by inviting short-term capital flows. The markets perceived that on the short time horizon, at least, Reuss was out of step with American policy.

Volcker's honeymoon, however, lasted only a little more than a month. The Europeans returning from their August vacations found Congress back in session, not terribly interested in the President's (or any other) energy program, talking idly about tax cuts to relieve the anticipated recession, really excited only about the putative candidacy of Edward Kennedy. Moreover, while Volcker's Fed was raising interest rates rapidly, all the measured money supplies were still going up at a fast clip, and, if past experience was any guide, some fraction of those increased M's would spill out into demand for foreign currencies. Suddenly, rising American interest rates no longer drew inflows of short-term capital. In September, the dollar weakened dramatically against the currencies of the European Monetary System—and against gold.

Publicly, the United States was unconcerned. (Treasury Secretary Miller professed himself "amused.") Out in the markets, though, through nominee banks all over the world, the Fed was spending the proceeds of the Carter bonds and marshalling swap lines to prevent a recurrence of the snowballing descent that had forced the President's hand on November 1, 1978. But the intervention system had an Achilles heel in the gold market, which had been inadvertently exposed by the Swiss decision of the previous October to break the link between the franc and gold. If the central banks had the power to prevent the rise of the European currencies against the dollar, holders of dollars who wanted out could park their funds in gold. A speculative burst in the gold market pushed the price near $400 an ounce.

Both the Treasury and the Fed refused to regard the panic in the gold market as a monetary phenomenon. Not only the United States, but the International Monetary Fund in the Second Amendment to its Articles had officially "demonetized" gold. The American gold reserve of 265 million ounces was officially a stockpile like, say, the stockpile of tin; when the Treasury held monthly auctions of that gold (cut back in the spring to 750,000 ounces from the 1.5 million ounces announced on November 1, 1978), it was no different from any other commodity sale. Certainly the auctions were not (heaven forfend!) a settlement of an international payments deficit through the transfer of reserve assets—though that was, of course, how the Europeans saw them. "Since there's no indication that central banks are involved in the buying," the Treasury's Lisle Widman told a *Time* magazine correspondent who asked about the gold frenzy, "we're not really concerned. This is the world of speculators . . ."

But if the world's central banks weren't buying gold (and some authorities, notably Edward M. Bernstein, thinks they were), they certainly weren't *selling* gold. Almost without exception, the nations of the world kept some of the reserves for their currencies and central banks in the form of gold. In the European Monetary System, 20 percent of the funds contributed to the reserves of the group as a whole were by treaty to be paid in gold. In total, the central banks and monetary authorities in mid-1979 held an admitted 1.187 billion ounces of gold.

Each nation valued its gold hoard its own way, from the derisory $42.22 per ounce the United States has imposed on itself by law to the 80 percent or so of recent market prices which is common procedure in French-speaking countries. Most of the world's central banks had made up for their losses on their dollar holdings in 1978 by revaluing upward the gold reserves on their books. ("The difference between gold and tin as commodities," said Geoffrey Bell of the British banking house of J. H. Schroder, director of the new Rockefeller study of the monetary system, "is that central banks don't hold their reserves in tin.") Valued at two-thirds of market price in mid-September 1979, the central banks' gold holdings amounted to roughly 60 percent of the world's total monetary reserves—and this after a quarter of a century of mounting American deficits which left dollars scattered all over the place.

But what made the movement into gold a monetary phenomenon was something more subtle: the large buyers of gold (especially the Arabs) had no intention of holding onto the metal forever. They were sophisticated people guided by experienced economists, and sooner or later—probably sooner—they would want to earn interest on their assets. What was obvious to the market if not to the U.S. government, and deeply disturbing, was that the purchasers of gold in the big run-up of 1979 would not be returning to dollars. Gold was a way station for them: they were waiting to see which of the currency options had earned the Gresham's Law preference.

On September 16, the finance ministers of the Big Five—the United States, Germany, Japan, Britain and France—met in Paris, supposedly secretly, to wrestle out a program for monetary cooperation to be adopted at the forthcoming annual meeting of the International Monetary Fund, to be held in Belgrade two weeks later. In an atmosphere of galloping gold prices and impending currency panics, the meeting failed. (Asked the next week whether the United States had changed any of its positions in Paris, Under Secretary Anthony Solomon said, "No." Anyone else change positions? "No.") The three biggest French "private" banks, all government-owned, were of course privy to the fact and dimensions of the failure, and the markets erupted. Having bid gold above any likely sustainable price in the first three days of the week, dollar-holders on Thursday turned their attention to the Swiss franc and the German mark.

Very heavy intervention in the preceding weeks had cost the United States the entire proceeds of the three sales of Carter bonds denominated in marks and francs, and had required the expenditure of large new swap lines. Washington decided that the *real* problem was not the weakness of the dollar but the strength of the mark and franc, and that the proper resolution of the crisis was revaluation by these key currencies. To expend increasingly scarce American reserves to hold down the mark and franc would be "inappropriate." Despite concerns on the trading desk in New York that a drop in the dollar's value vis-à-vis the mark might provoke a tidal wave of flight from American currency—"There is *no* support level for the dollar below one mark, seventy pfennig," said one of the most experienced and important actors in the market—the Treasury ordered the Fed to cease its purchases of marks and francs.

Volcker at this moment put a foot wrong, forcing an increase in the Federal Reserve discount rate against the publicly announced opposition of three of seven Governors. Discount rate increases have a symbolic rather than a real effect on American markets (even when they are borrowing heavily at the discount window, banks raise thirty times as much money in the Fed Funds market as they borrow directly from the Fed). The symbolic significance of a split vote was far greater than the significance of the increase itself—especially when Congressman Reuss and Senator Lloyd Bentsen, Chairman of the Joint Economic Committee, took the occasion to advise Volcker that interest rates had gone as high as they should go.

On September 19, the dollar in one day lost 2 percent of its exchange value against the Swiss franc and the currencies of the D-mark bloc; even the weak Japanese yen rose by 1 percent, sympathetically. The Germans and Swiss pumped out marks and francs—immense quantities, because only their intervention kept the other EMS currencies rising in tandem with the mark. (The Germans probably bought more French francs than dollars in the market the week of September 17.) Over the weekend of September 23, the mark was revalued by 2 percent against its companions in the European Monetary System (5 percent against the suffering Danish krone), and an announcement was made that the EMS central banks would cooperate closely "with the monetary authorities of third countries" to maintain the new parities. Of course.

1

In May 1979, Otmar Emminger had proclaimed more or less ex cathedra that if the dollar again went into a nosedive, the Bundesbank would do little to help maintain its exchange value. In July, shrugging off an appeal from OECD, he raised the German discount rate by a full percentage point in the face of what looked like an accelerating decline in the dollar. He had his reasons. In 1978, both the Germans and the Swiss had vastly expanded their money supplies in the course of acquiring the dollars others were reluctant to keep. A theory had supported this activity: because the effective "money supply" of a country is quantity times velocity, increases in the quantity the government produces will not produce inflationary effects if velocity slows down at the same time. When foreigners are acquiring a currency for reserve purposes rather than for spending—socking that currency away pursuant to the dictates of Gresham's Law—its circulation is likely to slow down, mitigating and perhaps even eliminating the inflationary effects of expanded numbers.

By making it more difficult for foreigners to inject the newly created money into the domestic economy (for example, by forbidding foreign ownership of local securities, by imposing the "bardepot" or a negative interest rate on foreign-owned deposits in domestic banks), the authorities can apply a brake of unknown frictional force to velocity of circulation. In 1977 and 1978 the Bundesbank overshot its monetary growth targets by roughly one half, and until the end of 1978 showed no ill effects for it in the price indices. It was on such a theory that Leutwiler printed $4.5 billion of Swiss francs in three days in October 1978, to restore the cross-rate between the mark and the franc to bearable levels.

But in the first half of 1979, both Switzerland and Germany began to experience much higher inflation than the populace of either country is prepared to bear. The natural scapegoat was the previous year's overexpansion of monetary quantities—indeed, that expansion was probably not just the scapegoat, but the real villain. When the dollar came under attack again in July 1979, then, the European central banks were reluctant to defend it, and though there was "coordination" with the Europeans the Fed had to push the stone back up the hill pretty much by itself. At first the Carter administration had refused to intervene at all in the markets (except, perhaps, to "correct disorderly conditions"); then the United States had begun to stabilize exchange rates in the New York market; now, with great wear and tear on everyone, the Fed was working with nominees everywhere in the world, buying dollars in Hong Kong and Singapore, Bahrain, Zurich, Frankfurt, and London, as well as on the home territory.

THE FATE OF THE DOLLAR

The crisis in September had forced the European central banks back into the markets in a big way: the new policy, too, had failed. Once again, at considerable risk to their domestic anti-inflation programs, the Germans and the Swiss had been forced to pour money into the world to keep their currencies convertible at a price their exporters would live with. "The great wheel" of international money, as Adam Smith called it, had turned full circle; the need to keep it going had once again overwhelmed concern about the direction it had taken.

Emminger's threat had implied a willingness to witness the abandonment of the dollar as the world's reserve, vehicle, and intervention currency. Nobody will long use as a reserve a store of value that can rapidly lose purchasing power at any moment. But it is by no means clear that this option really exists—that governments and central banks, even in joint maneuver across the face of the globe, can determine which currencies will have which international functions. The Swiss, the Germans, and the Japanese have all fought tenaciously to prevent the use of their currencies as alternatives to the dollar, but through the 1970s the franc, the D-mark and the yen were steadily taken into central bank portfolios as reserves.

Markets will ultimately decide what currency or currencies serve reserve and vehicle functions. West Germany can force these markets to abandon the dollar (so can Saudi Arabia) by making conditions so chaotic that business can no longer be done. But where does the world go then? "To the moon?" asked Zijlstra of the Netherlands Bank. Is *any* domestic consequence from German efforts to prop the dollar really going to be as damaging *to Germans* as the collapse of the dollar-based trading system in which Germany has become the largest exporter? If not, can the Germans in a crunch be anything but conservators of the dollar?

The answers to those questions are obvious, but two other questions arise. Given that private markets determine which currencies will serve which purposes, can the Germans, even in concert with the Americans, the Japanese, and the other Common Market nations, really preserve the centrality of the dollar if the private markets reject it? The authoritative answer is no, provided by a central banker in a position to know (who would not enjoy being named in this context). "If the markets now decide the dollar has had it," he said in late spring 1979, "they will simply overwhelm central bank intervention."

The other question is what *can* be rolled into place to substitute for the dollar—and to this question no answer has been found. The failure of private or governmental enterprise to create a substitute for the dollar was in 1979 the greatest single source of the currency's strength, but also over the longer term the greatest cause of its weakness. Triffin had said it all, back in 1959.

2

South Korea was the best economic success story of the 1970s, with GNP, exports, and imports doubling every six years or so. The South Koreans earn yen and dollars through the sale of textiles, electronic components, cheap objets d'art (to the Japanese) and toys (to the Americans). They earn Saudi riyals through the design, management and staffing of big construction projects in the Persian Gulf. Except that the Saudis actually pay in dollars (of which they have a bagful), there would be no point to paying in riyals because the Koreans would immediately convert them. There are no money markets in which the riyal can be lent or invested because the payment of interest is un-Arabian. There are no Moslems in South Korea to demand riyals for their trip to Mecca. And Saudi Arabia exports nothing but oil, which is paid for not in riyals, but in dollars.

The riyal, then, is not a viable reserve currency for South Korea (it may be for Yemen)—but both the yen and the dollar are viable. If the Koreans want to buy beef from Australia, they can use yen just about as conveniently as they can use U.S. dollars—the Bank of New South Wales will not demand that a Korean customer convert his yen to American dollars before he can acquire Australian dollars. Anyway, for practical purposes, the yen and the dollar are immediately convertible to each other without restriction in money markets throughout the world. Interest can be earned on yen: the immense deficits of the Japanese government are funded by the sale of bonds (mostly longer-term instruments which sop up savings, rather than short-term instruments that can inflate the money supply). The Japanese do not encourage foreign holdings of such paper, but it would be available to the South Korean central bank if desired.

Still, the South Koreans keep their reserves overwhelmingly in dollars. The reasons are various. The market for dollar-denominated debt instruments is much deeper and broader than the market for yen-denominated paper—there is simply no problem about buying or selling hundreds of millions of dollars of U.S. Treasury bills in a single telephone call. (After all, the U.S. national debt is represented by roughly $600 billion of salable paper.) There are always sellers and always buyers of huge quantities, and very large transactions don't move prices much. Moreover, the U.S. market makes no distinction between foreign and domestic customers, while the Bank of Japan keeps an eye on all foreign-owned bank deposits and bond holdings and can change the rules at any time. The Koreans have long-standing cultural-political difficulties with Japan, which was the occupying power—and oppressor—of Korea for forty years of this century. And the Koreans are dependent on the United States for military protection.

Still, the fact remains that in October 1978, the Korean dollar holdings were worth about 20 percent less in terms of yen than they had been worth at the beginning of that year. (Conversely, if the Koreans had been holding their reserves in yen, they would have been worth 25 percent more dollars.) By mid-1979, the balance had been restored; as against the yen, the dollar had regained its value. But any indication that the dollar might collapse again would be a powerful inducement for the Koreans to switch their reserves from dollar-denominated to yen-denominated paper. And their sale of dollars for yen in the exchange markets would help depress the dollar, making the prophecy self-reinforcing—which is one of the reasons exchange markets in an era of floating rates don't work the way the theories predicted.

Cross the Pacific and the Andes now to Brazil, another country with hypercharged economic growth. Brazil earns a wide variety of foreign currencies through the sale of coffee, iron, rubber, oranges, diamonds, soybeans (the Japanese put the Brazilians into the soybean business in a big way after President Richard Nixon briefly embargoed the export of this Japanese staple from the United States in an effort to break a bubble in prices in the soybean futures markets). Here the cultural-political factors run the other way, with traditions of resentment of the United States. Brazil has long had close commercial and cultural ties with Germany and France; and in the 1970s the German influence on Brazilian trade grew increasingly strong. The Volkswagen (locally assembled) is the Brazilian car, and it is to Germany rather than the United States that Brazil looked when shopping for nuclear reactors to reduce its dependence on imported oil.

Having wavered between sterling and the dollar through the interwar period, Brazil in the 1950s and 1960s kept its reserves all but exclusively in dollars. But the volume of its trade with Germany makes the mark a viable alternative, provided ways can be found to purchase German government paper and earn interest on deposits in German banks. In 1978, Brazil "diversified" substantially out of dollars by speculative means—borrowing heavily to secure dollars from the Eurobanks, and converting the proceeds to D-marks.

Most of the former French colonies have always been part of a "franc bloc," keeping their reserves in French currency and doing their banking through Paris. Right after the war, of course, most of the British Commonwealth, Iran and the Gulf sheikhdoms, Greece, Egypt, and others kept their reserves in sterling—indeed, there is still money from a "sterling bloc" on deposit in Britain, serving reserve functions for countries like Nigeria, Iraq, Kuwait, India, and Malaysia. East European countries were expected to keep their reserves in "transferable rubles," though in the 1970s they became dollar borrowers and holders of both dollars and marks. As noted some chapters back, countries like the Netherlands, France, and Switzerland have always liked to keep at least half of their reserves in gold—and at least 20 percent of the reserves backing the European Monetary System were contributed in gold (which in fall 1979, after the explosive rise in the gold market, worked out to 60 percent of the value of the reserve fund), though in theory gold is now and forever "demonetized." And then there are the Special Drawing Rights of the International Monetary Fund, on which the Fund—using the earnings on its holdings of all currencies—will pay interest at a rate four-fifths that of the weighted average of rates in the United States, Britain, Germany, France, and Japan.

"A reserve currency," says an expert at the International Monetary Fund, "is any currency accepted as such by the country holding it and the countries with which it trades." The events of the 1970s have in fact created an international monetary system with multiple reserve currencies. There is probably nothing new about this. Historians have stressed the centrality of the London market and the pound in the nineteenth century, but there was always a franc bloc that included not only the French colonies and protectorates in Africa and Asia but also those parts of Eastern Europe that were self-governing—and Czarist Russia was as likely to do its banking business in Paris as in London. In the early years of this century, the financial markets of Berlin grew to the point where the Reichsmark became a currency in international use. In the 1920s, the dollar and the pound were coexisting reserve currencies worldwide, and after its stabilization by Poincaré, the gold franc regained much of its prewar role. What may seem peculiar to future historians is not the emerging multicurrency reserves of today but the overweening hegemony of the dollar in the period 1945–68.

But the earlier systems were built on groupings of geographical continuity and colonial possession. They had an international unit of account through which all transactions between the blocs could pass (specified weights of gold and silver). They were operated in an era when international trade formed a far smaller component in national economies, when governments were far less pervasive in societies, when banks provided a far smaller portion of the money supply, when communications were slow or limited in content (or both).

What gave the dollar its supremacy was the preponderant position of the American economy in world trade, the stability of the American currency in its purchasing power, and the fact that the dollar really was "money" in Vespasian's sense—like gold, it was no respecter of persons or nations: it didn't smell. All other currencies were national properties, to be used by foreigners only under national restrictions, but in the United States prior to 1963, all dollar holders or dollar borrowers were equal. And when the Kennedy administration imposed its tiny dollop of capital controls in the form of an Interest Equalization Tax on securities sales by foreigners, the worldwide banking systems made possible by telecommunications created a dollar market abroad, beyond the reach of the American authorities.

Today only the third of these conditions still serves the dollar. West Germany has surpassed the United States in the value of its foreign trade, and Japan will do so soon. The purchasing power of the dollar has rapidly eroded through the 1970s, with no end in sight. But the American capital markets, freed from all controls by the Nixon administration in 1974, are still open to foreign use as no other capital markets in the world. Meanwhile, the closely linked, unsupervised offshore dollar market has become the most active financial market in history, with something like $15 *trillion* a year crossing back and forth through the computer in the basement of the New York Clearing House that every day balances the dollar books of the international banks.

What the dollar has going for it internationally, then, is very simply its utility. Quite apart from all the questions that agitated the meetings in 1972–74 to reform the international monetary system, the SDR cannot substitute for the dollar because impossible institutional change would be required at the IMF, the central banks and the private banks. The development of the Ecu in this direction would require years of experiment in denominating bank loans and deposits in an artificial unit that businessmen cannot spend anywhere. One can imagine an artificial international currency that could perform the functions now performed by the Eurodollar—the French engineer and new town developer Jacques Riboud, for example, has worked through a program for a "Eurostable," a unit of account *and of payment* that would maintain a level purchasing power in its exchange rate with the currencies of all the countries in which banks were permitted to create it. But the authorities (and the bankers) will have to get much more scared than they are now before so drastic an innovation can be seriously considered.

The multicurrency reserve system we now have is an unending tug of war between Gresham's Law preferences for "strong" currencies as the best long-term investment and utilitarian preferences for the dollar as the most usable currency for today's transactions. To maintain such a system requires an interest-rate differential that keeps the reward to lenders and the cost of dollars to borrowers higher than it might be if only American domestic needs were considered.

Whether such dedication to maintaining the value of the dollar will last—whether, indeed, there can be any politically acceptable (as opposed to market-dictated) solution to the American dilemma—remains uncertain. The current account deficit had been the weight pushing the dollar down in 1977–78, and it was still there in 1979—though the *reported* deficit was reduced in the Commerce Department figures by a new piece of obfuscation worthy of Lyndon Johnson himself. (Prior to 1979, the foreign earnings of U.S. international corporations had been credited to the plus side of the services account only when the money was repatriated; starting in 1979, profits abroad were taken into American receipts when earned, even if the money was never converted to dollars but immediately reinvested on the spot by the foreign subsidiary. "I wonder," said Edward Bernstein, "who they think they're kidding.)

Though investment by foreigners in the United States was still expanding in 1979, drawn by the bargain prices of a still-undervalued currency, the deficit in capital flows persisted. On Wall Street, hungry brokerage houses and increasing numbers of bank-trusteed pension funds had begun seeking to diversify their customers' and beneficiaries' investments through the purchase of foreign securities. Official reports for the first quarter of 1979 indicated growing direct investment (especially in Europe) by American-based multinational corporations. Profits, it seems, were higher in Europe.

As the American economy moved toward recession in the spring, Miller as Federal Reserve Board Chairman had urged Congress to keep the fiscal ship on an even keel, permitting monetary policy to stimulate and constrain. Unconscious of the degree to which the inflow of funds from the Eurobanks during the high interest rate period had frustrated the Fed's attempts to restrict credit expansion in the boom (none of the statistical aggregates that purport to measure the various "M" 's for Money included the Eurodollar deposits by branches of American banks), Miller had been equally unconscious of the degree to which a collapsing dollar, undermined by the flight of money to higher yields abroad, would make it impossible for the Fed to stimulate the economy out of a slump through its traditional procedures. Paul Volcker is exquisitely conscious of such problems, having lived with them since George Champion summoned him to the president's office at Chase in 1957. That was why the markets reacted so enthusiastically when Volcker took over the Chairman's job.

But personality and understanding, as the events of September demonstrated, can carry a currency so far and no farther. Essentially, what the United States was counting on to carry the dollar in the early part of the 1980s was a replay of the 1975 recession. During that downturn, the reduction of demand for foreign goods (coupled with enormous sales of agricultural produce abroad) yielded a large current account surplus for the United States, eliminating the pressure on the dollar in the exchanges and permitting a major reduction in interest rates without a major drain of dollars. Economic history has not been repeating itself in recent years, however, either as tragedy or as farce. (Each time around, we seem to get a different tragedy followed by a different farce.) In the early 1980s, the burden on the American balance of payments from the cost of oil imports is going to be extremely heavy. If sizable deficits persist through a severe American recession, the international monetary system may be subject to strains it cannot possibly withstand.

3

Before this storm breaks, it would be wise to make what technical changes are possible to reduce the role of the dollar in international markets. Some significant part of the weakness of the dollar—and thus of the international monetary system—results from the abuse of the world's easy access to American financial markets. Bank lending creates money. If most of the world's trade and investment are financed through loans denominated in dollars, there will ultimately be a global oversupply. The problem existed but was not troublesome in the 1960s because the dollars could be *used* only for one of two purposes: the maintenance of the dollar-based foreign financial system itself, or expenditures in the United States. (Significantly, one of the few dollar-denominated markets outside the United States was the London gold market.) Both those conditions disappeared in the 1970s, and the problem is now central.

The great drop in the demand for dollars to run the financial system is the result of technological change. As late as the 1960s, the biggest European banks were still entering their business in paper ledgers, with ranks of clerks in green eyeshades, and they moved their paper around through the mails. The need for transaction balances was heavy, and great quantitites of exported dollars were immobilized as necessary grease for the system. By the mid-1970s any bank large enough to participate in Eurolending was fully computerized, with money represented as blips on tape and moving over wires (or via satellite) to the computers of the fellow on the other side of the transaction. Though many customer transactions still required a look at a piece of paper that had to be physically transported, "cash management" experts had moved into Europe as into the remote corners of the United States, teaching the wonders of payable-through drafts, zero-balance banking, lock boxes, automatic transfer, and the like. The need for privately held dollars to keep the system functioning was cut by at least three-quarters and maybe more.

Far more serious, of course, is the growth of foreign markets where commodities are purchased for dollars, thereby creating locations outside the United States where dollars can be spent. Now entire trade transactions can be financed and accomplished without reference to the American economy, and while the dollars created in the process are not really claims on the United States, they look like such to their recipients and—thanks to the heavy involvement of American banks in the interbank process—would have to be validated as such somehow if push came to shove. Over the next years, if everybody does what he says he is going to do, the Chinese will be borrowing massively in dollars for the purpose of purchasing mostly in Japan, Germany, Britain, and France. From the American point of view, that makes no sense at all—it isn't even American banks doing most of the lending. (The first loan actually closed with the Chinese was by Britain's Midland Bank.)

Sooner or later—better sooner—the United States must put an end to this system of easy Eurodollar creation. Today, perhaps 25 percent of the Eurocurrency market is denominated in currencies other than dollars (Euromarks, Euroyen, Eurofrancs, Euroguilders, Eurosterling). That figure has not changed much with the years, which is discouraging, because it means that the increase in Eurodollar lending and borrowing has been more rapid than the increase in loans in other Eurocurrencies as the exchange value of the dollar has declined. The United States, which now plays no larger role than Germany or Japan in world trade, must seek to push the nondollar component in this market to 50 percent or more.

THE FATE OF THE DOLLAR

Almost everyone (the dissenters are concentrated in the executive offices of the international banks) agrees on the need to "control" the Eurodollar market. No doubt the market served the world well in the mid-1970s, and the absence of regulation saved money for borrowers, earned money for lenders (though there can be some disagreement about whether the earnings have truly compensated for the risks, and the books are far from closed). But the dangers are now much too great, starkly revealed by the panicky wash of dollars out of private hands and into official accounts during the massive depreciation of fall 1978, and the reflow out of official holdings to the private market in spring 1979.

Different suggestions have come from different experts at meetings of the Organization for Economic Cooperation and Development, the Bank for International Settlements, the International Monetary Fund and various foundation-sponsored think tanks. (A Rockefeller Foundation study group opened its work in February 1979 with a sad statement by Johannes Witteveen, former managing director of the IMF, that *nobody* has a "clear and complete understanding" of how the present international monetary system really works.)

The American proposals, worked up mostly by Governor Henry Wallich, involve extending the reserve requirements the Fed now imposes on domestic deposits of American banks to *all* deposits in Eurocurrencies in banks of *all* national origins. Each country would police the worldwide operations of its own banks. This system is no longer working very well in the United States, however, and finds few parallels abroad, where authorities normally supervise their banks' lending policies or liquidity ratios rather than sequestering reserves from them. As "borrowed reserves" could be acquired internationally through the London Interbank Market (as they are acquired domestically through the Fed Funds market), it is by no means clear that reserve requirements would restrain lending internationally any more than they have, in recent years, in the United States.

The Germans have suggested that each nation require its banks to maintain minimum capital ratios (the proportion of a bank's liabilities that represent investment in the bank by its owners rather than the bank's borrowings or deposits by its customers), and enforce the requirement against each bank's total worldwide activities. This looks more to the safety of the system—decreasing the likelihood that a major international bank could fail—than to the inflationary potential of offshore lending, but it would exert some constraint on money-creation, too. The French won't have it: their four largest banks are all state-owned and have invisible capital ratios.

The Japanese, in their usual nonassertive way, have called attention to their own established system for policing the foreign-currency operations of their own banks, which involves requiring the banks to fund term loans with term deposits to some ratio set from time to time by the central bank. That ratio has been as high as 100 percent; at this writing in mid-1979 it is 70 percent, but looks likely to climb again in the near future. This suggestion, unfortunately, is anathema to the British, with their long-established system of asset controls (compelling the banks to keep fixed ratios of their loans and investments in short-term money-market instruments)—and, of course, the British are making the money from the fast turnover in the London interbank market.

Nothing will work, in any event, without an IMF "substitution account" to absorb a sizable fraction of the dollars currently on the books of central banks and governments abroad. It is that backup supply of dollars, fluxing and refluxing from and to the private markets, that makes the creation of Eurodollars look so safe to the Eurobanks. In the IMF substitution scheme the central banks would surrender their dollars in return for interest-bearing credits denominated in Special Drawing Rights. The United States would pay interest (originally the thought was that the interest would be in SDRs, too, but the first round of negotiations brought agreement that interest could be paid in dollars), and might under some very long-range program pay off the principal. Further depreciation of the dollar would then produce losses for the United States, which would see the size of its dollar obligations rise; under the present system, depreciation of the dollar produces losses for the foreign holders.

A substitution account (first proposed by the Bank of America in a formal response to the Nixon bombshell of 1971) was placed on the table by Johannes Witteveen as one of his last acts as managing director of the IMF in spring 1978; it was brushed aside as pointless and worthless by Blumenthal. In January 1979, Henry Reuss and Jacob Javits issued a joint statement urging the administration to reconsider, and Blumenthal told the Joint Economic Committee that he *had* reconsidered and the United States was now prepared to negotiate a substitution account. But when the IMF produced a working document as a basis for negotiations, the Treasury found it most unsatisfactory.

The unanswered question in the debate over the substitution account is exactly what assets the United States is prepared to transfer to neutralize—it cannot possibly at this moment pay off—the enormous dollar holdings of the outside world. A substitution account, Treasury Under Secretary Anthony Solomon told the Alpbach Economic Forum in Austria in August 1979, "would have to incorporate an appropriate balancing of the rights and obligations of participants in a wide variety of circumstances, and—a particularly thorny question—an equitable division of any costs arising from its operations." The Paris meeting of finance ministers in September 1979, called to establish a coordinated position that would enable the October meeting of the IMF to place real momentum behind the creation of a substitution account, failed on this issue, provoking the frenzy in the gold market, the revaluation of the D-mark, and further erosion of the world's confidence in the capacity of its governments.

There are informed opponents of the substitution account idea. Until 1979, the Germans distrusted it as an American scheme to make possible continuing American deficits—but eventually the Bundesbank decided that this risk had to be taken to maintain the hope that the mark would not be used by the world as a reserve currency alternative to the dollar. The New York Fed would rather see the dollar stay the sole reserve, but held "in what the

Swiss call 'firm hands.' " But no hands are that firm any more—and there are $200 billion in the infirm hands of the LDCs. "When you get to $200 billion," Geoffrey Bell comments sagely, "we're talking about real money."

In any event, the indirect benefits to the United States from the creation of a large substitution account far exceed the costs Solomon is calculating. Once a substitution account is in place and adequately filled with money no longer available to the market, the United States could regain control of its currency simply by prohibiting American banks and their foreign branches from lending in any overseas market for any period shorter than, say, thirty days. This would knock out the assured source of dollars for the London interbank market, deprive the Eurodollar system of its homemade private lender of last resort, and force both wider spreads and new caution in London and Luxembourg.

Defending the unregulated Euromarket, Dennis Weatherstone of Morgan Guaranty told the first meeting of a Rockefeller Brothers study group on international finance that "in the absence of this market a large portion of world credit demand would have been satisfied through other channels, including foreign lending by parent banks in domestic currencies." That's the ticket: let's bring the boys home. If all the statements are true about how the deposits in the Euromarket are longer term than deposits at home, the elimination of overnight and one-week lending from New York shouldn't even cause much disruption.

Loans for foreigners could still be financed through an overnight market—the Fed Funds market—*in* New York. But the American monetary authorities would know what was being done with their dollar, and could through their normal open market operations exercise the sort of influence a central bank is supposed to have over the creation and use of its nation's currency. The hunch here is that an international dollar market directly rather than (as now) indirectly linked to the New York market would be considerably less frenetic than what we have experienced—it is hard to imagine, for example, an increase of $21.5 billion of loans to foreign banks and branches and foreign governments *in a single quarter* (which is what happened in the fourth quarter of 1978) if all the dealing had to be open and aboveboard in the United States. As a bonus, this sort of control would give the Eurobanks new reasons to hunt up marks, yen and Swiss francs (perhaps pounds and French francs, too) as sources of funds for loans.

Some means must be found to make the markets realize in more than a speculative way that the world has moved into an age of multiple currency reserves. Such a system may be undesirable—C. Fred Bergsten, the Assistant Secretary of Treasury for International Monetary Affairs in the Carter administration, has said it is "the worst possible approach to reform." We must not, Anthony Solomon said at Alpbach, "fall by default into an unregulated multiple currency system." But, as Benjamin Cohen of the Fletcher School responded, "It profits little . . . to denounce what is unavoidable."

4

The Belgrade meeting of the IMF in October 1979 marked the end of the dollar's dominion over the world's currency markets— and of American leadership in international monetary affairs. On their way to Belgrade, Volcker and Miller had stopped in Germany to lunch with their opposite numbers, and had found themselves essentially receiving instructions rather than negotiating a compromise. Doubtless with the approval of their European allies—and of the Arabs—the Germans told their visitors that the world would no longer permit the export of American inflation, that the $500 million worth of marks the Germans had printed to help the dollar stay above water the previous week was the last such infusion of help the Americans could expect, that the problem was now one for the United States to solve in the only way it could be solved, by suppressing demand in the American economy until prices began stabilizing. A previously scheduled press conference to follow the lunch was cancelled, though Under Secretary Solomon met with the press more casually and told them that it's always darkest just before the dawn.

At Belgrade, the American representatives found themselves under sustained and universal attack. Failing American agreement to accept the exchange-rate risk for a substitution account in SDRs, the rest of the world was unwilling to give even a meaningless "approval in principle" for the idea. American efforts to blame the Arabs or the Germans for the disarray in the gold and currency markets were simply laughed aside. The twin facts of life were that the United States through domestic controls kept the price of gasoline to American consumers at roughly half the level in the rest of the world, and that American interest rates were actually below the rate of inflation in the United States. All the statistical data said that Americans were losing faith in their own currency. The society had gone debt-happy: individuals, corporations and governments were taking on debt at a dizzying pace, and in proportion to their incomes Americans were saving less than one-quarter as much as the Germans or French or Japanese—even less than the British. Under these circumstances, how *could* the rest of the world be expected to hold dollars as reserves?

Volcker took two days of this in Belgrade and then fled, leaving Miller alone to praise the "courage and intelligence" of President Carter's economic policies in his formal address to the meeting. The currency markets stabilized and gold prices began to drop in the face of rumors that a new "dollar support package" was in the making. Clearly, Volcker, returned to Washington, was doing *something*. On Friday, October 5, the markets went into a tailspin as the rumor spread that he had resigned. Though the rumor was denied by Federal Reserve spokesmen as "ridiculous," it is not unlikely that a threat was uttered. Argument and analysis alone could not have created the atmosphere *in terrorem* that persuaded the three Governors who had dissented from a one-half-point rise in the discount rate only two weeks before to go along now in a unanimous vote to raise the discount rate a further full 1 percent—and persuaded the White House to welcome the move.

The discount-rate rise was part of a package that otherwise had virtually no international component. Indeed, one element of it was the restoration of Chairman Martin's reserve requirement on Eurodollar deposits from branches—for the American affiliates of foreign banks as well as for the U.S. banks themselves—which would act to discourage the repatriation of Eurodollars and might weaken the dollar on the exchanges. Taking perhaps a leaf from the German book, Volcker without any formal statement to that effect was saying that domestic considerations would have to take precedence over the foreign exchange markets, that interest-rate increases which merely drew capital flows from abroad would hurt rather than help the campaign to control inflation, and that the Fed was prepared to take foreign-exchange risks over the short run in the interests of a more effective control over credit in the U.S. banking system over the long run. It was an immensely exciting and courageous decision, especially as nobody in the stock market and very few bankers were likely to understand it. President Carter did, though—he answered a question about the Volcker program most intelligently at a press conference three days after its announcement; and, for a wonder, Congressman Reuss was persuaded not to criticize.

Assuming that Volcker had no prearranged quid pro quo from the Europeans (which seemed likely: if he had, some blabbermouth at Treasury would have talked about it), the post-Belgrade package of Federal Reserve actions represented a return to the tough-minded, we-take-care-of-ourselves attitudes that had characterized Connally's operation of the Treasury Department—not, on consideration, a surprising development, because Volcker had been Connally's *eminence grise*. Though the package appeared to be responsive to European demands, it actually raised before the Europeans a collection of rather difficult problems. The reserve on Eurodollar deposits meant that there would be no short-term capital flows to relieve central banks of the need to support the dollar in the markets in the medium term. And another part of the plan—the imposition of reserve requirements on Fed Funds purchased from any source but another member bank of the Federal Reserve System—would disrupt the free and easy concourse

between the London interbank market and the American overnight markets, reducing in effect the liquidity of the Eurodollar
system, which still serves as the common credit source for the European Economic Community.

The entire scheme was a gamble of considerable dimensions. It
might not work domestically, coming into an election year when
politicians hate the idea of anybody hurting for money; it might
not work because the genie of liability management has got out of
the bottle, and the Fed can no longer control through bank reserves the substitution of credit for money at the margin. The
business could simply go abroad. By increasing the reserves
banks must hold on their domestic Certificates of Deposit to 14
percent when the new CD represents an increase in borrowed
funds over the totals on the books in October, the Fed gave the
offshore banking system (where CDs can be offered without any
set-aside for reserves) a very large advantage over the domestic
banking system in soliciting such deposits. A scenario could be
written in which the result of the Fed's action would be a massive
dollar outflow and the transfer of considerable lending activity
from the domestic market to the Eurodollar market (either
directly or through commercial paper). But *American* banks will
have less incentive to play such games—and it is the participation
of the American banks in the London interbank market that
makes possible its expansion.

Though the thrust of the Fed's fall 1979 changes was predominantly domestic—and Volcker used the foreign exchange crisis to
club his opponents into acceptance of domestic proposals they
might otherwise have prevented—there was an underlying message for the rest of the world. As best he can, Volcker intends to
reduce the utility of the dollar internationally. The means to be
employed are quite different from those suggested earlier in this
chapter, but the ends envisaged are not dissimilar.

Implicit in the Volcker program is an acceptance of multiple
reserve currencies as a fact of life, to be taken into account rather
than merely analyzed. If the dollar becomes less useful internationally, it is assumed that the proprietors of marks, yen, French

327

francs, British pounds and Swiss francs will increase the international utility of their currencies in parallel with the growth of their reserve functions. The hope, ultimately, to quote Alexander Lamfalussy, the new chief economist at the Bank for International Settlements, must be that "multiple reserve currencies will force coordination of the economies."

The mechanism by which that coordination can be forced is still not clear, though the run-up of gold prices in fall 1979 (resolving the Triffin dilemma) did open the door to the return of a use of gold as a source of automaticity in international monetary relations. (It is at least arguable—and at the end of a long road I would argue—that a multicurrency reserve system requires an external *numeraire,* which in present conditions can only be gold.) What is entirely clear is that Volcker's domestically-oriented response to international pressures proposes an end to the era in which the United States pretended that the world's problems were its problems and behaved in a way that made its problems the world's problems.

As a deficit country requiring help to finance its imports, the United States can scarcely give the marching orders for the cooperative, negotiated international monetary system that now must be designed. That's fine: we will have enough on our plate in America in the 1980s to exhaust our digestive (let alone our mental or political) capacities.

10 / The Fate of the Dollar

My father administered the German currency reform after the war, for Allied Military Government. I was at the press conference where he announced the new German mark. A reporter said, "What's the backing for this new currency? Where's the gold?" My father said, "There isn't any gold backing. The value of this currency depends on the willingness of the German people to show self-restraint, because they want their money to keep its worth." The reporter shook his head and said, "Never work."

But that's the only backing any currency ever has.

> —Jack Bennett, executive vice-president, Exxon; former Under Secretary of the Treasury

* * *

There has always been a kind of noblesse oblige in the ordinary American's reactions to foreigners. They had nothing *we* needed; their quarrels were not ours; their habits were dirty; their statesmen were unprincipled; their history was bunk. Except (naturally) in Britain, their money was flimsy, funny stuff—paper that tore and coins that would scarcely sink in a fountain. Most of them did not even speak English. Nevertheless, we wished to be nice to them, and in addition to shipping them some of our manufactures and crops, we would accept some of their goods for sale in our markets. There were even a few things—British woolens, French wines, Belgian linen, Dutch cheese, German cameras,

329

Italian olive oil—that we conceded might be better than our own. At least for a while.

Anyone born fifty years ago in the United States—and the leadership of the country is still primarily in the hands of those born before 1930—was conscientiously taught in school that the United States was not *completely* self-sufficient: in addition to tropical products like coffee and bananas and rubber (but we could make that synthetically) there were some rare minerals like manganese and chrome which America had to import. In the 1930s, export promotion was considered a praiseworthy activity because the production of the exports employed workers who might otherwise be without jobs. But the notion that the United States had to import to maintain its standard of living is something very few older Americans find it possible to absorb even after some economic preacher has convinced them that it's true. Even younger Americans rarely have much gut feeling for the idea that the United States is no longer an independent, self-propelled, self-contained economic entity. And the notion that the *dollar* is no longer a dominant currency somehow worth more than others still seems to nearly all Americans like the repeal of a law of nature.

Yet there it is: the United States can no longer write the rules of the game before it agrees to play. We must now trade to survive, like Britain or Japan. And the United States enters this interdependent future with its strength mortgaged by thirty years of policy, charity, folly, arrogance, greed, and incompetence. There is lead to be got out of American shoes and American pants if the United States is to compete in arenas where the race is truly to the swift.

This does not mean that the United States is in any sense "bankrupt" or powerless to protect its interests. Kindleberger's bank still has assets considerably greater than its borrowings—and the domestic economy has assets that can painlessly be sold to foreigners for the dollars they honestly accumulated by selling us all the oil and television sets and automobiles and clothing we consumed without paying for them. ("We need to export securities as well as goods," Douglas Dillon said as long ago as 1963.) But just as official indebtedness must be shrunk through the IMF substitution account, Kindleberger's bank must be cut back in size.

With the improvement of capital markets abroad, the advantages American corporations have enjoyed through their easier access to dollars will be—and should be—diminished. The decline in dollar holdings overseas which is a vital part of international monetary reform will necessarily be accompanied by a reduction of American privately owned assets abroad. This process need not be painful—many American multinational corporations would be happy now to take their money and run—but it wants help. U.S. Ambassador to Austria Milton Wolf has proposed tax inducements to persuade American corporations to repatriate more of their profits and sell off more of their foreign holdings. As in all economic affairs, the carrot is more likely to be effective than the stick.

By the same token, the best way to reduce new American investment abroad is to improve the prospects for profit in American investment at home. The erosion of the dollar abroad has the same causes as the erosion of productivity at home. The costs of overregulation and of taxing the efficient to subsidize the inefficient are felt not only in domestic inflation but in an internationally depreciating currency. Quite apart from all the technical questions—overriding even the concern about the trade deficits—the vacuum under the dollar was formed by the world's loss of faith that American government and political process had the will to stop domestic inflation.

Yet the American institutional structure is strong. The United States has clean and efficient capital markets and long-established, well-conceived government regulation of those markets. What has gone wrong is a generation of neglect of the need for investment, the use of governmental process to achieve public purpose by imposing unacknowledged private costs, a willingness (nay, eagerness) in the academic and political community to beat down what Keynes described as "the animal high spirits of businessmen," and an abuse of the regulatory agencies by interest groups (especially supposed "public interest groups") seeking to use them to achieve missions far removed from their established purposes.

Few Americans understand—few have studied—the institutional apparatus of American government, with its pervasive, delicately balanced systems of "checks and balances." These systems were designed to restrict the power of government and to provide the political equivalent of economic process (a "marketplace of ideas," Justice Holmes called it) to assure that intensities of feeling as well as masses of votes would have standing when government action was contemplated. Such institutions are, almost deliberately, unresponsive to the exigencies of time—and their elephantiasis in the postwar period has increased their sluggishness. In a period of instantaneous communications and the sudden impact of economic decisions from many points on the globe, the American Congress solemnly adopts overall budgets (complete with asserted receipts) for an annual period that will have its midpoint a year from the date of the adoption. All sorts of "impact statements" are demanded before anything new can be done, and the equity jurisdiction of the courts has been expanded to permit judges to enjoin virtually anything they decide they don't like. And then we wonder why our policies are out of phase with reality.

In the Carter administration, confusion was compounded by the failure to understand that the agencies regulating economic activity and advising on government policy are designed to be in conflict with each other, to check and balance, to bring differing viewpoints on questions of great importance to the attention of political leadership. With a kind of consistency that appears planned—though it was really a run of bad luck—President Carter appointed to the leadership of these institutions men whose beliefs and backgrounds gave them attitudes at odds with the positions their agencies were designed to take, and thus with the stream of information and proposals rising to their desks from their own subordinates. The result was to make the economic advice that came to the President essentially trivial, like newspaper editorials, lacking the gravity and force that only institutional experience and support can provide. And this was a President totally unfamiliar with the terms and rationale of economic debate, who needed all the help he could get.

Virtually every senior economic position in government was unsuitably staffed, by men whose high ability made their disagreement with their roles the more debilitating. Richard Cooper as Under Secretary of State for Economic Affairs, for example, had for some years maintained in his academic publications the need for floating exchange rates. ("I've never been a free-floater," he said recently. "My view of floating rates is Churchill's view of democracy—the worst system except for all the others.") But the State Department in American government is a force for stable relations with foreigners, for as little unpredictable change as possible. The research done in the bureaus of economic affairs, which the Under Secretary is supposed to present on the higher levels of government, all tends to denigrate floating rates and advocate a return to some kind of exchange-rate peg. Cooper in council argued against the evidence prepared for his own use, for the very good reason that he disagreed. He quibbled about Carter's November 1 dollar support program (he was out of the country when it was adopted), against the background of a vast sigh of relief through the State Department.

Similarly, the Council of Economic Advisers prepares forecasts for the President of expected economic activity in the private sector, against which plans for government policy should be measured. But President Carter appointed as its chairman Charles Schultze, a man whose experience and interests lay almost entirely in the stage beyond his job—in the analysis of government activity itself. (He had been Lyndon Johnson's budget director.) The result was the damaging mismatch between the economy as predicted by the Council for 1978 and the economy that was actually in being, and that was thus driven beyond its capacities by violently overstimulative government policy.

The institutional position of the Treasury Department had

been fudged by Secretary Michael Blumenthal's immediate pre-
decessors—especially William Simon and George Shultz—who
had injected the Department into economic policy-making to an
unprecedented degree. Treasury's first function is to fund the
government, which gives the Department a split personality,
hoping for a strong currency abroad (to reduce the costs of government activity overseas) and low interest rates at home (to hold
down the burden of servicing the national debt). Blumenthal,
Ph.D. in economics, superbly successful as a trade negotiator and
a businessman, considered himself primarily an economic policy-
maker, and in this role he looked for a depreciated dollar to help
employment, then for high interest rates to control inflation.

At the Office of Management and Budget, the President started
off with Bert Lance, and then moved on to another friend from
Georgia. . . .

The worst problem, however, was at the Federal Reserve System. Here, too, functions had been confused in the previous administrations, because Arthur Burns as Chairman considered
himself a political actor rather than an executive technician with
political accountability. Moreover, the Federal Reserve had become a focal point in the Congress for those who wished to bend
existing institutions of government to serve new and potentially
contradictory functions. But William Miller was a businessman
pure and simple, whose view of money was that it facilitated economic activity. Given the diminishing effectiveness of the tools
available to the Federal Reserve in the performance of its established functions—because the international banks were running
rings around national monetary policy—the arrival of these attitudes in the Chairman's job was little short of disastrous.

1

With the switch from Miller to Volcker in July 1979—forced
on an administration *in extremis*—the institutionally correct attitudes (and skills) came into the Chairman's job. But the confu-

sion of roles in the making of American monetary policy has been building for a long time and has now become almost institutionalized itself. Robert Anderson says that when he took the job as Secretary of the Treasury to President Eisenhower, "I asked myself, What was my *primary* responsibility? And I said, You have got to maintain the value of the currency, because if you don't, you impair the willingness of people to accumulate. And you are responsible for the currencies of the Allied countries." But in fact the Secretary of the Treasury, in the American system, is *not* responsible for the money supply. He is responsible for financing the work of the government and managing the debt. The question of whether he can force the Federal Reserve System to monetize that debt (to purchase the paper itself by creating new money in the banks) was resolved against him in the Accord of 1951 which Anderson himself negotiated. It is quite possible for a government to run large deficits without inflating the currency (the Japanese do it with some regularity), if the paper that represents that deficit is purchased by the public with its savings rather than by the banking system with created deposits.

The idea that a decline in the value of the currency will impair the willingness to accumulate is theoretically correct, but until recently American behavior belied the theory. Inflation led to an *increase* in people's savings, apparently because they hoped to maintain the real value of what they had in the bank. This attitude, extremely helpful to the monetary authorities combatting inflation, was a casualty of the 1970s. Two-thirds of the way through the decade, former Chairman Martin said to Arthur Burns that he was concerned about the savings ratios. Burns demurred with the comment that the numbers looked strong enough. "Yes," Martin replied, "but people aren't saving any more to send their kids to college. They don't think they can do that now. They're saving to buy a piece of land in Virginia. That's a very different kind of savings—you have to keep an eye on the quality of these things, too." And so it proved.

Once all the plausible farmland has been cleared and cultivated, accumulation is a necessary activity for any society that hopes to expand its economic production: without a stream of capital formation, the real value of labor input will decline. (It makes no difference whether the society is capitalist, socialist or fascist: political organization affects the modes of accumulation and the efficiency of allocation, not the need.) But accumulation and capital investment are the aspects of economic life which governments find most difficult to stimulate. Moreover, the benefits of investment by definition lie in the future, and governments in a democracy feel an urgent need to get reelected today. The tendency is always to spend more now, with the hope that some of the money will trickle up into savings and investment.

After a decade of inflation, this "money illusion"—discovered by David Hume more than two centuries ago though generally linked with the name of Keynes—simply doesn't work anymore. Americans now react like Europeans to a general increase in both income and prices, and try to beat inflation by purchasing before the price goes up again, not only reducing their savings but increasing their borrowings. And the "Phillips curve" which purports to show a trade-off between inflation and unemployment doesn't work either. Employment may rise with inflation, but unemployment does not fall, because the labor supply becomes elastic—that is, more people (especially women, obviously) come into the job market, trying to defend the purchasing power of the family's income by adding to its earnings. In any event, Keynesian economics presumes excess savings and underemployed productive resources; it clearly doesn't apply to the situation we face in the United States over the full decade of the 1980s—though there will doubtless be bad, perhaps very bad, years.

The role of the Federal Reserve is to encourage private accumulation by maintaining the value of money. In an interdependent world, this role includes the maintenance of the foreign exchange value of the dollar ("the single most important price in the world, since so many other prices here and abroad are influenced by it," as Paul Volcker said in a speech delivered the day President Carter announced his anti-inflation guidelines). The source of decision making in international monetary operations should be transferred from the Treasury to the Fed. If there are losses, the Fed does not need to seek appropriations (or even explain what happened to the Exchange Stabilization Fund); its huge profits from issuing the currency can easily absorb the losses and are indeed a wholly appropriate source for funding them.

In the system of checks and balances that supports American government, the Fed's constituency is the community of lenders. To affirm the Fed's primary mission of maintaining the value of money does not prevent the government from pumping up the economy; it merely assures public debate on public matters. In the end, the Treasury's ability to issue government paper can overwhelm the central bank's ability to control whatever we wish to call the money supply, if that is what the nation wants.

But it is a great—potentially fatal—mistake to make the Fed the "partner" of the administration. Chairman Martin was right when he said he could take actions to protect the country in 1965 when Henry Fowler was helpless, because Fowler was a subordinate and he wasn't. All over the world, for just these reasons, central banks are kept separate in some degree from the political process. We appoint Governors of the Fed for fourteen-year terms to shoo away politicians. Even Communist countries have found it administratively useful to give at least some insulation to the operations of their central banks.

In the Humphrey-Hawkins bill of 1978, Congress has gone a long way toward the disaster of making the value of the nation's money, the expression of the store of national resources, a function of transient government policies. Those sections should be repealed. The Federal Reserve should be given a goal of maintaining within a margin of perhaps 2 percent to 3 percent the measured purchasing power of the dollar in the home economy. (Martin hit that target on average for nineteen years, under five Presidents.) If that goal is to be altered in any given year, it should be by special resolution of Congress, to place the blame for inflation where it belongs.

Avoidance of deflation is in truth a more important goal than restricting inflation—and can be built into the law. But actually

337

stimulating the economy on the downslope of the business cycle should be the job of the government, not the central bank. (And please God everyone will remember that the stimulus should be timed to mitigate declines and not to accelerate recoveries.)

The central bank must monitor and smooth the impact of government actions in the financial market. This is all but impossible from Washington, which doesn't know from markets. Quite apart from the need to get central bank operations out of that politically poisonous atmosphere—where people who have serious work to do are forever being buzzed by the growing swarms of Presidential and Congressional staff assistants whose sole purpose in life is to get their principals reelected—the Federal Reserve Board for constructive reasons should be moved to New York. And the President and Congress should assure that those appointed to the Fed understand that their function is to preserve the value of the dollar unless specifically instructed otherwise—and that this will often require, in Chairman Martin's charming metaphor, taking away the punch bowl just as the party gets going.

The collection of new reserve requirements and definitions voted by the Board in October 1979 are a serious effort to control inflation, nothing less than a counterrevolution to roll back the credit-creating excesses of the revolution in banking that began in 1960. But counterrevolutions are chancy; and in the end the Fed may have to return to the forms of asset control that it imposed on the banks to head off the threat of hyperinflation in 1951—to regulations that raise down payments on mortgages and shorten terms on car loans, and restrict the use of credit in mergers and take-overs and in stock-market and commodity operations generally. The hunch here is that the Fed will also need new powers to prohibit from time to time loans that carry a variable interest rate, to compel both borrowers and lenders during accelerating economic movement to accept more of the discipline of risk. A government that insures depositors in banks against loss cannot abdicate all responsibility for policing systemic effects of the use of their money. On the evidence of October 1979, Volcker left to his own devices would have the knowledge and imagination to manage this problem without the economic disaster of direct credit allocation by ignorant and unimaginative governments in Washington.

2

Of the changes in attitude and behavior required of Americans to make this mess come out right, these pages are not the place to speak. It is getting to be an oft-told and dreary tale, anyway.

The day these words are being written, another of those Yankelovich studies got publicized, pointing out that Americans are increasingly interested in "self." That's fine, so long as it's understood that a society mostly interested in self isn't going to eat quite so well as it expects, or drive around so much in cars, live in houses with 1600 square feet of living space, go on pleasure trips to far-off places, clean up so much of its air and water, or reduce the numbers of people living in poverty.

In the modern world, where commodities are traded at uniform price all over the globe, one nation lives better than another mostly because its people have skills and organization and capital equipment to multiply the value of the skills. That capital equipment is there because previous inhabitants saved and invested some part of their Gross National Product. If the savings stop, or the government eats them all, the standard of living will decline—and not all the economic stimulus programs or labor contracts in the world can stop the decline. A newspaper columnist pointed out with some anger, also the week of this writing, that the Japanese, who lost the war, somehow "can save 25% of their income." It's not "can"—the average Japanese still lives much less well than the average American—it's "do." If Americans refuse to make provision for their own future, nobody else will do it for them.

There are encouraging signs. The 1979 Report of the Joint Economic Committee "focuses on the underlying issue of the capacity of the economy over the long term"—the first time in twenty years that this group has not stressed programs of demand stimulus or distribution. Foreigners have responded to the undervalued dollar by making investments in America—especially in the Southeast (and in the Southeast, especially in South Carolina, where the populace is rapidly learning to speak German). American exporters, too, did well with the undervalued dollar in early 1979 (though the combination of a still-stimulative federal budget and heavy exports accelerated the American inflation). Walter Hoadley of Bank of America believes that foreign investment will produce an urge for exports more potent than the United States has ever known before: "The foreign investor has an export mentality, expects to export twenty, thirty, forty percent of what he makes in this country. American manufacturers will copy, because they'll be afraid of losing shares of market."

But the country has a long way to go. A senior official of the British Treasury noted recently a special advantage enjoyed by the Germans, the Japanese, and the French: "Having lost the war—the French *think* they did lose the war—they know that nobody owes them a living." In the United States, as in Britain, it is still widely believed that consumption can somehow be separated from production—that it is the union contract or the budget appropriation or the fee schedule rather than the work performed that provides the income.

After a decade of grossly insufficient savings and investment, Americans in the next few years are going to have to get used to living a little less well than they lived before—because either imports must be diminished or domestic production exported to pay for them, because resources must be set aside from consumption to pay the costs of the capital investment the nation now really must make. The first half of 1979, when an increase in total employment produced a decrease in the national product, sounds a siren of warning.

The only question is how this (slight) reduction in the American standard of living is to be accomplished. Monetary means alone, as the Federal Reserve demonstrated throughout 1979, are now literally impossible: there are simply too many dollars outside America in the parallel Eurodollar system, which will be brought home to keep the credit markets expanding and to frustrate the Fed's restrictive policies. The higher the interest rates are pushed, the greater the inflow of funds. Only fiscal restraint—tax increases (which may inhibit desired investment) or actual reductions of government expenditure—remains plausible as a way to contract demand. In the absence of reduced demand, the reduction of American consumption will be accomplished by inflation, making everyone's salaries and savings worth less in real terms. Inflation of the dimensions necessary to keep the cost of living rising more rapidly than incomes (which is what is required, if consumption is to be reduced by this route) does great damage to the social fabric at home and to American influence (and the dollar) abroad. And then deep recession overkills demand, reducing income and consumption far more than necessary. But that is the route we took when the President made his Economic Report in January 1978. President Nixon had led us down the same path in 1972.

3

International programs will work right only if domestic activities are managed with reasonable competence; and among the international problems the choice of "exchange-rate regime" turns out not to be salient. The fact of convertibility dominates all other elements, transmitting economic decisions into the world market with frightening efficiency. Anything the world will take in payment without applying too severe a discount will serve as reserves under conditions of general convertibility. As Yeo and de Larosière concluded, pegged rates can be viable only if governments manage their own economies soundly, and if the governments manage the economies soundly floating rates will be stable. Some form of pegging, however, would be preferable, to sound alarm bells when imbalances grow dangerous and to use IMF bridge financing resources efficiently.

THE FATE OF THE DOLLAR

In a series of speeches in 1978, Henry Wallich blamed the exchange-rate turmoil of that year on "dissynchronization" of the leading economies—the fact that growth rates were so different in the United States, Germany, Japan, Switzerland, and the United Kingdom. Dissynchronization creates a Gresham's Law preference, he argued, for the currency of the economy that is growing less rapidly, and this preference (a "bond effect," endangering the value of the principal of a loan in the currency it runs against) will overwhelm the interest-rate differentials that might otherwise draw funds into the currency of the country that is growing most rapidly. On the other hand, Wallich somewhat gingerly pointed out, close synchronization of the world's leading economies, as in 1972–74, can create a simultaneous worldwide inflationary boom and fearful bust, as everybody gets greedy together and then gets scared together.

What makes Wallich's argument suspect is the failure to distinguish between consumer-led growth and investment-led growth. The former does indeed make a currency undesirable as a haven for a store of value, but the latter does not. In retrospect, it seems entirely plausible that the pause in the recovery in Germany and much of the rest of Europe in the second half of 1977 was necessary to persuade the labor unions not to grab (as the Swedish unions, in what they later admitted was a disaster, had grabbed) for too high a proportion of the growth. In a mature economy capable of generating its own savings, future income is likely to be greater if government seeks to maintain the value of the currency and encourage accumulation—rather than to stimulate incessantly, which seems to be the only weapon in the economic arsenal any American government likes to use. Demand restraint and currency stability also have the virtue of making capital available if desired to the economies of the Less Developed Countries.

As convertibility and instant communications link the industrial economies ever more tightly, other government policies in many areas will have to be reconciled across national boundaries to yield the benefits of world trade and economic specialization without which few nations today can hope to improve the living standards of their people. Not the least of the problems of the United States in international trade, for example, has been its reliance on income taxation for more than 55 percent of central government revenues, and on capital levies (real estate taxes) for more than half of local government tax receipts. Such taxes are built into the cost structures of American industry, and affect export prices. The European Value Added Tax, by contrast, is external to production costs and does not appear in exporters' prices.

Domestic subsidy programs become increasingly troublesome as economies are more closely intertwined. In the 1970s, a crisis of overcapacity in the steel industries struck all the developed countries. The British government accepted losses ranging up to $1 billion a year to keep the nationalized British Steel Corporation going; the United States instituted a variable import levy to protect local production; the Japanese stockpiled everything from structural shapes to tankers; the Germans took a strike; the French accepted political hoo-hah up to and including the firing of guns at police stations in Lorraine. In each country, with the honorable exception of France, politicians publicly discussed what was obviously an international problem from an exclusively domestic viewpoint: the subject was not talked about as a need to share shrinkage, but as a need to fight off foreigners.

With the passage of time, an increasing share of the world's technically simple industrial production (textiles, shoes, basic machine tools) and of its labor-intensive production (especially consumer electronics) has been shifting to countries that previously had no industrial base. The result in the developed countries is a low ceiling on wages in those industries, and eventually a loss of jobs, anyway. The political pressures to prevent the job losses are heavy—and since the LaFollette movement no consumer group has organized against the tariffs and quotas that make them pay more and often enough accept a lower quality than could be bought from abroad. (Ralph Nader clearly has a different agenda.) Meanwhile, because the radical rhetoric of the

"New International Economic Order" has nothing to do with the situation under discussion, the LDCs find it impossible to get their points across: they were clobbered in the Multilateral Trade Negotiations.

As the East European countries uncomfortably learned in the 1970s, the ceiling on economic development is low without participation in world trade. A nation raises its income by concentrating its labors on those activities it performs most efficiently. Investment broadens and deepens the "comparative advantage" a nation enjoys, raising its relative standard of living; innovation makes possible continuing wage disparities between the labor forces of the different nations in an interdependent world. This is why all the once "planned" economies are now in retreat from planning—because planning is the enemy of innovation, and without innovation, over time, real wages in wealthy societies will diminish as the less wealthy societies master the techniques.

Internationally, we are in some danger of validating the Marxist economics that never predicted anything right in national economies: there could be competition among nations to lower export prices by reducing real wages. In effect, though neither the British nor American authorities who got clever in the exchange markets realized it, this is what depreciation of the currency does. There are also dangers of competition by pollution, as factories that must meet stringent emission controls find their goods overpriced by comparison with those produced where regulations are slack. And there are dangers of interest-rate wars, with countries seeking to avoid the chill of currency depreciation or domestic contraction by applying a stream of hot money.

The most serious problems now as always are the tariff walls, quotas and subsidies by which governments seek to protect their inefficient industries from foreign competition. If some smart fellow years ago had learned to grow bananas in a heated shed in Maine, Americans would probably be paying a hell of a price today for bananas to keep out low-cost competition from Central America. Food prices in both Europe and Japan are ludicrously high by comparison with the United States because the Common

Market and the Japanese have determined to shield their less efficient dairy farms and orange groves and chicken coops from the
importation of low-priced foreign products. Japanese television
sets and American hand-held calculators cost twice as much as
necessary in the Common Market; sugar is overpriced in the
United States; and so are a whole crowd of chemicals, not to
mention steel. The lists are endless.

Not all of this discrimination is avoidable. The older generation in Europe remembers what it meant to go hungry. Quite
apart from the social considerations that argue for the maintenance of a farming community, no nation likes to be more dependent on foreigners for its food than it must be. If higher prices
now are needed to maintain sugar production in the United
States, the fact is that a source of domestic sugar was useful to the
country during the big sugar scare of 1974–75. There is some
question whether it makes sense in terms of national security to
have *all* radio communications equipment for the country made
in Japan, or by multinational companies in Taiwan, Hong Kong,
Korea, Singapore, and Mexico.

Especially where state-owned or state-sponsored industries are
involved in world trade, there is a constant danger of predatory
behavior. Russian shipping—even after one discounts for the ap-
palling living conditions which the Soviets can force on their sail-
ors—sells for less than any private shipper can afford to charge
because the Russian government is paying a price to establish a
position. Polish golf carts are being sold for less than cost, and so
is British steel. The American semiconductor makers who are
screaming about an expected assault on their markets organized
by the Japanese trading companies are certainly paranoid—but
as an analysand once said of Dr. Wilhelm Reich, they may be
justifiably paranoid.

Internationally, we need rules of the game, and ways to discipline violators. Obviously, subsidies to domestic producers whose
continuance is regarded as a national interest will be cheaper to a
nation's consumers and less disruptive of world trade than tariff
barriers (but such industries should then be forbidden to export).

345

The MTN negotiators in Geneva did, in fact, develop an impressive collection of codes; it remains to be seen whether they will be enforced. There is always a temptation to "preserve jobs" domestically by freezing out imports—and these days there is even "scientific" proof that such self-defeating gestures will be beneficial, from university economists who program their computers to show splendid results when the home country jacks up tariffs and the rest of the world refrains from retaliation.

But you can't live higher than the value of your production over a period of time—though you can pretend to do so for a while by invading your inheritance. Europeans looking at America speculate about the "loss of innovation" as the root cause of the decline of the dollar. On a relative basis, of course, the American lead has greatly shrunk: foreigners win an increasing proportion of our patents, and introduce an increasing proportion of new products and processes. But on an absolute scale, the United States is still doing fine: microminiaturization, computerization, communications devices, servocontrol systems, space technology, chemical creation and recombination, medical machinery—these are the areas of the leading edge, and all of them are areas where American contributions are still the world's strongest. There are problems of attitude: any nation will fall behind if it makes heroes of its crusaders, entertainers, lawyers, and journalists rather than its scientists, inventors, and developers—if it insists on *always* ranking the values of cleanliness, safety, and "fairness" above those of efficiency, output, and investment.

Barring the return of dramatic political instability in Europe (always a significant source of strength for the American financial markets), there is no way the dollar can regain the position it held in the 1950s—just as there is no way the United States can ever again be economically as self-contained as it was in the 1950s. Reliance on foreign need for American military protection, which can still be exploited for economic advantage, will eventually erode both the military position and the economy. It may well be that the margin between the American standard of living and that in other developed countries (already much diminished) must disappear, and even incline to American disadvantage. There are signs that for a while we will need an undervalued currency (that is, a currency that will buy more at home than its exchange-rate equivalent will buy in other countries) if our exports are to be competitive in world markets—and to the extent that this statement is true we must expect domestic inflation that will lower domestic purchasing power until it reaches a sustainable position in a band of parities. The United States is now one nation among many, with not quite so many obligations as it once assumed—and with many fewer privileges.

What is vital is not to fritter away the sources of American strength—from the foreign investments to the work habits of the people—in search of fashionable chimeras. You can't redistribute the national income by political intervention unless you produce, you can't clean up the environment unless you produce, you can't lead an alliance unless you produce. Government, for all its majestic force and command of blarney, is not a producer. If these self-evident truths have been forgotten (and casual perusal of the culture and its politics could argue that they have been), then the decline of the dollar will prove, as price changes so often do prove, a harbinger of an unpleasant future. If the cultural-political evidence is merely fun and games, ready to be shucked off as part of the response to a challenge, the United States still has the resources both human and natural to sustain its standard of living, its charitable self-image, and its freedoms.

The weakness of the dollar is partly technical, partly systemic, partly an expression of worldwide political and economic change that cannot be escaped and should not be fought. What has made the condition so difficult to treat is a kind of utopian self-indulgence, a refusal to make choices and to pay bills, in the American polity. Supported by evidence that the United States intends to make its goals fit its opportunities—and to implement policies that fit its goals—the rest of the industrial world, in its own self-interest, will be happy to cooperate with American plans to wring out the excess liquidity in the world's monetary basins. The dollar will not be almighty ever again; but it can be sound.

Apologia and Acknowledgments

The origins of this book go back, no doubt, to John Williams' course on Money and Banking and Joseph Schumpeter's seminar on European Central Banking, which I "took" 35 years ago. Its immediate background, of course, is the work I did for my reportorial study *The Bankers,* published in January 1975. But its proximate cause was in the work I began in mid-1977 toward a book about diplomats and diplomacy.

Among the most obvious reasons for the low efficiency and effectiveness of American international policy in that year was the decline of the dollar on the international exchanges. In January 1978, as the dimensions of the problem grew, I went to the Treasury Department to inquire about the degree of concern there, and how the liaison with the State Department worked. And I found to my astonishment that on the working-stiff (Deputy Assistant Secretary) level, which was as high as I then penetrated, there was no concern at all. The exchange value of the dollar had been placed in the all-knowing hands of the marketplace; the State Department, like everybody else, would have to learn to live with the market's decisions. Certainly there was no thought that any aspect of American domestic economic policy might have to be changed to maintain the exchange value of the currency.

This was a profitable visit, as a personal matter. I was going off for several months to the Western Pacific, and a few days after my trip to Washington I armed myself for the voyage by purchasing yen-denominated rather than dollar-denominated travelers' checks, which cut my travel expenses by roughly 10 percent as the months passed. On my return to the United States at the end of April, I found that the sickening slide of the dollar in the late winter was now regarded as an aberration, like the bad weather: the markets had stabilized, the dollar was if anything rising on the exchanges, and in general the Treasury felt it was not to worry. I began to suspect that Treasury attitudes were being in-

349

fluenced by the ease of funding the very high domestic budget deficit in a period when the United States had a high international payments deficit. An administration still committed to low interest rates would have found it damned inconvenient to peddle to the public that stream of new Treasury bills, notes and bonds—but the foreigners needed a place to park all those unwanted dollars they were accumulating, which took care of the problem. Temporarily.

I wrote an article accusing the Treasury (and the country) of cheating its creditors, and *Atlantic Monthly* published it under the title of "The Incredible Shrinking Dollar." It took some courage for *Atlantic* to publish the piece, because the experts they consulted said they couldn't understand what was troubling me. (It also, I learned when I began work on this book, had taken courage for me to write the piece, because the subject was much more complicated, and its history much more interesting, than I had realized.) In any event, as the predictions in the *Atlantic Monthly* piece began to come true toward the end of summer 1978, I proposed a book on the subject to Truman M. Talley, who had published *The Bankers*. Doubleday, to which I was contracted for the diplomacy book, generously postponed my delivery schedule to permit me to write first on the dollar.

During the course of work on this book, I was able to interview six Secretaries of the Treasury and six Under Secretaries; three Chairmen of the Federal Reserve Board and a Governor of the Board; the present and past managers of the foreign exchange department at the Federal Reserve Bank of New York; the heads of the Danish, Hungarian, Dutch, and German central banks and highly placed specialists at the Swiss and British central banks; the permanent undersecretary of the British Treasury; the chairman of the House Banking Committee; the U.S. Treasury attaches in Bonn, London, Rome and Tokyo (and the British Treasury attache in Washington); the chairmen and/or foreign exchange department heads of four of the largest international banks; the present and immediate past chief economists of the Bank for International Settlements; the managing director of the

International Monetary Fund and his deputy; the chief economist and chief counsel at the IMF; such distinguished academic experts in the field as Robert Triffin, Robert Aliber, and Edward Bernstein—and many others. I am grateful to all of them.

Winston Lord graciously made available to me the library facilities of the Council on Foreign Relations, where a high fraction of the printed material cited was found (especially the Congressional hearings). I am grateful also to the New York Public Library, the New York University Library, the library at the International Monetary Fund, and the Kennedy Library in Waltham, Massachusetts.

A number of experts, friends, and sons read all or part of this book for me in manuscript, and made suggestions for its correction or improvement. Among them were Jean-François Berheim, Arthur Burns, James Burtle, Frank Deastlov, Deborah Ishlon, James Mayer, Thomas Mayer, Charles Ramond, Henry Reuss, Robert Roosa, Murray Rossant, Paul Volcker, and Thomas O. Waage. By no means all suggestions or corrections were accepted—though all were carefully considered, and many were made—and *all* responsibility for what's wrong with this book is mine, though the credit for what may be right about it should be diffused.

For his sake and mine, the dedication to Henry Reuss should be explained. He obviously does not agree with what prescriptions this book offers, nor with all the analysis. The dedication is a professional tribute, from a writer who has often had to plow through the endless parochialisms, irrelevancies, lunacies, hotdogging, and special pleading that characterize the transcripts of Congressional hearings on nearly all other subjects. The hearings Reuss has organized and personally supervised on this subject are models of what the legislative investigating process should be, and a pleasure to read (including the Chairman's own contributions). They were a great help to me, and the dedication of a book seems an appropriate acknowledgment.

Notes

Chapter 1
From Power and Glory to Glut

3 Crowther quote: Richard N. Gardner, *Sterling-Dollar Diplomacy,* McGraw-Hill, New York, 1969 edition, pp. xliii–ix.

10 Staff report, in *Staff Papers,* Committee on Foreign Economic Policy, Washington, 2/54, p. 472.

12 Report to Budget Bureau, in *The Balance of Payments Statistics of the United States,* Report of the Review Committee for Balance of Payments Statistics, Washington, 4/65, p. 102. Hereafter, Bernstein Committee.

16 Triffin figures, in Robert Triffin, *The Future of Floating Exchange Rates: Free? Managed? or Mismanaged?* The Exchequer, Boeing Computer Services, Morristown, N.J., 1978, unpaginated.

17 Bergsten quote: C. Fred Bergsten, *The Dilemmas of the Dollar,* Council on Foreign Relations-New York University Press, New York, 1975, p. 177.

19 Triffin quote: Robert Triffin, *The World Money Maze,* Yale University Press, New Haven, 1966, p. 61.

21 Bagehot quote: Norman St. John-Stevas, ed., *The Collected Works of Walter Bagehot,* Vol. III, The Historical Essays, Harvard University Press, Cambridge, 1968, pp. 202–3.

Chapter 2
Truth and Money

23 R. S. Sayers, *Central Banking After Bagehot,* Oxford University Press, London, 1957, p. 4.

23 Keynes, *Essays in Persuasion,* W. W. Norton, New York, 1963, pp. 183–184.

26– Machlup: "The Mysterious Numbers Game" (1962), in Fritz Machlup, *Inter-*
27 *national Payments, Debts and Gold,* New York University Press, New York (paper), 1975 (second ed.), pp. 141–166, esp. 145–153.

28 Marx: Karl Marx, *Capital,* Charles H. Kerr & Co., Inc., Chicago, 1906, Vol. I, p. 144.

29 Triffin: Robert Triffin, *Gold and the Dollar Crisis,* Yale University Press, New Haven, paper, revised ed., 1961, p. 21.

29 Ruggles' scheme: see Ernest N. Paolino, *William Henry Seward and American Foreign Policy,* Cornell University Press, Ithaca, N.Y., 1973, pp. 76 et seq.

33 footnote: see Charles P. Kindleberger, *The World in Depression, 1929-39,* University of California Press (paper), Berkeley, 1975, pp. 66–70.

35 Keynes "do without": op. cit., p. 293.

35 "sleep": ibid., p. 294.

35– Keynes: ibid., p. 285.
36

36 Stimson: Henry Stimson with McGeorge Bundy, *On Active Service in Peace and War,* Harper & Brothers, New York, 1948, p. 216.

37 Hull: in Dean Acheson, *Present at the Creation,* W. W. Norton, New York, 1969, p. 10.

38 Roosevelt: in Lester V. Chandler, *America's Greatest Depression,* Harper & Row, New York, 1970, pp. 164–165.

39 Chamberlain quote: in Richard N. Kottman, *Reciprocity and the North Atlantic Triangle, 1932–1938,* Cornell University Press, Ithaca, N.Y., 1968, p. 206. Kottman, however, does not accept the conclusion. "The notion that Anglo-American trade negotiations were conscious attempts to build a barrier to Axis expansion was largely the creation of journalists. Secretary of State Hull certainly entertained this ambition, but London did not reciprocate." p. 208.

40 Block: Fred L. Block, *The Origins of International Economic Disorder,* University of California Press, Berkeley, 1977; "national capitalism," p. 38; "relative prosperity," p. 64; "German domestic program," p. 28.

40– de Souza Costa: in Gilbert P. Verbit, *International Monetary Reform and the*
41 *Developing Countries,* Columbia University Press, New York, 1975, p. 95.

41 Keynes: in Gardner, op. cit., pp. 79–80.

43 White: in Joseph Gold, *The "Sanctions" of the International Monetary Fund,* American Journal of International Law, Vol. 66, No. 5, Oct. 1972, p. 737 @ 743.

47 Morgenthau: in Gardner, op. cit., p. xxvi.

50 Verbit: op. cit., p. 81.

Chapter 3

Eisenhower's Conservatives

53 Treasury spokesman: in Triffin, *World Money Maze,* p. 232.

55 aid role: Staff Papers, Commission on Foreign Economic Policy, Supt. of Public Documents, Wash., 1954, p. 7.

55 concealed dollar gap: Report of the Commission on Foreign Economic Policy, p. 5.

55 free trade: ibid., p. 44.

55 convertibility: ibid., p. 73.

56 Baruch quote: Minority Report of the Commission, p. 12.

56 Jacobsson: ibid., p. 13.

59 Triffin quote: Triffin, *Gold and the Dollar Crisis,* p. 61.

59 Madison quote: from Federalist #10, in Cooke, ed., The Federalist, Wesleyan University Press, Middletown, Conn., 1961, p. 65.

61 Triffin quote: *Gold and the Dollar Crisis,* p. 232.

61 Machlup quote: Fritz Machlup, op. cit., p. 239 et seq.

61 Fekete quote: Janos Fekete, *Some Reflections on International Monetary Problems and East-West Economic Relations,* National Bank of Hungary, Budapest, 1977, pp. 69–70.

63 Radcliffe quote: *Report of the Committee on the Working of the Monetary System,* HMSO, London, 1969, para 687, p. 251.

67 Monnet quote: Jean Monnet, *Memoirs,* Doubleday, 1978, p. 428.

67 DeGaulle quote: Charles DeGaulle, *Memoirs of Hope; Renewal and Endeavor,* Simon & Schuster, 1971, pp. 137–8.

69 Shultz quote: George P. Shultz and Kenneth W. Dam, *Economic Policy Beyond the Headlines,* W. W. Norton, 1978, p. 107.

72 Tobin quote: James Tobin, in *Guidelines for International Monetary Reform,* Hearings of the Subcommittee on International Exchanges and Payments of the Joint Economic Committee, 1965; part 2, Supplement, p. 224. Hereafter, "1965 Hearings."

73 Emminger quote: Otmar Emminger, *The D-Mark in the Conflict Between Internal and External Equilibrium, 1948-1975.* PRINCETON ESSAYS IN INTERNATIONAL FINANCE No. 122, June, 1977. Princeton University, N.J., p. 48.

74– Gardner quotes: Richard N. Gardner, *Strategy for the Dollar,* Foreign Affairs
75 April 1960 p. 433 @ 435, 439.

75 Gardner quotes: ibid., p. 438.
75– Anderson quotes: Robert B. Anderson, *The Balance of Payments Problem,* For-
76 eign Affairs, April 1960, p. 419 @ 428.
77 Anderson quotes: ibid., pp. 427, 426.
80 Gilbert quote: 41st Annual Report, Bank for International Settlements, Basle,
Switzerland, 1971, p. 17.
80 Kennedy quote: from Robert V. Roosa, *The Dollar and World Liquidity,* Ran-
dom House, New York, 1967, p. 266.
82 Coombs quote: Charles A. Coombs, *The Arena of International Finance,* John
Wiley & Sons, New York, 1976, p. 27.

Chapter 4
Kennedy's Improvisers

85 Kennedy quote: in Roosa, op. cit., p. 319.
85 Schlesinger quote: Arthur M. Schlesinger, *A Thousand Days,* Houghton-Mif-
flin Co., Boston, 1965, p. 654.
86– Task force quotes: Report to Honorable John F. Kennedy of Task Force on
87 the Balance of Payments. Mimeo (at JFK Library, Waltham, Mass.); "highest
priority," p. 9; "cost-price spirals," p. 2; "surveillance," p. 2; "gold markets,"
p. 5.
87– Solomon quote: from Robert Solomon, *The International Monetary System,*
88 *1945–1976,* Harper & Row, New York, 1977, p. 39.
88 Sproul Committee quote: in Roosa, op. cit., p. 297.
89 Kennedy quote: in Solomon, loc. cit.
89 Treasury quote: *Maintaining the Strength of the United States Dollar in a
Strong Free World Economy,* U.S. Treasury Dept., Washington, 1968, p. 58.
90 message to Germany: in Emminger, op. cit., p. 14.
91 Emminger quote: ibid., p. 15.
95 Treasury quote: from Henry H. Schloss, *The Bank for International Settlements,* The Bulletin, NYU Graduate School of Business Administration, September 1970, p. 22. Other material for the preceding pages has been taken
from this pamphlet.
99– central bank plan and announcement: Coombs, op. cit., p. 19.
100
102 Johnson quote: *Outlook for the United States Balance of Payments,* Hearings
Before the Subcommittee on International Payments and Exchanges, Joint
Economic Committee, 1962, p. 219. Hereafter, 1962 Hearings.
105 "close to $400 million": Sherman Maisel, *Managing the Dollar,* W. W. Norton,
New York, 1973, p. 207.
107 Coombs quote: Coombs, op. cit., p. 63.
108 Harrod quote: in Triffin, *World Money Maze,* p. 349.
108 Roosa quote: Roosa, op. cit., p. 68.
108 Jacobsson quote: in Machlup, op. cit., p. 122.
109 bananas: *The Balance-of-Payments Statistics of the United States,* Report of
the Review Committee for Balance-of-Payments Statistics to the Bureau of
Budget, April 1969, p. 24. Hereafter, Bernstein Committee.
111 "unsatisfactory": ibid., p. 2.
112 all foreign holdings: ibid., p. 109.
113 Kennedy quote: 1962 Hearings, p. 55.
114 Reuss quote: *U.S. Payments Policies Consistent With Domestic Objectives of
Maximum Employment and Growth,* Report of the Subcommittee on International Payments and Exchange, Joint Economic Committee, 1962, p. 7.

116 production abroad: Nasrollah S. Fatemi, Thibault de Saint Phalle and Grace M. Keefe, *The Dollar Crisis,* Fairleigh-Dickinson University Press, New Jersey, 1963, pp. 176–178.

116 Blough quote: ibid., p. 174.

117 Cohen figure: *The United States Balance of Payments,* Hearings Before the Joint Economic Committee, 1963, pp. 192 et. seq. Hereafter, 1963 Hearings.

118 Houthakker quote: *Factors Affecting the United States Balance of Payments,* Compilation of Studies, Joint Economic Committee 1962, p. 299.

119 Roosa quote: ibid., p. 343.

119 Roosa quote: 1962 Hearings, p. 121.

119–Roosa quote: 1963 Hearings, pp. 129–30.

120

122 Dillon quote: ibid., p. 28.

Chapter 5
Johnson's Warriors

125 Johnson quote: Lyndon B. Johnson, *The Vantage Point,* Holt, Rinehart & Winston, New York, 1971, p. 321.

128 Johnson quote: in Roosa, op. cit., p. 321.

129 Johnson quote: ibid., p. 348.

129 Commerce Dept. quote: Treasury Dept., *Maintaining the Strength,* p. 158.

134 Kenen quote: 1962 Hearings, p. 132.

136 Reuss quote: *Off Dead Center,* A Report to the Joint Economic Committee by Rep. Henry Reuss and Rep. Robert F. Ellsworth, 1965, p. 13.

137–Brookings quotes: Walter S. Salant et al., *The American Balance of Payments*
138 *in 1968,* Brookings Institution, Washington, 1963, pp. 78, 153.

138 Brookings quotes: ibid., p. 23.

138 JEC quote: *U.S. Balance of Payments,* Report of the Joint Economic Committee, 1964, p. 7.

139 Tobin quote: 1963 Hearings, p. 566.

142 Maisel quote: Maisel, op. cit., p. 214.

143 Reuss quote: 1962 Hearings, p. 6.

143–Kindleberger quote: Charles H. Kindleberger, *Europe's Postwar Growth,* Har-
144 vard University Press, Cambridge, Mass., 1967, pp. 124–125.

146 Brooks quote: John Brooks, *Business Adventures,* Weybright & Talley, New York, 1969, p. 353.

150 Kindleberger quote: *Gold Cover,* Hearings of the Senate Banking and Currency Committee, 1968, p. 168.

150 Johnson quote: *Maintaining the Strength,* p. xvii.

150 Zijlstra quote: in Coombs, op. cit., p. 166.

151 Cooper quote: Richard N. Cooper, Introduction to Fred Hirsch, *Money International,* Doubleday, Garden City, L.I., 1969, p. xviii.

155–Johnson quotes: *Maintaining the Strength,* pp. xii, xiv, xv, xi.
156

156 Kindleberger quote: *Gold Cover* Hearings, p. 171.

159 Bernstein quote: *New Plan for International Monetary Reserves,* Hearings of the International Payments and Exchange Subcommittee, 1967, p. 99.

159 DeGaulle quote: DeGaulle, op. cit., p. 135.

161 Fowler quote: *Maintaining the Strength, A 1968 Progress Report,* U.S. Treasury, Washington, 12/68, p. 5.

161 Gilbert quote: Bank for International Settlements Annual Report 1968, Basle, p. 37.

162 Bernstein quote: Edward M. Bernstein, *Flexible Exchange Rates and Balance of Payments Adjustments,* EMB Ltd., Washington, 12/11/68, p. 3.

Chapter 6
Nixon's Nationalists

165 Nixon expletive: *The New York Times*, 8/6/74, p. 1.
166 Nixon fact: *RN, The Memoirs of Richard Nixon,* Grosset & Dunlap, New York, 1978, p. 516.
170 revolution in banking: see Martin Mayer, *The Bankers,* Weybright & Talley, New York, 1975.
171 Nixon quote: in Coombs, p. 206.
171 Houthakker I: 1962 Hearings, p. 163.
172 Houthakker II; *The Balance of Payments Mess,* Subcommittee on International Payments and Exchange, 1971, p. 259. Hereafter, 1971 Hearings.
172 Houthakker III: in Coombs, op. cit., p. 208.
173 Little quotes: in Joan Sneddon Little, *Eurodollars: The Money Market Gypsies,* Harper & Row, New York, 1975, p. 231.
175 Bernstein quote: in Edward M. Bernstein, *Quarterly Review and Investment Survey,* Roland, Model & Stone, 2nd Quarter 1971, p. 7.
176 Bronfenbrenner quote: 1971 Hearings, p. 246.
177 Bronfenbrenner quote: Martin Bronfenbrenner, *A Japanese-American Economic War?,* Carnegie-Mellon University, Pittsburgh, 1971, p. 13; in 1971 Hearings, p. 228.
179 Connally quote: 1971 Hearings, p. 264.
179–Volcker quote: ibid., p. 102.
180
180 Houthakker quote: ibid., p. 253.
180 Klopstock quote: ibid., p. 294.
180 Gilbert quote: ibid., p. 295.
182–Peterson quote: Peter Peterson, *The United States in the Changing World*
183 *Economy,* Government Printing Office, Washington, 1971, pp. 5, 8, 41.
184 Dillon quote: 1963 Hearings, p. 84.
186 Reuss quote: *Action Now to Strengthen U.S. Dollar,* Report of the Subcommittee on International Payments and Exchange, 1971, pp. 7, 9, 11.
189 Camp David: see William Safire, *Before the Fall,* Doubleday, Garden City, L.I., pp. 509 et seq.
189 Crossman quote (fn): Richard H. S. Crossman, *Diaries of a Cabinet Minister,* Vol. II, Holt Rinehart & Winston, New York, 1976, p. 579.
189 Nixon quote: op. cit., p. 520.
191 Aliber quote: Aliber, loc. cit.
191 Cooper quote: in Hirsch, op. cit., p. xxix.
193 Machlup quote: Machlup, op. cit., p. 169.
195 Jay and Connally quotes: "Mr. Connally Spells Out U.S. Conditions for an Early Removal of 10PC Surcharge," by Peter Jay, London *Times,* 10/1/71, p. 21.
203 Reuss quote: *Removal of Gold Cover,* Hearings of House Committee on Banking & Currency, 1968, p. 25.
208 BIS quote: 43rd Annual Report, Bank for International Settlements, Basle, 1973, p. 21.

Chapter 7
Ford's Ideologues

221 CEA quote: 1975 Economic Report of the President, p. 194.
222 Schultz quote: Schultz & Dam, op. cit., p. 122.
222 Williamson quote: John Williamson, *The Failure of World Monetary Reform, 1971–74,* New York University Press (paper), 1977, p. 69.
223 profits on seignorage: Bergsten, op. cit., p. 215, estimated a maximum of $1 billion per year, "probably much smaller and . . . declining."

NOTES

224 Posthuma quote: in Tom DeVries, "Jamaica, or the Non-Reform of the International Monetary System," *Foreign Affairs,* April 1976, p. 577 @ 604.
226 Gilbert quote: 39th Annual Report, Bank for International Settlements, in Schloss, op. cit., pp. 26–27.
227 Williamson quote: Williamson, op. cit., p. 143.
228 IMF quote: 1978 Annual Report, International Monetary Fund, Washington, p. 44.
230 CEA estimate: 1975 Economic Report, pp. 194 et seq.
230 CEA quote: ibid., p. 140.
231 production drops: ibid., p. 129.
232 CEA quote: ibid., p. 21.
232–Bernstein figures: *The Trade Deficit, Capital Movements and The Floating Dol-*
233 *lar,* EMB, Ltd., Washington, 5/26/78, p. 5.
233–Friedman quote: 1963 Hearings, pp. 455–6, p. 459.
234
235 Rolfe and Burtle quote: Sidney Rolfe and James L. Burtle, *The Great Wheel,* McGraw-Hill (paper), New York, 1975, p. 143.
235 Kindleberger quote: 1962 Hearings, p. 182.
236 Cooper quote: Richard N. Cooper, *The Economics of Interdependence,* Council on Foreign Relations, McGraw-Hill, New York, 1968, p. 14.
236 Machlup quote: Machlup, op. cit., p. 201.
236 Solomon quote: Solomon, op. cit., p. 321.
237 convertibility: see Joseph Gold, *Use, Conversion and Exchange of SDRs Under the Second Amendment of the Fund's Articles,* International Monetary Fund, Washington, 1978, pp. 59–61.
238 Fowler quote: *The IMF Gold Agreement,* Hearings before the House Subcommittee on International Economics, 1975, p. 5. Hereafter, 1975 Hearings.
239 Williamson quotes: Williamson, op. cit., pp. 74, 75, 74.
242 Reuss quote: 1975 Hearings, p. 2.
243 Ossola quote: in Robert D. Mundell and Jacques J. Polak, eds., *The New International Monetary System,* Columbia University Press, New York, 1977, p. 38.
243 A first-class demolition of floating theories was available but not used in the debate. In 1947, the English economist Joan Robinson had proved the impossibility of the "equilibrium" Friedman insisted would be attained automatically: "There is no one rate of exchange which is the equilibrium rate corresponding to a given state of world demands and techniques. In any given situation there is an equilibrium rate corresponding to each rate of interest and level of effective demand ... The notion of *the* equilibrium exchange rate is a chimera. The rate of exchange, the rate of interest, the level of effective demand and the level of money wages react upon each other ... and no one is determined unless all the rest are given." [JOAN ROBINSON, THE FOREIGN EXCHANGES, ESSAYS IN THE THEORY OF EMPLOYMENT, OXFORD UNIVERSITY PRESS, 2nd ed., 1947; cited in Machlup, op. cit., p. 125] Yet "every economist in the country," Paul Volcker says with some disgust, "conservative or liberal, said floating rates would solve the domestic problem."
243 Machlup quote: Machlup, op. cit., pp. 43–44.
246 Pardee quote: Scott Pardee, *How Well Are the Exchange Markets Functioning,* Federal Reserve Bank of New York Quarterly Review, Spring 1979, p. 49 @ 50, 51.
248 Ruth Pleak quote: Ruth E. Pleak, *An Analysis of the FASB's Treatment of Foreign Currency Translation,* in Management Accounting, 9/77, p. 29 @ 31.
248–Alan Teck quote: Alan Teck, "Beyond FAS No. 8: Defining Other Exposures,"
249 Management Accounting, 12/78, p. 54 @ 55.

249 John Y. Gray quote: John Y. Gray, "Translating Foreign Currency Transactions and Financial Statements," *The CPA Journal,* 6/77, p. 31 @ 35.
249 Kramer quote: "Banks Cash In on FASB-8," *Business Week,* 12/6/76, p. 104.
251 Fay and Young quote: Stephen Fay and Hugo Young, "The Day the Pound Nearly Died," Sunday *Times,* 5/14/78, p. 33 @ 34.
252 Yeo quote: ibid.

Chapter 8
Carter's Incompetents

257 Palk quote: ibid., p. 24.
257 Economic Report: 1978 Economic Report of the President, p. 42.
259 Robert Solomon quote: *The International Monetary System: Progress and Prospects,* The Atlantic Community Working Group on the International Monetary System, Westview Press, Boulder, Col., 1977, pp. 38–9.
259 Laurence S. Klein quote: in *Hearings of the Joint Economic Committee on the Economic Report of the President,* 1977, Washington, p. 183.
260 Blumenthal quote: ibid., p. 135.
263 Blumenthal quote: "Candid Reflections of a Businessman in Washington," *Fortune* magazine, 1/29/79, p. 36 @ 37.
264 Wallich quote: 1963 Hearings, p. 497.
265 Peterson quote: Peterson, op. cit., Vol. II, Background Materials, p. 19.
266 1972 study: The 1979 Joint Economic Report, p. 142.
268 import figures: ibid., p. 151, with estimates for footnote.
269 Kindleberger quote: Charles Kindleberger, "Protected Markets and Economic Growth," *in Factors Affecting the U.S. Balance of Payments,* pp. 162, 170, 171.
270–Tobin quote: 1965 Hearings, Vol. II, Supplement, p. 224.
271
271 Chesterton quote: *A Song of Self Esteem,* in G. K. Chesterton, *Collected Poems,* Dodd, Mead & Co., New York, 1932, p. 371.
271–Anthony Solomon quote: in *The Trade Deficit: How Much of a Problem? What*
272 *Remedy?* Hearings Before the Subcommittee on International Economics, JEC, 10/11/77, pp. 43, 47.
272 Reuss quote: ibid., p. 81.
272 Subcommittee report: *Living with the Trade Deficit,* Report of the Subcommittee on International Economics, JEC, 11/18/77, pp. 4, 5.
273 "modest 3%": "U.S. Said to Decline to Step in Further in Support of Dollar," *The New York Times,* 12/10/77, p. 31 @ 33.
273 Leutwiler quote: *The New York Times,* 12/14/77, Sec. IV, pp. 1, 9.
274 News story: "Carter Suggests Action to Bolster Dollar Abroad," by Clyde H. Farnsworth, *The New York Times,* 12/22/77, p. 1.
274 Comment: "Heavy Pressures on the Dollar, But Is There a Rally Ahead," by Leonard Silk, *The New York Times,* 12/22/77, p. 3.
277 "unsettling": 1978 Economic Report of the President, p. 57.
277 "savings": ibid., p. 81.
277 "concern" and "economic forces": ibid., p. 21.
277 "speculative activities": ibid., pp. 21, 22.
277–"large countries": ibid., p. 125.
278
278 Schultze: JEC Hearings, 2/1/78, p. 3.
279 Bolling quote: ibid., p. 2.
279 staff report: ibid., p. 385.
279–Reuss quote: ibid., p. 385.
280
282 Volcker quote: Federal Reserve Bank of New York Annual Report for 1978, p. 19.

NOTES

285 Cameron quote: Donald O. Cameron, *FX: An Inside View of the Foreign Exchange Market,* Chase Bank, New York, 1976, p. 9.
286 Swiss industrialist: Dr. Robert Lang, "A Testing Time for Machines and Metals," *Credit Suisse Bulletin,* Winter 1978–79, p. 11.
293 Holmes quote: "Monetary Policy and Open Market Operations in 1978," *Federal Reserve Bank of New York Quarterly Review,* Spring 1979, p. 49 @ 64.
296 Robert Solomon quote: Robert Solomon, "The Dollar Bounce," in *The New Republic,* 11/11/78, p. 15 @ 16, 17.

Chapter 9
The State of the Dollar

297 Prosser quote: William L. Prosser, "Lighthouse No Good," in *Journal of Legal Education,* Vol. 1, 1948, p. 257.
297 Sayers, op. cit., p. 5.
300 mark-denominated bonds and interest rates: see Irwin Perry, *Money Market Letter,* Herzfeld and Stern, New York, 3/13/79.
320 Witteveen quote: "Rockefeller Foundation New Group Studies How Monetary Systems Work," *Foundation News,* Mar/Apr 1979, p. 11.
323 Weatherstone quote: Dennis Weatherstone, "No Clear Case for Control of the Euro-currency Market," *Financier,* April 1979, p. 30 @ 32.
324 Bergsten and Cohen quotes: Benjamin J. Cohen, *Organizing the World's Money,* Basic Books, New York, 1977, p. 246.

Chapter 10
The Fate of the Dollar

336 Volcker quote: *Dilemmas of Economic Policy,* Remarks Before the School of Banking and Money Management, Adelphi University, 10/24/78, Federal Reserve Bank of New York, p. 3.
339–JEC quote: 1979 Joint Economic Committee Report, p. 3.
340
342 "dissynchronization": see especially *Evolution of the International Monetary System,* Remarks by Henry C. Wallich at the Conference of the "Zeitschrift fuer das Gesamte Kreditwesen," Frankfurt, Germany, 11/10/78, Federal Reserve Board, Washington, mimeo.

Index

INDEX

INDEX